91°
International
Boundary
Dzongkhag (District)
Boundary
Paved Road
Unpaved Road/
under Construction
Capital
Dzongkhag (District)
Headquarter
Dungkhag (Sub-
district) Headquarter
Town, Village
Airport
Singye Dzong
28°
Lhedang
Khenpa
Dzong
LHUNTSHI
Lhuntshi
BUMTHANG
Nangnang
Kurjey
Jakar
Tashi
Yangtse
Ura
Sakteng
Radi
Dametsi
Tashigang
Mongar
Gyepozhing
TASHIGANG
GSA
Shemgang
MONGAR
Wamrong
Pemagatsel
SAMDRUP
PEMA-
GATSEL
27°
HUG
SHEMGANG
JONGKHAR
Daifam
Panbang
Lalai
Nganglam
Samdrup
Jongkhar
Bhangtar
91°

The Politics of BHUTAN

Retrospect And Prospect

The Politics of BHUTAN
Retrospect And Prospect

Parmanand

PRAGATI PUBLICATIONS
DELHI
1998

REISSUED 1998
First Published 1992

ISBN 81-7307-000-8

Published by Vinod Kapoor for Pragati Publications
9926 Library Road, Azad Market, Delhi 110 006

Printed by
D.K. Fine Arts Press Pvt. Ltd.
New Delhi - 110 052

For
My Daughter Ruma
and
Son Jayant

Contents

Preface

I

It was not for nothing that the world-famous scientist, Einstein, once said that politics "is much more difficult than physics". The fifth edition of the world-famous dictionary, *The Concise Oxford Dictionary Of Current English,* (1964), had while explaining this word, stated among other things, that to "talk politics is not practical politics" ("is too remote to be worth discussing"). Politics is, indeed, a multidimensional and multifaceted word and no one dimension or facet is often capable of telling the real story. It is, therefore, desirable to assess as many dimensions of politics as possible in any given situation. Even that may not be able to tell the ultimate truth, but it would certainly be a good guide in making us move in that direction.

The eighth edition of *The Concise Oxford Dictionary Of Current English* (1990) has described politics as "the art and science of government", "public life and affairs as involving authority and government", "a particular set of ideas, principles, or commitments in politics. . .","activities concerned with the acquisition or exercise of authority or government" and "an organizational process or principle affecting authority, status, etc. . ." *The Chambers English Dictionary* (1991) has defined the term as "the art or science of government","the management of a political party","political affairs or opinions","manoeuvring and intriguing","policy-making as opposed to administration" and "the civil rather the military aspects of government".

Dwight D. Eisenhower, the 34th President of the USA (1953-61), once said: "Politics is a profession; a serious, complicated, and in its true sense, a noble one". Charles de Gaulle, one of the most noted French statesmen and a former President, had once said: "Politics is too serious a matter to be left to the politicians". Nikita Khruschev, a distinguished Soviet statesman and one-time Prime Minister of the now dismembered USSR, had once opined: "Politicians are the same all over. They promise to build a bridge even where there is no river".

To the noted political scientist, David Easton, politics is the "authoritative allocation of values" for a society. Politics is, in fact, concerned with public goals and decisions. Moreover, politics is an instrument of conflict resolution in a society. Besides, politics involves interest groups. Politics, on the other hand, is the art of capturing, holding and wielding power. To an Indian Prime Minister politics was the art of "managing contradictions". Relevantly and significantly, the possession and use of power may not necessarily be for the selfish interests of its holders. It may be used for the benefit of the masses. Maybe all this enables politics to be described as the "art of the possible". All these and several other unmentioned facets and dimensions constitute politics.

II

The pages that follow try to understand, classify and analyse the politics of the small and beautiful mountain kingdom, i.e. Bhutan, keeping as many dimensions and facets of politics in mind as possible.

Chapter 1 introduces Bhutan or *Druk-yul* (the land of the Thunder Dragon) by discussing the meaning of the word, the location of the kingdom, unification thereof, various ethnic groups therein and the languages spoken. It also analyses the religious and cultural lives of the country. Besides, it deals with printing, painting, arts and crafts along with architecture. Moreover, it discusses food and dress habits of the people as also the national anthem.

The kingdom's political economy and the various changes and strides therein since the establishment of the state structure form the subject-matter of Chapter 2.

Chapter 3, entitled "The Political System", deals with the various structures and sub-structures that constitute the political system of the kingdom. It discusses the institutions like the *Druk Gyalpo,* the *Je Khenpo,* the *Lodey Tshogdey,* the *Lhengyel Tsok* and the administration at the district level. It also analyses the institution and functions of the Planning Commission. Moreover, it discusses the Royal Civil Service Commission and the bureaucracy. The Kingdom's unicameral legislature, the *Tshogdu,* also forms Preface part of this chapter. Bhutan's judiciary, political parties and pressure groups, the army, the police, the constitution, apart from Bhutan's place in global politics have been chosen for a critical analysis in this chapter.

Chapter 4, entitled "Monarchy And Monarchs", deals with the *modi operandi* and the roles played by the 4 Wangchuck Kings—Ugyen Wangchuck, Jigme Wangchuck, Jigme Dorji Wangchuck and Jigme Singye Wangchuck—in the overall development of Bhutan. The Monarchy, has thus far remained pivotal in the political system of the kingdom. It is playing a significant role even in the present context. And yet various observations made by the incumbent King from time to time makes one look at the monarchy with more care and caution, in a world where the institution is becoming rather uncommon. For instance, King Jigme Singye Wangchuck on one occasion said: "I do not believe that monarchy is the best system of Government". (*The Statesman,* Delhi, 27 October 1990, 6). One wonders whether any other ruling monarch would speak of the institution in the same fashion. On another occasion, the King stated: "The greatest weakness of monarchy is that a person who holds the high position of being a King is chosen by birth and not merit". (Idid., 23 November 1991, 6) Relevantly all socio-politico-economic reforms in Bhutan have thus far, emanated fror the monarchy. This fact has, *inter alia,* made this institution and various persons constituting it significant enough to deserve a separate chapter.

Chapter 5, entitled "Contrived Problems of State-building and Nation-building", deals with the problems created by a segment of Bhutanese from time to time as also with the efforts made by the powers that be to make Bhutan an integrated society. Indeed, the problem of national integration has become intense of late. Ironically, the problem has been created by that segment of the populace which has been given more than sufficiently in terms of values, liberties and privileges in Bhutanese society. More ironically, very many of those involved in the contrived problems are not even Bhutanese citizens. The extent of ham-handedness of the law-enforcing agency has also been analysed.

Chapter 6, entitled "Bhutan In Global Politics", assesses the process and impact of the mountain kingdom's internationalization. How, despite various encumbrances, Bhutan has registered its presence in regional and global politics, form the subject-matter of this chapter.

Chapter 7, entitled "Bhutan-China Relations : An Exercise In Tightrope Walking", is an analysis of the relations between the Asian giant and the small South Asian mountain kingdom over the years. Quite expectedly, dealing with China has not been an easy job for most of the countries and Bhutan is no exception. Yet, Bhutan has thus far proved its diplomatic mettle in dealing with China. More importantly, while dealing with the PRC, Bhutan has not offended India. The chapter also tries to visualize the prospects of the relations between the two in future.

In "Bhutan-India Relations:The Importance Of Being Matured"(Chapter 8), an attempt has been made to analyse the relations between the core South Asian state and the small mountain kingdom. In fact, the relations between the big and the small has proved to be assuming more and more maturity with the passage of time. Analysis has also shown how both have been careful not to hurt the feelings of each other. This has augured well for the relationship between the two countries and there is no reason why it should not continue to be so in future.

The last Chapter, "Retrospect And Prospect", analyses Bhutan's overall past and present and tries to visualize the socio-politico-economic scenario in future.

III

My two visits to Bhutan in October 1990 and October 1991, and interviews with various personalities, including His Majesty King Jigme Singye Wangchuck, Foreign Minister Lyonpo Dawa Tsering, Home Minister Lyonpo Dago Tshering, Planning Minister Lyonpo C. Dorji, Commerce Minister Lyonpo Om Pradhan, and others of the kingdom, enabled me to see, understand, analyse and assess the politics and political actors in *Druk-yul* in perspective. I also had the privilege of watching the proceedings of the *Tshogdu* (The National Assembly) during its 70th session for several days in October 1991. It was, if anything, quite educative.

I have received a great deal of encouragement and help from several people in writing this book. I must thank them for the same. I am thankful to Professor Ram Rahul, author of several books on Bhutan, for generating my interest in Bhutan's politics. I thank Dr. O.P. Gauba, Reader in Political Science, School of Correspondence Courses and Continuing Education, University of Delhi and Dr. N.K. Jain, Reader in English in the same institute, for constant encouragement to complete this work. I thank Mr. Subrat Sahoo, my former student at M.A. class of South Asian Politics (Political Science) and currently a Research Scholar in the Department of Political Science, University of Delhi, immensely for going through the manuscript meticulously and making several valuable suggestions.

I received several valuable documents from Mr. Sonam Tobden Rabgye, First Secretary (Press), Royal Bhutanese Embassy, New Delhi, which were of great help in writing this book. He was ever ready to answer or get answer for each and every query related to this work. I owe him deep thanks.

My wife, Usha, Reader in English, School of Correspondence Courses and Continuing Education, University of Delhi, daughter, Ruma, and son, Jayant, have been a constant source of inspiration, help and encouragement in completing this work. They always cooperated in creating a congenial atmosphere, something quite vital to completing a project like this.

Last but not least, my sincere thanks are due to Mr. Vinod Kapoor of the Pragati Publications, Delhi, for publishing this book on a priority basis.

Needless to state, I alone am responsible for the analyses, observations and conclusions mentioned in the book, as also for any errors that may have inadvertently crept it.

April 1992 PARMANAND

Acknowledgements

(Eminent persons and others whom the author interviewed or talked to in connection with collecting information for the book)

HIS MAJESTY DRUK GYALPO JIGME SINGYE WANGCHUCK

LYONPO DAWA TSERING: Foreign Minister, Royal Government of Bhutan, Thimphu.

LYONPO(DR.) T. TOBGYEL: Minister for Social Services and Communications.

LYONPO DAGO TSHERING: Home Minister.

LYONPO OM PRADHAN: Minister for Trade and Industries.

LYONPO C. DORJI: Minister for Planning and Chairman, Planning Commission.

HIS EXCELLENCY DASHO KARMA LETHO: The Ambassador of the Royal Government of Bhutan in India.

DASHO PASSANG DORJI: Speaker, *Tshogdu.*

DASHO LEKI DORJI: Deputy Minister, Ministry of Agriculture.

DASHO KHANDU WANGCHUK: Secretary, Royal Civil Service Commission.

DASHO NADO RINCHHEN: Secretary, Ministry of Communications.

DASHO RIGZIN DORJI: Secretary, Special Commission for Cultural Affairs.

DASHO DOPHU TSHERING: Chief of Protocol.

MR. TASHI PHUNGSOG: Secretary, *Tshogdu,* formerly, Director, Department of Information and Broadcasting.

MR. LEKI DORJI: Counsellor, Royal Bhutanese Embassy, New Delhi.

MR. SONAM TOBDEN RABGYE: First Secretary (Press), Royal Bhutanese Embassy.

MR. KINLEY DORJI: Editor, *Kuensel* (Bhutan's national newspaper).
MS. LEKI WANGMO: Deputy Director, Ministry of Foreign Affairs.
MR. KESANG WANGDI: Director, Admn./Finance, Ministry of Foreign Affairs.

MR. YONTEN GYELSTHEN: PRO/News Editor, Bhutan Broadcasting Service.

MS. RINCHEN CHODEN: English News Reader and News Coordinator.
MR. ASHOK RAI: News Reader, Nepali.
MR. C. DORJI: Protocol Officer, Ministry of Foreign Affairs.
MR. UGYEN WANGCHUK: Protocol Officer, Ministry of Foreign Affairs.

INDIANS
MR. B.C. KHANNA: Formerly, India's Ambassador to Bhutan.
MR. N. RAVI: Counsellor, Indian Embassy in Bhutan.
MR. G.N. RAO: Managing Director/Secretary, Chukha Hydro Power Corporation, Tasimalakha, Bhutan.

1

Bhutan: An Introduction

Bhutan is a very small country but is immensely beautiful and significant in every sense of the term. To many people, it comes as a surprise that a country such as Bhutan can still be found in the world today. In terms of the smallness of area (46,500 sq kilometres) and population (6,00,000),[1] Bhutan is second only to Maldives in the South Asian region. However, in terms of beauty and strategic importance it is second to none.

Meaning of "Bhutan"

The name of Bhutan seems to have been derived from the Sanskrit word "Bhotanta", which means "the end of the land of the Bhots or Bhotas". *Bhot or Bhota* was the term by which traditional India knew the Tibetans. In fact, Tibet was called *Bhotdesha.* Bhotanta (Sanskrit's Bhota+anta, i.e. end) would, thus, stand for the region that lay to the southern end or border of Tibet. However, this interpretation is not very much off the mark. This is revealed by the social, religious, ethnic and cultural character of the Bhutanese people, which can be fully appreciated and understood apropos of and in the framework of the ethnology and total cultural pattern and character of Tibet.[2] As for the Bhutanese themselves, they seem to prefer the word "Druk-yul" for their country, romantically translated as the "Land of the Thunder-Dragon". Druk, which means "dragon", comes from the name of the Drukpa school of Tibetan Buddhism which first brought unity to Bhutan in the 17th century. According to a legend, when in the 12th century, as the founder of the Drukpa sect, Tsangpa Gyalrey, was preaching to his disciples at Namkhiphu, some 20 miles west of Lhasa, they suddenly heard the sound of thunder in the winter sky. They interpreted it as a good omen and it was decided to establish a monastery at the spot at which the prayer meeting was being held. The monastery was named as Nam

Drukgar ("thunder in the winter sky") and the new sect as the Drukpa or Thunder Dragon sect. Under pressure of the reformist Gelukpa sect, some of the older sects found themselves stunk out of Tibet and sought fresh pastures for evangelical work outside their own country. The Drukpas, who had proceeded to Bhutan, were so successful in their missionary enterprise that the country of their adoption was soon established as the main stronghold of the Drukpa sect. As a result, the country came to be known as "Druk-yul".[3]

Location

Druk-yul or Bhutan is situated along the southern slopes of the great Himalayan range between 26°5' and 28°5' north latitude and 88° and 92° east longitude.[4] It is surrounded by the tableland of Tibet on the north and on the south it is bounded by the plains of the Indian districts of Jalpaiguri and Cooch Behar in West Bengal, and those of Darang, Kamrup and Goalpara in Assam. In the west and the east, Bhutan is sandwiched between the Chumbi Valley of Tibet, Sikkim and Darjeeling, on the one hand, and the district of Kameng of Arunachal Pradesh of India, on the other. The beautiful Himalayan kingdom is rectangular in shape.

In terms of location, Bhutan is a landlocked country, like the only other South Asian Himalayan state of Nepal. But even though it has been landlocked, mountainous and difficult of access, Bhutan was scarcely a closed country as far as its interaction with the neighbouring territories was concerned. With Ladakh, Lahaul-Spiti and Kinnaur in the west, Tibet in the north and Sikkim, Cooch Behar and northern Assam as her immediate neighbours, Bhutan wellnigh formed one ethnic and cultural unit and appeared to have maintained close contact with these areas since time immemorial. This was obviously facilitated by Bhutan's geographical location, her river valleys and mountain passes. However, the Bhutanese throughout their history have been suspicious of foreigners and influence thereof. A predominantly religious state, Bhutan has been scared of the influx of foreign ideas and the impact thereof on their religious practices and social usages. "Even in the matter of marriage alliances, we do not find in Bhutan the tendency that had been prevalent in Sikkim from upper-class families to seek for their children brides and bridegrooms from the aristocracy of Tibet".[5]

Bhutan's geopolitical and geostrategic importance is enhanced by the fact that it is a buffer between the two Asian giants—the People's Republic of China and India. On this count, Bhutan's smallness in terms of size and population becomes irrelevant.

Nature seems to have divided Bhutan into 3 main zones : the southern foothills, the northern Himalayan borderland and the central zone. The southern foothills, an area of dense tropical forests, rise above 1,500 metres (about 5,000 feet) above the plains and stretch for about 20 kilometres into Bhutan. In the northern region, the Himalayan range is generally not as high as it is in further west, but it still contains peaks rising above 7,500 metres (about 24,500 feet). There are about 6 major passes in this border area, all of which lead from Bhutan to Tibet.

The most important area of Bhutan, however, is the central zone because it includes much of the cultivable land. For this very reason it also contains the greater part of the population. This region is divided into quite narrow river valleys by mountain ranges which run from north to south. The Black Mountain range, traditionally regarded as the dividing line between western and eastern Bhutan, is the most notable of these ranges. Thimphu (the capital of Bhutan), Punakha (the old winter capital), Paro, Ha and Wangdiphodrang are the main valleys in western Bhutan. In eastern Bhutan, there are the valley districts of Bumthang, Tongsa and Mongar among others. Still further east in Bhutan are the Tashigang and Samdrup Jongkhar valley districts.

As for climatic conditions, like another Himalayan kingdom of South Asia, Nepal, Bhutan has a great range from subtropical to the arctic cold and freezing snows of the high reaches of the Himalayas.[6]

Almost the entire population of the mountain kingdom of Bhutan was concentrated in the main valleys of Ha, Paro, Punakha, Thimphu, Tongsa, Bumthang, Kurtoey and Tashigang and eastern Bhutan till the 1940s. Principal rivers, the Toorsa, Raidak, Sankosh and Manas and their tributaries, all flowing into the Brahamputra in the Indian territory, watered these valleys and eastern Bhutan. Of these rivers the Manas and its tributary, the Kuru, are the mightiest inasmuch as they carry the largest volume of water and drain the whole of eastern Bhutan and north-east region of India's part of Tawang.[7] Quite expectedly, however, this situation changed in the 1950s as people from outside Bhutan came to take up various jobs in that country.

Unification of Bhutan

Bhutan has not been an unified state, as it is today, since time immemorial. But before we delve into analysing the unification of Bhutan, it would be in order here to mention that there is no ethnic, paleobotanic, geographic or physiographic record of its prehistoric period which fall roughly between 500 BC and AD 500. Earthquake, flood, internecine warfare and fire destroyed whatever records that might have existed once. The accidental burning of the *dzong* (monastery-fortress) in Punakha (1832), which at that time was one of the Bhutanese capitals, and widespread destruction caused at the same site by an earthquake (1897), were primarily responsible for the destruction of the historical documents of Bhutan pertaining to that period. A number of stone tools and megaliths that are available, however, suggest that Bhutan was populated from a relatively early date—probably around 2000-1500 BC. Little, however, is known about the early history of Druk-yul. From the available artefacts, preserved in a small number of ancient monasteries, one finds that Bonism, "a shamanistic ritual, was followed in Bhutan prior to the advent of Buddhism. The Bon tradition and rituals are still practiced in some parts of Bhutan during the celebration of local festivals".[8]

If only one person were to be regarded as the founder of Bhutan, without doubt, it was Shabdung Ngawang Namgyal, who appeared in Bhutan from Tibet sometime in the 16th or the 17th century. The Shabdung was a lama of the Durkpa sect and was determined to establish order on a permanent footing in the country of his adoption. He quickly proceeded, crushing all opposition, obliterating all rivals and establishing himself up as the undisputed Head of state. Although he was mainly interested in enforcing religious discipline, he was a man of parts and multifarious interests. In fact, there was no field related to the administration where he did not make his mark and contribution. Shabdung Namgyal prescribed rules of conduct for all officers—religious and secular. He also laid down strict regulations for judicial and revenue administration. More importantly, he was responsible for dividing the country into administrative units, each under a local governor, but ultimately owing allegiance to the central authority.[9]

It is difficult to say when Shabdung Ngawang Namgyal, who was the son of the prince of the Drukpas (who was also the head abbot of the Drukpa school) died. It was probably because of the absence of a suitable successor that the Shabdung's death was kept a secret for many years—from about 1651 to 1705. The Shabdung's closest associate had announced that the ruler had shut himself away to meditate. The Bhutanese believed it because of the reputation of the Shabdung as a man of religion and magic. They thought he lived in isolation to an amazingly old age. While the mystery was being maintained as a secret, the borders of Bhutan were extended to the present limits. However, towards the end of the 17th century, there must have been some one who suspected the truth.[10]

After the death of Shabdung Ngawang Namgyal, who came to be known subsequently as Shabdung Rimpoche, his successive reincarnations continued to exercise supreme religious authority, the secular administration being entrusted to their nominee, known as the Deb Raja (the "King who dispenses bounty"), who was appointed on the recommendation of a Council of State. The administrative units were placed under officers of various ranks, depending on their size and importance. Tongsa and Dagana in central Bhutan and Paro in western Bhutan were the most important of these units and each of these was ruled by a Penlop (Governor). Significantly, all significant decisions were taken by the Shabdung on the recommendation of the Council of State (comprising the Deb Raja, the Penlops and other high-ranking religious and secular officers). However, the Penlops dominated the proceedings of the Council, and even the Deb Raja, though theoretically the nominee of the Shabdung, was in fact the creature of one of the senior Penlops, who happened to be the most powerful at that time. As the Deb Raja owned his office to the support of the Penlop, he virtually functioned as the latter's mouthpiece.[11]

Before the arrival of the Shabdung on the scene, Bhutan was a group of small states ruled either by royal clans or by powerful monasteries. At all times, however, it was important that the government should be seen to be supporting religion. According to one scholar, legends appear to suggest that till as late as the 7th century of the Christian era Bhutan was being ruled by chiefs of Indian descent, who were under the tutelage of the Kings of Kamrup, the last great of whom was Bhaskarvarman, a contemporary of the Indian king Harshavardhan and the Chinese pilgrim Hiuen T'sang. Bhutan, however, became free from the tutelage of Kamrup after the death of Bhaskarvarman and Harshavardhan. Probably, the Bhutanese took advantage of the political confusion that arose after the Tibetan invasion of Magadha. Within the next one century or so, the people of Bhutan accepted Buddhism as their religion.[12] We have already seen in the preceding paragraphs as to how Bhutan came to be unified under these circumstances. It augured well for the future of the country.

Ethnic groups

Though Bhutan is a small country in terms of population and size, its multiplicity and variety are not impoverished by this smallness. A number of ethnic groups inhabit the small-sized mountain kingdom of

South Asia. An ethnic group has been defined as a social group "having a common national or cultural tradition", "denoting origin by birth or descent rather than nationality", relating to race or culture".[13]

3 main ethnic groups called the Sharchops, the Ngalops and the Nepalese constitute the population of Druk-yul. The Sharchops were the earliest inhabitants and they reside mainly in eastern Bhutan. Their origin can be traced to the tribes of north Burma and north-east India. The Ngalops were the migrants from Tibet and they brought Buddhism with them to the mountain Kingdom. The Nepalese, predominantly belonging to Hindu religion, came to Bhutan much later—in the late 19th century or the early 20th century. The bulk of them came to Bhutan in the early 20th century. Mostly they came as labourers to work in the inhospitable climate of southern Bhutan. All the 3 groups had their distinct identity based on culture and religion. The Ngalops gradually became the governing elite by subduing the Sharchops and also by integrating them through conversion to Buddhism and inter-marriages. The Nepalese were confined to the south not being allowed to migrate or own property in the upper regions. The ethnic distinction and separation is also reflected in the country's geographical zones to a very great extent. The Sharchops live mostly in eastern Bhutan; the Ngalops inhabit the western and central Bhutan; the Nepalese live in southern Bhutan.

The 3 ethnic groups remained separated from each other not only in the geographical context but also in the contexts of history and realpolitik. Despite the rigid power apex, each ethnic group was, to a very great extent, left to itself in the social and cultural contexts. The existing economy hardly facilitated any interaction between the people of any 2 regions. Ethnic groups were, thus, left to lead their traditional way of life. However, in matters relating to monastic order the entire Buddhist community was under some kind of a rigid control exercised by the ruling group of the Drukpas.[14] Attempts were made subsequently even to incorporate the Nepalese segment of the Bhutanese society into the mainstream of the national life. A large number of jobs and opportunities were provided to them, at times much more in terms of the size of their population. But from 1990, there increased alienation on the part of the Nepalese, which at times seem to be challenging the very unity and integrity of Bhutan as a modern nation state. Ethnic distinctions in Bhutan have, in fact, become a matter of serious study for researchers and academics in this region.

Language

Just as on the front of ethnicity, on the front of language also we find that multiplicity—perhaps in a greater degree—is the reality and smallness again is no hindrance. A large number of languages are spoken in Bhutan. The main language of Bhutan is the "Dzong language" or Dzongkha, which is taught at all schools and is written in classical Tibetan script, for print purposes. The handwritten script of Bhutan is known as "Juyig" and is entirely different from Tibetan handwriting which is known as "Ume".

Dzongkha may have its origin in classical Tibetan, it varies greatly in pronunciation. Prefixes and end-letters, which become mute in the high Tibetan language, are still spoken or at least heard in the Bhutanese pronunciation. Different dialects' pronunciation spoken in different districts varies widely. In the south-east of the country, the Mon and Khen languages of aboriginal inhabitants of the Himalaya are still alive. Significantly, these old languages are a striking linguistic mirror of the rich Bhutanese tradition comprising treasures of local legends, songs and plays. 6 of these languages or dialects belong to the Dzongkha group. They are as follows:

1. Dzongkha, the language of the Dzongs, spoken especially in western Bhutan and the common language of Bhutan;
2. Tapadamteng, spoken in the south-west, near Buxa ;
3. Laya Lingzhi, the shepherd language of the north-west in Laya and in Lingzhi;
4. Tshalingpa, spoken in the Tshali area of the Shongar district and in eastern Bhutan;
5. Dagpakha, a Tibetan dialect of the north-eastern border; and
6. Mira Sagtengpa, Tibetan dialect of Tashigang in the farthest east of Bhutan.

The following 7 dialects are said to be belonging to the so-called Khen languages:

1. Mangdikha, spoken in the Mangdi district (Tongsa);
2. Gungdekha, an archaic language of the south, originally without relation to Khenkha but today added to the Khen group;
3. Khenkha, spoken in the Khen district south of Tongsa;
4. Bumthangkha, spoken in Bumthang and in whole of central Bhutan;
5. Tsamangkha, spoken in the east and north-east on the eastern border of Kurto;

6. Kurtopkha, especially spoken in Kurto; and
7. Salabekha or Yangtsepakha, spoken in the Yangtse district as also in Tawang and in south-east Tibet.

These languages or dialects are said to be without script but they are now transcribed into Ucan.

In addition, there are two dialects belonging to the Mon-group:

1. Monpakha in the south and south-east; and
2. Sharchapkha, spoken in the east and the south-east, especially spoken in Tashigang and Dungsam.[15]

Palpably, Bhutan is a babel of tounges and it appears striking in view of its small size and population. However, one could safely say that there are four main languages in Bhutan today:

1. Dzongkha, spoken in the western and northern Bhutan. It has been made the official language of the Kingdom;
2. Bumthangkha spoken in central Bhutan;
3. Sarchapkha, spoken in eastern Bhutan; and
4. Nepali spoken in southern Bhutan.

While Dzongkha, Bumthangkha Sarchapkha are written in the Tibetan Ucan script, Nepali is written in the Devanagari script. Hindi is not unknown in urban areas, thanks to the exhibition of Hindi films. In offices, English is used extensively. Communication in English among the Bhutanese elite has been facilitated because of their education in English medium schools as also because of the communication between the Bhutanese and European and American tourists.

An interesting aspect of the Royal Government's education programme is the development of the Dzongkha language. In the traditional education provided by the monks, in classical Tibetan was used as the medium of instruction. However, different dialects in different parts of the kingdom at times made the communication among Bhutanese themselves—especially those who did not know English—difficult. With a view to making the communication among the people more convenient, as also with a view to having a common language for the administration, the spoken language of western Bhutan was refined and developed. With a view to making it the official language of the country, it came to be called Dzongkha (or the language of the Dzong). True, eventually, some eastern Bhutanese could speak Dzongkha better than the western Bhutanese themselves, it did not succeed in replacing Tibetan as the written language of the country till very recently. Not only has Dzongkha been designated as the official language of the country, there is a special department working on Dzonghka textbooks for use in all Bhutanese schools. Nevertheless, because of the newness of the language and also because of maintaining educational links with India, English is still the language of instruction to a very great extent.

Religion

Religion, of course, cannot be said to be as important in man's life as language. Whereas one can do without a religion, one's life would become immensely difficult without a language. It is, therefore, said that language is one of those ideas which have helped mankind civilize itself. But religion also occupies a place of paramount significance in man's life in many a Third World state. Religion assumes greater significance in the life of a man or a state, if religion becomes basis of the state at one point of time or another. Religion has been described as "the belief in a superhuman controlling power, esp. in a personal God or gods entitled to obedience and worship", "the expression of this in worship", "a particular system of faith and worship", "life under monastic vows".[16] Seen in the framework of this description, Bhutan could be said to be a religious state since the time of its unification under the leadership of the Shabdung, as we saw earlier. In fact, the impact of religion was far-reaching even before the arrival of the Shabdung on the scene.

Before the advent of Buddhism in Bhutan, there existed a religion which would always remain somewhat difficult to describe. "Bhutan's original religion has been called *Pon* and perhaps broadly falls in the category of Animism. One is inclined to believe that this original religion must be entirely based on nature worship".[17] With the arrival and impact of Buddhism, most of the rituals of Ponism got replaced, suppressed or superseded. But some aspects of nature worship which Ponism professed were duly incorporated in the Mahayana Buddhism which Guru Padmasambhava introduced in the 8th century AD. The religion known as Mahayana or Northern Buddhism continues to flourish freely and vigorously in Bhutan, as it does nowhere else in the world since the People's Republic of China took over Tibet in the 1950s. Only other country in South Asia, where Buddhism is given immense prominence is Sri Lanka. But the Buddhism is of the Hinayana (Theravada) sect. In yet another Asian country, Thailand, Theravada Buddhism is the state religion. Though Laos was declared officially a secular state in 1975, an estimated 58% of the population adhere to traditional Theravada Buddhism. In Combodia (Kampuchea), too, the traditional religion is Theravada Buddhism.[18] Thus, Bhutan stands incomparable on this count.

The religion of Bhutan today is basically and primarily a sect of Mahayana Buddhism allowed by the process of evolution to develop and establish distinct faith of the land, which may be called the national Church of Bhutan. To some, the real historical period of Bhutan begins with the introduction of Buddhism in the 7th century AD. Since then Buddhism has always played an important role both in Bhutan's history and people's life. Mentionably, religion and secular powers were not clearly separated till the 17th century, when Shabdung Ngawang Namgyal, as we saw, established a new dual system of government. To this day it is palpable that the *Je Khenpo*, the head of religious affairs in the kingdom, holds a prominent place in the social and cultural life of the Bhutanese people.

Albeit the two most sacred and historically significant Buddhist temple—Kyerchu and Byampsa—were built in the 7th century, it was not till the visit of great Indian saint Guru Padmasambhava (AD 746) that Buddhism took firm roots in Bhutan. Padmasambhava converted a king (Sendha) reigning in the Bumthang valley to Buddhism, after which the faith gradually spread over to other regions of Bhutan.

One significant feature of Guru Padmasambhava's religious policy was his incorporation of the Bon deities into the Buddhist pantheon, having, as the legend suggests, bound them through oaths not only to serve the Buddhist faith, but also in the process to become its protectors. This development had a significant psychological impact inasmuch as it lent a sense of continuity to the beliefs of the new adherents and satisfied the needs of their stage of consciousness.[19]

The growth of Buddhism in Bhutan was contributed by another incident—which occurred in Tibet—as well. With the emergence of the anti-Buddhist king Langdarma in the northern kingdom of Tibet, a wave of religious persecution and political turmoil shook the country. As a result, the 9th and 10th centuries witnessed an exodus of monks to Kham in eastern Tibet and Bhutan. In fact, the latter was quickly recognized as a *Balyul* (sacred hidden land of spiritual treasures) that had received the blessings of Guru Rimpoche. Among the umpteen monks and Tibetan religious preachers who took shelter in Bhutan, many rose to eminence through their mystic practices and contributed significantly to the several schools of later Buddhism in the Himalayan region. Significant among them were the Kadampa, the Kagyupda, the Sakyapa and the Gelugpa that emerged with the revival of the religion in Tibet in the 11th century. A special feature of the religious history of this period was the appearance of *Tertons* (Treasure-Discoverers) in Paro and Bumthang, who revealed, at predestined, opportune moments, texts and sacred objects hidden for posterity by Guru Padmasambhava and other saints.[20]

Another significant event occurred in the first half of the 13th century. A spiritual figure called Phajo Drukgom Zhigpo (1208-1276) reached Druk-yul. He is considered as a very significant figure in the kingdom because he was the forerunner of the Drukpa Kargyu traditions, which ultimately gained a place of great prominence in the country. Scarcely had Phajo Drukgom Zhigpo arrived in Bhutan when he had to face the hostility of the Lhapas, who were already firmly established in western Bhutan. However, Phajo Durkgom Zhigpo finally won in the struggle and married a woman from the Thimphu valley. He was blessed with 4 sons, who spread the Drukpa Kargyu traditions of the country. Nevertheless, the Lhapa school continued until the 17th century, when it was completely crushed by Shabdung Ngawang Namgyal.[21]

Though the Himalayan Kingdom of Bhutan has no written constitution, the core of the state there is represented through the Monarchy and Buddhism. We have already seen that the religion of Bhutan today is basically a sect of Mahayana Buddhism, allowed by the process to develop and establish a distinct faith of the land which may be called the National Church of Bhutan. The present-day Bhutanese belong mainly to the Nyingmpa and Kargyupa sects. The Drukpa sect of Buddhism is the real foundation of the national church of Bhutan today.[22]

In the religious scheme of the kingdom, some 5,000 Lamas[23] occupy a place of prime significance. They dominate and guide the religious life of the people. They are supposed to devote their entire life to prayer and meditation. They have no means of livelihood and they turn to depend upon the charity of the people. Relevantly, the Royal Government of Bhutan also makes contributions for the maintenance of the Lamas who run the numerous monasteries of the National Church, always housed in the dzongs of Bhutan (which are the centres of administration, politics and religion). The centre of activity of the Lamas is the monastery and almost every village of Bhutan has a monastery of its own. The trained Lamas take a leading part in numerous festivals throughout the year. More significantly, the Lamas are exempt from any kind of taxation.[24]

Doubtless, there has been some significant change on this front mainly due to the development on the economic front. B.S. Das, for instance, writes:

> Another significant social change has been in the age-old pattern of sending the brightest son to monkhood. Being a monk was not only considered a sign of prestige but an obligation. This practice is dying

out and the clergy's source of monkhood is drying up. Thus the economic development is changing the entire value system.[25]

Another group of writers observe:

> There are today three to four thousand monks. A few years ago, there were fifteen thousand. But even during the reign of Jigme Dorji Wangchuck, father to the present King Jigme Singye Wangchuck the demand for admission to the monastic life slackened. The late Monarch had reduced the subsidies to the state monasteries substantially. Instead of one-fourth of the state budget, the monks have received only five per cent from the treasury in the last few years. Even the private monasteries have only scant means at their disposal. Like the state monasteries, they live mainly on a share of the harvest of their tenants.[26]

Significantly, on way to mountains, one passes prayer-walls. Pious Buddhists have let stone tablets into them bearing the holy mantra, the invocations, "Om Mane Padme Hum" "Oh, thou jewel in the lotus", "Buddha is the heart of man". Where the long prayer-flags fly, printed with the same mantras the dwellings of the monks are not far away. According to the faith of the Lamas, the wind carries the words into space, to the Bodhisattvas, the men destined to Buddhahood who have chosen the sacrifice, the renunciation of Nirvana. By comparison, they want to save others from the wheel of reincarnation. Gratefully, people bring their offering to their images. In the "chorten", the shrines in memory of the Buddha, the copper prayer-wheels revolve. They are driven by the force of the rushing mountain streams. Murmuring, the monks gather for circumambulation of the sanctuary. Everything moves, so that the mantra is carried further.[27]

Buddhism, thus, is one of the strong conditioning forces in the Himalayan Kingdom of Bhutan. It belongs to the daily life of its inhabitants. The Bhutanese have refused to do away with their past and tradition like an old garment. And in no way Buddhism is a tolerated remnant of past centuries. It has penetrated deep into the psyche of the Bhutanese. We have already seen how the Mahayana sect of Buddhism—comprising mainly the Nyingmpapa and Kargyupa sects—is in existence in Bhutan only. This may have made the Bhutanese more motivated to preserve and protect their religions from all kinds of onslaughts—including modernization.

It should not, however, be forgotten that in south Bhutan, Hinduism is the main religion. Of course, some Nepalese, too, follow Buddhism. Of late, there have been complaints by some Hindus of south Bhutan that their religion is hindered by the state apparatus. However, these allegations have been found to be baseless and motivated by many objective observers.

Bhutan's culture

Culture has been defined as "the art and other manifestations of human intellectual achievement regarded collectively","refined understanding of this", "intellectual development", "the customs, civilization, and achievements of particular time or people" and "improvement by mental or physical training". [28] Thus,when we talk of any culture, we, willy-nilly, imply the linkage between the past and the present in various aspects of human life, like, dances, painting and printing, arts and crafts, architecture and the like. Culture occupies a place of prime significance in man's life in a variety of ways. It makes him appreciate all that was good in the past and also impels him to retain that in the present.

In Bhutan's context, we would try to delve into its dances, printing and painting, arts and crafts and architecture etc. with a view to having a clear perspective of its culture.

Dances: Bhutan still retains its folkloristic treasures having their roots in the dawn of history. It has been possible because the country had been able to maintain some kind of isolation to its cultural advantage. Revealingly, between 1774 and 1921, only 13 diplomatic missions visited the country. Visitors to Bhutan are generally enthusiastic about the gay festivals and folk dances as also the performances of religious mask dances. The art of folk dance is believed to be as old as Bhutan itself. It is a peculiar dance of the Bhutanese practised in every remote village and in the courts of the Dzongs. This dance is usually performed under the guidance of a dance-master. The dance-master also acts as a medieval choreographer during various important festivals.

The performace of the sword dance is also considered very important important in Bhutan. It is generally displayed by the headman of the village. The sword dance is joined by the round-dance of the men who for this event are dressed in ancient armour. The ancient armour consists of the sword and buckler shields, covered by rhino skin. These dances are generally performed either on the occasion of the New Year, which according to the Moon Calendar, falls in February or on the foundation anniversaries of a monastery. Significantly, on these occasions the religious mask dances as well as other dramatic plays——dating back to the 8th century——

are also performed. Relevantly, the costumes and the precious wooden masks belong to the monasteries. They are kept in the protective Deities' temples and given out only for dance ceremonies. Educationally, all these dances and mask plays are considered very significant. They try to drive the lesson home that the victory of good over evil is inevitable. They also stress the short duration of all mundane and the material values.

An orchestra of monks plays the accompanying music for the religious dances with big and small drums. Long and short trumpets and clashing cymbals are also used by these monks.[29]

Archery: Archery is a very popular and loved national sport in Bhutan. Each village has its own archery range. Relevantly, it is impossible to imagine any important festival taking place without a high spirited competition in archery. Year-round contests continue in the field of archery. Most of the Bhutanese try to excel in archery from their childhood and many of them are skilful archers in the true sense of the term. An outsider might be unnerved at the sight where competition goes on but a number of local stroll without any concern near the targets during competitions.

Other sports: Apart from archery, which has now become wellnigh known internationally, there are a number of national sports which preoccupy the Bhutanese. *Degor* is a traditional sport in which a round flat stone is thrown at a target. *Kenshey* (wrestling) is not uncommon. So is *Pung-do* (shotput). In *soksom* a spear, held at either end, is thrown at a target. In *khuru* the projectile is small and dart-like, with a sharp nail at one end and feathers at the other. In *sherey parey* (a contest of strength), one man holds the opponent, who must free himself in order to score victory.[30]

Among the sports, which the Bhutanese have accepted and adopted from outside, are soccer, basketball, volleyball, golf, badminton, tennis, table tennis and horse-racing. King Jigme Singye Wangchuck is himself an avid enthusiast of basketball and participates in it publicly. The King used to play soccer when he was the Crown Prince.

Printing and Painting

Ancient and old Bhutanese blockprints are, without doubt, mines of information on the early history of these regions. The best known printing sites were located in the Dzongs of Simthokha and Punakha. The Dzong of Punakha was once famous for editions of the Tibetan Holy Scripts. The wooden printing blocks were, however, generally destroyed by fire which also burnt the framework of architecture of the temples and houses. However, rare copies of the country's prints are now being collected for the Bhutan Museum.

The rock monastery of Bumda, situated above the Tiger's Den monastery in the north of the valley of Paro, takes special care of the art of painting. Temple halls and altar corners in Bhutan are often decorated with religious picture rolls. On the other hand, the Bhutanese painters are famous for their wall-paintings, including the series of Cosmic Mandals, which covers the walls right and left of the entrance of the temple of Paro Dzong or like the frescoes of the temple of the Protective Deities in Kunzangda in Bumthang.

It must be mentioned here that the Himalayan kingdom of Bhutan is also famous for its beautiful embroidery. In *Tankas,* which could be called religious scrolls, we have the best specimens of embroidered paintings of gods and goddesses in artful combination of colour. The *Tankas* involve a high degree of skill and artistic imagination.

The *Tankas* are available in various sizes and one of them is reproduced in colour to indicate the mastery of its artistic pattern. Goddess Tara and Guru Padmasambhava as also Lord Buddha are the usual deities depicted in *Tanka* paintings. Without doubt, the *Tanka* art is an ancestral inheritance; it is very much alive today; it is patronized by those who care for the culture of the state.

It would be of relevance to mention here that some of the masterpieces of wall-paintings depict the legends of Lord Buddha's life as also the events leading to the nirvana of Siddha Lutsoka, a Brahmin from Bengal. This, to a great extent, indicates the influence of India not only on Bhutan's art but also its religious philosophy. It is generally stated that the Ajanta methods have greatly influenced the techniques of applying colours on the walls as well as on the line drawing and composition of figures.

Needless to state, Bhutan is a treasure house of precious and colourful traditions. It is significant to note that despite all kinds of impact of modernization on the small kingdom, the Bhutanese have, by and large, preserved their cultural heritage in the fields of printing and painting. Perhaps, it is because of this, along with other factors, of course, that Bhutan and the Bhutanese have succeeded in maintaining and retaining their identity.[31]

Bhutanese arts and crafts

Both India and China (especially its Tibetan part) have influenced Bhutan's art and craft. Bhutan is well known for it articles of brass and bronze. Bhutan's art industry covers a wide range of activity, beginning with artistic production of objects of gold, silver and copper. It includes production of steel weapons like swords and daggers. Thimphu and other centres of culture like Paro have been from ancient times producing crafts which had been produced in Indian religious cities like Varanasi. But the indelible imprint of Bhutan was always visible on the Bhutanese products. One example of this special art of Bhutan has been reproduced in colour along with 3 miniature paintings of Lord Buddha, Goddess Tara and Guru Padmasambhava.

Moreover, production of temple bells, swords, daggers and knives in charateristic and distinct Bhutanese designs could also be said to be the outcome of excellent craftsmanship. Indigenous methods were used to extract steel from charcoal iron in olden days. The Bhutanese craftsmen have also excelled in bronze casting and fine metal works of all types. Probably, in the early 16th century, a bronze foundry operated in the Punakha Dzong for production of bronze casting for which Bhutan has become famous. India's influence seems palpable on this front as well.

Another Bhutanese industry centres round the manufacture of casting bells with very fine tones. The composition used for the best bells includes a large quantity of silver. However, these bells are made of small size. The largest bell is not more than 24 inches in diameter. Bhutanese women have an old tradition of producing not only woven strips of cotton, but also of sheep's wool, which is rain-proof and wind-proof. Weaving, in fact, is the national industry of every household. It may be seen as a cottage industry, where considerable art is displayed in producing designs and patterns, which rank as the speciality of the country. In fact, every Bhutanese home has a room meant for weaving in which wool, silk and cotton textiles are produced along with floor carpets.

Beautiful needle-work pictures of saints produced on hanging banners at display in various monasteries is another special feature of Bhutan's art and craft. Apparently, innumerable pieces of coloured silk and brocades are applied in a most artistic manner with elaborate stitches of all kinds. On the other hand, an artistic industry is based on the use of split cane. Excellent baskets are produced in this field. Apart from basket weaving, one comes across the production of mats, finely woven of split cane. Apart from being durable, they are amazingly fine and soft and flexible. They can be rolled up into a quite small space.[32]

In Bhutan, great encouragement and patronage was provided since time immemorial to all kinds of industries, especially in the spheres of arts and craft. It augured well for their growth and progress. The non-colonization of Bhutan, on the other hand, contributed to the well-being of the art and craft industries in the kingdom. Without doubt, Bhutan had succeeded in making its mark in this field.

Architecture

Bhutan seems to be very rich in the sphere of architecture. In fact, the architectural forms in Bhutan are quite diverse. Chortens (stupas), mani-walls, temples, monasteries, fortresses, palaces and village houses constitute a landscape, quite unique to Bhutan. Chortens are erected in the memory of an eminent lama or to protect against evil spirits at dangerous places such as crossroads and passes. They are of 3 styles: huge stone chortens (often white-washed), small stone chortens (common throughout central and eastern Bhutan, often protected by a wooden superstructure), and chortens whose outer structure is a square stone tower with a red stripe at the upper level and shingle roof. The third kind of chorten is primarily widespread in western Bhutan. Some of the chortens are linked together by mani-walls. These are stone walls that support a multitude of stones carved with sacred formulas. However, mani-walls may also stand by themselves without chortens.

Wood is used in good quantity in Bhutan's architecture. Windows have distinctive trefoil-shaped tops and elaborate lintels, which are painted with geometrical motifs. In olden times, the use of nails was unknown but has of late become more common. Though fires frequently destroy temples, monasteries, fortresses and houses, they are generally rebuilt in their original mode.

Temples are usually plain and simple one-to-two storied buildings with a wide red stripe at the upper level of the walls and a glided roof ornament. They may also contain a small courtyard. Inside the temple the walls are covered with paintings and the space is generally divided by pillars into an antechamber and a shrine. One of the earliest forms of the Bhutanese architecture, they have survived commendably till date.

As for the Bhutanese monasteries (gompa), these are of two architectural types: the cluster type and the dzong type. Probably, the cluster type is more ancient. It consists of a core of one or two temples, around which small houses of habitation and meditation are built for the monks who stay there. A monastery of dzong type is built like a fortress with a main tower housing many temples and a surrounding outer wall that serves as habitats for the monks.

The Bhutanese fortress, the castlelike dzong, with its gently tapering walls, classic lines, large courtyards and beautiful galleries, in fact dates back to the 7th century. They were designed and constructed in such a manner that they were self-sufficient and could withstand siege. Its main purpose was to hold off potential attacks by the Tibetans and the British from the north and the south respectively.

The basic pattern of a dzong is a main tower (tuse) and a courtyard, surrounded by walls, that houses monks' quarters, kitchens and administrative offices. Gasa Dzong and Kimtokha Dzong fall under this category. Very few dzongs, however, strictly follow this pattern. The buildings of palaces, on the other hand, seem to have coincided with the advent of the monarchy at the beginning of the 20th century. Found mainly in Bumthang-Tongsa area, their basic pattern is very similar to that of a dzong. However, palaces have much less severe architecture than dzongs. Relevantly, they are profusely decorated with woodwork and even the outer walls are pierced by numerous beautifully carved and gaily painted windows.

Significantly, the dzongs have all been built to a general pattern handed down from generation to generation. In fact, no plans are drawn and no nails used. As late as 1962-70, when the Tashichho Dzong in Thimphu was rebuilt to house the state's government, this time-honoured tradition was faithfully followed. Within the framework of this ancient pattern, the architecture of each dzong varies in harmony with the surrounding terrain.[33]

It is, in fact, heartening to note that the Royal Government of Bhutan has shown its seriousness in continuing and preserving the architectural heritage. As on other fronts, Bhutan is determined to maintain its identity in the region and the world. Successive 5-year Plans of the kingdom, including the present one, have allocated funds for the protection of these national treasures and for the fostering of the ancient skills of building and design.

Food habits

The distinguishing Bhutanese diet comprises rice, dried beef, or pork and chillies sometimes cooked with dasthi (soft white cheese made from cow's milk with a view to giving a special flavour). The preference for chillies on the part of Bhutanese is quite well known. Bright and red chillies for the purpose of drying are kept on the roofs of houses in Bhutan and is a rather common sight in the kingdom.

Sooja (tea) is the most popular beverage. It was originally made by every household from indigenous leaves. Its preparation now, however, has become wellnigh a cottage industry and takes the form of tea balls called *jhari*. The required quantity of leaves is left in water and allowed to boil. Once the desired and common colour is obtained through heat, the liquid is transferred to a vessel (which is generally made of bamboo or wood). Now butter, salt or soda is mixed with it. Occasionally, milk is also mixed for the purpose of adding flavour to it. Finally, the tea or *sooja* is poured into kettle, and is now ready to be served.[34]

The food habits of the southern Bhutanese, however, differ from the central, western and eastern Bhutanese. The Southerners' food habits generally resemble these of the ethnic Nepalese of Nepal and Sikkim and Darjeeling. They generally prefer rice, mutton curry and the meat of buffalo.

Dress habits

More often than not, the Bhutanese are distinguished from the rest of the people by their typical dress. The official dress (which is also worn by most of the Bhutanese) in the kingdom is *gho*. The *gho* is tied around the waist by a woollen or cotton belt. The belt is called *kera*. A pouchlike fold in the front of *gho* substitutes for a pocket to keep various objects. A multipurpose dagger, generally used for slicing betel nuts or chopping wood, is tucked into the belt. A non-Bhutanese coming into contact with a Bhutanese in this typical dress might get frightened in the first go. But it takes little time to discover that the Bhutanese are peace-loving and violence generally does not fit into their psyche.

Women in Bhutan wear *kira*, a long robe, but fixed near the shoulders with a pair of silver brooches, or komas, and held together at the waist by a broad cloth belt, called *kera*. *Tyogo*, a loose-sleeved shirt is worn over the *kira*. Bhutanese women are fond of various kinds of necklaces.

However, in southern Bhutan, predominated by the Nepalese, the dress pattern is different. Men and women generally wear the typical Nepalese costumes or shirts and trousers and saris and blouses and salwars and kameezes etc. There has been serious resentment on the part of ethnic Nepalese against wearing *gho* and *kira*. However, Nepalese men and women living outside southern Bhutan seem to have accepted *gho* and *kira* without demur.

National Anthem

The Kingdom's national anthem praises the country and the protector who guards the teachings of the dual system. The ruler is described as "precious" and "glorious". While it talks of the flourishing doctrine of

Buddha, it wishes peace and happiness for the people. The exact words of the national anthem are as follows:

In the Thunder Dragon Kingdom
Adorned with sandalwood
The protector who guards the
Teachings of the dual system
He, the precious and glorious ruler,
Causes dominion to spread
While the unchanging person abides
in constancy
As the doctrine of the Buddha
flourishes
May the sun of peace and happiness
shine on the people.[35]

Summing-up

To sum up, we can safely suggest that though Bhutan is a small and landlocked country, it is immensely beautiful and attractive. Anyone with any sense of appreciating beauty and nature is bound to be attracted to Bhutan. Many Western tourists are thrilled at the sight of Bhutan. Likewise, many tourists from the underdeveloped world find the country so simple and yet so attractive.

True, Bhutan was not colonized by the British colonial masters in India and to that extent it trails behind its giant neighbours in terms of education, modernization etc. But the very fact that such a small country and the people could maintain and retain their identity against heavy odds adds to that country and its people a pride. Bhutan has achieved a regional and international personality of a peaceful, friendly, stable and non-controversial country. In any case Bhutan's history from its unification to the present day is fascinating and also shows how the people of India and Bhutan had interacted in the past.

The mountain kingdom's richness in the spheres of art, architecture, paintings and sports etc. is immense. Bhutan has made great strides in various spheres of life and they are bound to cause heart-burning among many. As such, powers that be in Bhutan are cautious against fast economic and political development. And, yet, Bhutanese have no grouse against their governing elite on the economic front. Most of the Bhutanese, if anything, seem satisfied with the existing socio-economic system.

Notes and References

1. Earlier Bhutan's population was estimated to be about 1.4 million. But of late authorities of Bhutan insist that their country's population is around 6,00,000. King Jigme Singye Wangchuck told me in an exclusive interview in October 1990 at Tashichho Dzong in Thimphu. Also see *Kuensel*, Thimphu, 15 June 1991, 2.
2. Manorama Kohli, *India and Bhutan: A Study in Interrelations 1772-1910*, Munshiram Manoharlal Publishers Pvt. Ltd., New Delhi, 1982, 1.
3. Nari Rustomji, *Bhutan: The Dragon Kingdom in Crisis*, Oxford University Press, Delhi, 1978, 5.
4. Dasho Rigzin Dorji, *A Brief Religious, Cultural and Secular History of Bhutan*, The Asia Society Galleries, New York, 1989, 9.
5. Nari Rustomji, n.3, 9.
6. Aung San Suu Kyi, *Let's Visit Bhutan*, Burke Publishing Company Limited, London, 1985, 9-12.
7. See Manorama Kohli, n.2, 2.
8. See Dasho Rigzin Dorji, n.4, 9-10.
9. Nari Rustomji, n.3, 5-6.
10. Aung San Suu Kyi, n.6, 20-23.
11. Nari Rustomji, n. 3, 6.
12. Manorama Kohli, n.2, 6.
13. *The Concise Oxford Dictionary of Current English*, Oxford University Press, Delhi, 1990, 401.
14. B.S. Das,"Economic Development and Social Change in Bhutan" in Urmila Phadnis, S.D. Muni and Kalim Bahadur, eds., *Domestic Conflicts in South Asia; vol. 2. Economic and Ethnic Dimensions*, South Asian Publishers New Delhi, 1986,84.
15. Nagendra Singh, *Bhutan: A Kingdom In The Himalayas* (Revised Second edition), Thomson Press India Limited, New Delhi, 1978, 65-67.
16. *The Concise Oxford Dictionary Of Current English*, n.13, 1015.
17. Nagendra Singh, n.15, 69.
18. See J. Denis Derbyshire and Ian Derbyshire, *Political Systems of the World*, Allied Publishers Limited, New Delhi, 1990.
19. Dasho Rigzin Dorji, n.4, 10.
20. Ibid., 10-11.
21. Ibid., 11.
22. Nagendra Singh, n.15,73.
23. V.H.Coelho, *Sikkim and Bhutan*, Indian Council of Cultural Relations, New Delhi, 1967,81.
24. Nagendra Singh, n.15,73-74.
25. B.S.Das,"Economic Development And Social Change In Bhutan", paper presented at the seminar on "Domestic Conflicts in South Asian States: Emerging Trends", Centre for South, Southeast and Central Asian Studies, School of International Studies, Jawaharlal Nehru University, New Delhi on 18-20 October 1984,21.
26. Gisela Bonn And Giselher Wirsing, *India And The Subcontinent: An Introduction To India, Pakistan, Bangladesh, Nepal, Sikkim, Bhutan*, Oxford & IBH Publishing Co, New Delhi, 1974, 105.
27. Ibid., 105-6.
28. *The Concise Oxford Dictionary of Current English*, n.13, 282.
29. Nagendra Singh, n.15, 67-8.
30. The Royal Government of the Kingdom of Bhutan, *Bhutan: Himalayan Kingdom*, Thimphu, 1979,16.

31. Nagendra Singh, n.15, 68-9.
32. Ibid., 61-5.
33. See Dasho Rigzin Dorji, n. 4, 25-7 and The Royal Government of the Kingdom of Bhutan, n.30, 21.
34. Dasho Rigzin Dorji, Ibid., 27-8.
35. See Ibid., 7.

2

Political Economy

The concept of political economy today occupies a place of great significance in the realm of comparative political analysis. It is, to a very great extent, the key to understanding, explaining and analysing a political system. It is because of this significance that a new approach called the political economy approach has been introduced to the study of comparative political analysis both in the developed and the developing countries of the world. The study of the political economy of any country, to a very great extent, throws light on the stability or otherwise of the political system *per se*.

Comprehending the term

It is time and place to have a clear view of the concept itself, its manifestations and connotations. The term "Political economy" has been described as "economics (as an academic study)".[1] It has also been defined as "the study of the economic aspects of government".[2] It has been viewed as "the study of the way in which a government influences or organizes a nation's wealth".[3]

Before the 19th century, the term was used to refer to the study of economics in general, but almost entirely in terms of national economies. Later usage, however, narrowed the term to allude to the study of economic policy, the linkage between, political and economic factors in public policy and related matters.[4] Roger Scruton has dwelt upon the term in the following words:

> In contrast to domestic economy, political economy studies the economic behaviour and interest of the entire state. The term was introduced in 1613 by A. de Monchrestien, and became established in English usage with James Steuart's *Inquiry into the Principles of Political Economy, 1767*. It survives from subsequent eighteenth and nineteenth century usage, but retains the word 'political', an implication

that factors other than economic may be relevant to questions of political economy.[5]

He has very rightly focused that:

> Welfare economics is an example of a theory of political economy, which attempts to build into its conception of 'welfare' some idea of the 'politically acceptable' which is not just reducible to the 'economically efficient'. The term is current among Marxists and thinkers of the New Left in order to denote systems of economics which take seriously the political implications of the science, and which (in contrast to 'mainstream economics') attempt describe arrangements which are radically different from the capitalist market. ..[6]

To sum up the discussion on the concept of political economy, thus, we may say that it has assumed significance in view of the fact that it studies the economy of the state as opposed to the study of economy of home. It is also significant to note that at one point of time distinctions were made between a science and an art of political economy, the former being regarded by many economists as a body of pure theory of universal validity, the latter as the application of the theory to the problems of the nitty-gritty of the world with or without the aid of other social sciences. Besides, the term has also assumed importance in view of the fact that it focuses on progressive and welfare economy, as opposed to the general economics. In a word, the politics and the economics of the state are linked together in political economy.

Some special features of Bhutan's political economy

While discussing some of the special features of Bhutan's political economy, we will do well to have a bird's eye view of its geographical features because they are willy-nilly interlinked and effect each other. Bhutan is a very small and immensely beautiful country of 46,500 sq kilometres (18,000 square miles). It lies in the eastern Himalaya and has natural mountain barriers. To the north, it is separated from Tibet by the Himalayan range. Its western and eastern limits, which border on Indian territory, are also marked by mountain barriers. To the south, the point at which the foothills rise from the plains separate Bhutan from the Indian states of West Bengal and Assam. Bhutan has a great range of climatic conditions, from the subtropical to the arctic cold and freezing snows of the high reaches of the Himalayas.[7]

Nature seems to have divided Bhutan into 3 zones:1) the southern foothills, 2) the northern Himalayan borderland and 3) the central zone. The southern foothills, where dense, tropical forests are to be found, rise about 1,500 metres (nearly 5,000 feet) above the plains and stretch from about 20 kilometres (12.5 miles) into Bhutan. To the north of Bhutan, the Himalayan range is not, in general, as high as it is further west, but it still contains peaks rising above 7,500 metres (24,500 feet). In this border area, there are about 6 major passes all of which lead from Bhutan to Tibet.[8]

The most important area of the country is the central zone. It consists of much of the cultivable land and therefore the greater part of the population. This region is divided into quite narrow river valleys by mountain ranges which run from north to south. The Black Mountain range is the most notable among these, as it is traditionally regarded as the dividing line between the western and eastern Bhutan. The main valleys in the western part of the state are Thimphu (where the modern capital is located), Punakha (the old winter capital), Paro, Ha and Wangdiphodrang. The eastern Bhutan comprises the valley districts of Bumthang, Tongsa and Mongar among others. Still further, east Bhutan has the districts of Tashigang and Samdrup Jongkhar.[9]

Significantly, Bhutan is a country of great physical beauty. The valleys are green, fertile and well-watered by rivers and streams. Both the Pho Chu and Mo Chu rivers run through the Punakha valley, while the Paro Chu and Ha Chu flow through the valleys of these names. Likewise, there are rivers in the country's other main valleys. Mentionably, more than half the area of Bhutan is still covered by forests. Oak and other deciduous trees grow at the lower altitudes. Higher up, there are coniferous trees. Above the grasslands, there are the alpine tundra (treeless area) and snowy peaks of the Himalayas.[10]

Mentionably, Southern Bhutan presents a picture quite unlike the popular idea of a Himalayan state. Its hot tropical forests and savannahs (grassy plains) are filled with elephants, tigers and buffaloes and with the golden langur monkeys which are to be found only in Bhutan. The rainfall is heavy and temperatures are also, indeed, much higher, averaging between 15 degrees celsius and 30 degrees celsius all the year round. In some of the central valleys, too, summer temperatures can rise to almost tropical levels, though the winters are very cold and the autumn and spring months are pleasantly cool.[11]

The primacy of agriculture

Bhutan is primarily and predominantly an agricultural country, where a large number of population (93% labour force) is involved in agriculture for its livelihood. The Bhutanese peasants' lives have not changed greatly since the time of their country's unification in the 17th century. They still cultivate their fields using traditional methods. There are few farming tools and ox-drawn ploughs are clusmy. Agriculture creates a need for labour which has led to practice of the sharing out land between relatives for short periods. People from other places also come to help in the fields in return for a share of the crop. In the old days, there were serfs or peasants who lived on the land and were made to work on it. Curiously, if the land was taken over by a owner, the serfs came under his authority.[12]

However, nowadays there are no great landowners and most people work on their own plots. The government is buying up large estates from the monasteries, to which they belonged traditionally. The government thereafter is distributing them among the people who have been cultivating them. In the event, there are a few peasant families who do not own land. Any family desirous of holding some land can petition the King and the request is invariably acceded to. Obviously, this argues well for the welfare-oriented political economy in the Himalayan kingdom.

Besides, the Government of Bhutan runs agricultural development programmes. Irrigation, improved methods of cultivation, distribution of seed and fertilizer, and help with the transport of harvested crops are among the ways in which the government assists the peasants. However, it is rather difficult to bring about rapid changes. Traditional ways still continue in the sphere of animal husbandry, as in that of agriculture. The number of animals that can be bred in Bhutan is limited by the available feed and pasture-land. Cattle are grazed in the central valleys during the summer, while the yak and sheep are taken up to the high alpine pastures. As the severe winter sets in, the yak and sheep are brought down to lower altitudes. In the valleys, the cattle are kept in the stalls.[13]

Advantageous land-man ratio

Bhutan presents the happiest land and man ratio in the whole of South Asia. The ratio is better in comparison to many other Asian states. When its population was estimated about 1.446 million in 1985, its population density per kilometre was 31. Now that its population is estimated to be around .6 million, its population density per kilometre would be reduced to 12.90. The land and man ratios in other Asian states based on the 1985 figures are as follows:

Table: 1[14]

State	Population density per square kilometre
Afghanistan	28
Bangladesh	723
Brunei	41
Burma (now Myanmar)	56
Cambodia	40
People's Republic of China	110
India	239
Indonesia	90
Japan	326
North Korea	169
South Korea	440
Laos	17
Malaysia	48
Maldives	600
Mongolia	1
Nepal	123
Pakistan	127
Singapore	4,195
Sri Lanka	249
Taiwan	544
Thailand	102
Vietnam	188

It would be relevant here to mention that Bhutan has of late been insisting that its population stands only at 0.6 million. In an interview to an Indian weekly, King Jigme Singye Wangchuk stated:

> . . .Also, our official population figure is 1.3 million, but actually, it is closer to 6,00,000. People think Bhutan deliberately gave a wrong figure in the Seventies, when we joined the United Nations. But in truth, someone had told my father that if he gave a figure less than one million, we would not be taken seriously by the UN.[15]

Per capita income

Bhutan's per capita income in 1988 was $ 190, according to the

World Bank Atlas for 1990.[16] According to the World Bank reports of 1983 the figure was $ 80 and, as such, Bhutan was described as a least developed country.[17] Needless to say, these figures were of relevance and significance when Bhutan's population was estimated to be around 1.4 million or more. It was not for nothing that King Jigme Singye Wangchuk said in an interview:

> Yes. Incidentally, our per capita income is over $400, not $150 as projected. It might be the highest in South Asia.[18]

Also Significant in this context becomes another statement of the Druk Gyalpo (King) about economic development and per capita income. In an interview the Druk Gyalpo averred:

> No. We consider the per capita contentment of people the yardstick of development. Gross national happiness is more important than gross national product. We are aiming at a perfect blend of modernisation and culture.[19]

An authoress has rightly observed that much publicity has been given to this remark made by King Jigme Singye Wangchuck but that perhaps "sums up the practical way in which the Bhutanese seem to be handling the choices and problems which confront them as they take their place among the nations of the twentieth century".[20]

A welfare state

Bhutan has, by any large, grown into a welfare state. A welfare state is a political system where the state assumes responsibility for the promotion and the protection of the social security and welfare of its citizens by universal medical care, insurance against sickness and unemployment, old age pensions, family allowances, public housing etc. on a "cradle to grave" basis. Social insurance was introduced in Germany in the 1880s and in Britain before 1914, but a comprehensive scheme (and the term "welfare state") was first adapted by the British Labour Party Government of 1945-50. Similar provision is made by the states in many other parts of the world, including Western Europe and Scandinavia. Critics of the welfare state assert that its beneficiaries become less industrious and self-reliant. It is also alleged that the element of personal choice is so restricted and that of state control so enhanced as to create a modern version of serfdom. However, despite these criticisms, the trend today is towards more and more welfare in various political systems of the world.

Paul Matthews, who worked as the Resident Coordinator of UN Systems in Bhutan for a tenure of 4 years, is of the opinion that Bhutan has become a welfare and service state. In an interview to *Kuensel,* Bhutan's national weekly newspaper, he said:

> I think that identity is not only related to cultural patterns, but also the quality of life. Here is a country which is, by and large, well run and well administered, where social services are made available to all corners of the country free of charge or virtually free of charge, where citizens can aspire to improve living standards, and where there is a common concern for the beautiful country that has been inherited and a desire to maintain it. I think Bhutan has an opportunity even to find an important role for itself on the world stage, as a world leader in environmental issues. For example, if you have a country that is environmentally intact and where people care for their physical environment, where they enjoy equitable services and opportunities, I think that itself finds a very distinctive and enviable identity among the developing countries.[21]

During my visits to Bhutan in October 1990, and October 1991, I learnt that Bhutan's Royal Government has been giving generous help to farmers to improve their productivity. The production of apple, orange, potato, cardamom,etc. has increased tremendously. Besides, education, board, lodging and stationery are free in Bhutan's schools and colleges. Bhutan's hospitals provide free treatment.[22] The emergence of Bhutan as a welfare state in this part of the globe, if anything, is heartening and reassuring. One hopes more and more countries of this region would try to follow the example set by Bhutan. Could the recent developments in Pakistan on the economic front be said to be a case in point? One will have to wait for some time to find an answer to this question. But attempts seem to be afoot. Bhutan might emerge as a trend-setter in this regard.

Constraints of industrialization

In Bhutan, industrialization is subject to a number of constraints. There is a shortage of local labour. Managerial experts and entrepreneurs are few. Besides, the size of the market at home is limited. The government's industrial policy, formulated taking these factors into account, aims both at optimal utilization of indigenous raw materials and at the gradual development of an industrial and commercial infrastructure. Incentives to private enterprise include financial assistance in the form of 3 to 5 years' tax holidays and low interest loans, and the provision of facilities such as water supply, power and communication in specially established industrial estates. There are at present 3 industrial estates, at Phuntsholing, Gaylegphug and Samdrup Jongkhar.

Unlike so many countries of the world, Bhutan faces underemployment. Shortages of manpower, both skilled and unskilled, are currently met by importing labour from neighbouring countries. This in itself is a big problem, for a large number of labourers try to overstay in Bhutan even after their contracts expire. Plenty of land and availability of several other facilities also seem to make them overstay. This, at times, results in law and order problems in the kingdom.

Trade policy of Bhutan is at a stage when the country must buy a great deal of materials from outside. It is oriented towards narrowing the gap between imports and exports. With a view to helping the Bhuatanese farmers obtaining the maximum benefit from their produce, a government organization has been set up to purchase and collect produce for export. On the other hand, steps have been taken to create facilities for storing, packing and grading agricultural produce, and an Export Division has been set up at Calcutta (India) to find and develop export markets. Besides, licences are issued to traders at nominal rates and low-interest loans are made available. With the launching of a number of business and industrial training programmes, the shortage of local expertise appears likely to be alleviated in the near future.[23]

Forestry and minerals

More than two-thirds of the kingdom is covered with valuable forest. At lower altitudes, sal is plentiful. In the central belt, the hills are cloaked with oak which gives way in the higher reaches to conifers, pine, fir, suruce and larch. The potential for forestry development is considerable. With the construction of highways to the south, exploitation of this natural resource has become quite feasible. Priority is being accorded to the survey and demarcation of forests and to the introduction of the most modern methods of harvesting and reforestation. In the last decade, a number of small private industries have sprung up which include saw-milling operation and factories manufacturing furniture, matches, tea chests and pencil slats. In the public sector, the government is planning a commercial plywood unit in the near future. Studies have revealed the possibility of a range of other forestry-related industries, such as paper, resin, turpentine and lemon-grass oil.

Until the early 1960s, no geological investigations had been undertaken in the kingdom. With the assistance of the Geological Survey of India, systematic surveys and searches for economically exploitable minerals were started. The country's mineral resources have been found to include dolomite, limestone, coal, graphite, gypsum, marble, lead, zinc and copper. Of these, only dolomite, limestone and coal have been mined to date. Because of the necessity of the large amounts of capital, all mineral-based industries are government-operated. They include a cement factory near Samchi, which has made Bhutan self-sufficient in cement and produce surplus for export, and projects for mining marble and slate. Plans for the processing of lead and zinc, graphite and magnesium carbonate are presently under consideration.[24]

Hydroelectric power

The harnessing of Bhutan's swift-flowing rivers and waterfalls has been, not without reason, seen as an important key to the country's economic growth from the beginning of the first development plan. The cornerstone of the hydroelectric development in Bhutan is the huge Chukha project which lies on the main route between Phuntsholing and Thimphu. With the commissioning of the first 2 units of the Chukha Hydel Project during 1986, Bhutan substantially increased its electricity generation, and became a significant exporter of electricity to India. The final 2 units of the Chukha project were commissioned during 1988. Total installed capacity at 1988-89 was 346.4 MW, of which 341.2 MW were generated from hydro power, 4.8 MW from diesel generating stations and 0.4 MW from micro hydel. In the 12 months ending June 1989, total electricity generation was 1,544 MW of which 1,541.1 MW was from the Chukha plant. A total of 1,396 (90% of the electricity generation) was exported to India. Total sales to consumers in Bhutan amounted to 123.3 MW representing consumption per head of population of only 90 units. Some 20 towns and 171 villages have now been electrified with total consumers being 14,092.[25]

In November 1990, the Government of India and the Royal Government of Bhutan signed a Memorandum of Understanding for Chukha II and Chukha III hydroelectric projects. The Memorandum was signed by L.L. Mehrotra, Secretary in the Ministry of External Affairs and Dasho Karma Letho, Bhutan's Ambassador in India, in the presence of His Majesty King Jigme Singye Wangchuck of Bhutan and Prime Minister Chandra Shekhar of India. An official spokesman said the Memorandum of Understanding represents a significant milestone in Indo-Bhutan relations.[26]

The detailed project reports for both the projects are to be prepared with Indian expertise at an estimated cost of Rs. 10 crores. When completed, the projects would make a major contribution to the welfare and economic development of the people of Bhutan. Significantly, the surplus power generated by the projects would be exported to India. Naturally, the outstanding success of the Chukha Project (Project 1) has generated keen interest in Bhutan for setting up 2 more large hydro projects on the same Wangchu river—Chukha Phase 2 and 3.

Chukha 2, called the Tala hydroelectric project, is a run-of-the river scheme and is expected to have an installed capacity of 1000 MW. Its estimated cost will be around Rs. 800 crores. The Wangchu Reservoir scheme (Chukha 3) involves the construction of a rock-filled dam and is estimated to have an installed capacity of 500-600 MW. The preliminary cost estimates will be around Rs. 800 crores.[27]

Several major bilateral projects have been executed in Bhutan by Indian agencies on a turnkey basis. The most important of these projects is the 336 MW Giant Chukha Hydel Project designed and built entirely by Indian engineers and technicians. Relevantly, the Chukha Hydel Project is one of the biggest and the most prestigious projects undertaken abroad with India's assistance. It has been completed at a relatively low cost of Rs. 247 crores. This project is a triumph of Indian engineering. It involved the construction of a dam to divert the waters of the Wangchu river in West Central Bhutan through a huge tunnel (inside the heart of a mountain), leading to a powerhouse, also built completely underground. These technically demanding specifications were negotiated successfully by Indian engineers and technicians. Over 8,000 technicians and workers were engaged in this endeavour.

The Chukha Hydel Project was inaugurated in October 1988 by the Indian President, R. Venkataraman, and King Jigme Singye Wangchuck. Today, the Project has emerged as the most important revenue source for the Royal Government of Bhutan.[28] G.N. Rao, who was appointed the Managing Director of the proposed Chukha Project Corporation by King Jigme Singye Wangchuck, and who was very much involved in the building up of the project from the beginning, said recently that the project was "one of the most economically constructed projects in the world". With the close coöperation, he had received from the Royal Government, especially Project Acting Chairman Lyonpo Dawa Tsering, Rao added that the project was completed far more efficiently than it would have been possible in most other countries.[29]

Transport and communications

Till recently, the only wheeled vehicles in the mountainous kingdom were simple carts used to carry heavy loads, the only methods of transportation being ponies, mules, yaks and of course, feet. In contrast, today, an impressive web of roads curls up the steep valley walls and across breathtaking mountain passes, reducing the span of journeys from several weeks to a few hours. Mentionably, work on the first road, from Phuntsholing near the Indian border, to Paro and Thimphu in the central highlands, began in January 1960. With as many as 10,000 people working on construction at a time, 145-km road was completed within 15 months. About 1,550 km of highway and arterial roads cross Bhutan today. Routes run north into the western and central regions, not only from Phuntsholing, but also from Gaylegphug, and into the east from Samdrup Jongkhar. A major east-west road across the Pele La Pass in the Black Mountains links the valleys of Ha, Wangdiphodrang, Punakha, Tongsa and Tashigang.

Significantly, the Royal Government Transport Service started functioning in 1962 with a view to carrying both passengers and goods. Its network spreads across the country and to the Indian Border towns in Assam and West Bengal. Since 1976, a new organization called the Transport Syndicate has been operating the carrier service.[30]

By June 1989, there were 2,280 kilometres of motorable roads in the kingdom, of which 1,761 kilometres were black topped. In 1988, there were a total of 7,002 registered vehicles in Bhutan. Bus Transport combines both public and private enterprises. Government buses carried1.2 million passengers in 1988-89.[31] Without doubt, the importance of road transport has grown with the expansion of the road network; there are now extensive bus services between most centres in the kingdom.

Civil Aviation arrived in Bhutan with the establishment of Druk Air Corporation and its commencement of operations in 1983 on the Paro-Calcutta sector. Services were extended to cover the Paro-Dhaka sector in 1986, Paro-Delhi in 1988, Paro-Bangkok and Paro-Kathmandu in 1989. A total of 8,700 passengers were carried by Druk Air during 1987, an increase of nearly 12% over the 1986 figure.[32]

In 1962, Bhutan began its regular postal service. Today it serves all but the most remote areas. Postal and other communication facilities were limited prior to 1962. Telephone services have also been considerably expanded and telex exchanges installed in Thimphu and Phuntsholing. An extensive civil wireless system also exists servicing many remote centres. Post offices in Bhutan handled a total of 6.4 million items of mail during 1988 of which 3.2 million were domestic, 2.8 million were of neighbouring countries and 0.3 million overseas.[33] A microwave station connected to the Indian network in Hashimara was installed in Thimphu. Wireless communication, teleprinter and telegraph services are also available.[34]

Till recently, the media was still in a fledging state. A small radio station in Thimphu broadcast local news and educational programmes twice a week in Dzongkha, English and Nepali. However, the radio station at Thimphu, the first short wave broadcasting station of Bhutan, began broadcasting programme from 15 March 1991. An example of Indo-Bhutanese friendship, the entire complex comprising studios, a 50-KW transmitter and other equipment representing the state of the art technology has been installed by All India Radio in a very short span of 4 years, notwithstanding the difficult terrain and climatic conditions. India provided to the Royal Government both financial and technical assistance to the project which has cost Rs. 8.5 crore. On its part, All India Radio has not only trained in its Staff Training Institute some technical personnel from the Royal Government of Bhutan, but is also providing on a continuing basis the service of its engineers for the upkeep and maintenance of the equipment installed including a FM link, ancillary structures and as outdoor broadcasting van.[35]

Education

The kingdom initiated the development of a comprehensive education system in 1961. Prior to 1961, there were virtually no modern education facilities inside Bhutan, apart from the traditional education given in the monasteries. One comes across an extensive network of schools and other educational institutions in Bhutan today, which are spread throughout the kingdom. In fact, many schools have boarding facilities for students living in areas far from the nearest school. While the medium of instruction in schools is English, Bhutan's national language Dzongkha, is taught as a compulsory subject from primary to college level. Moreover, school curricula also include religious instructions, training in traditional arts and crafts and agriculture. The Department of Education of the Royal Government of Bhutan maintains an extensive range of data on students, schools, and teaching personnel.

In 1988, there were in all 180 schools throughout the country; of these 150 were primary schools, 21 junior high schools and 9 high schools. In addition, there is a college and several other technical and vocational institutions. Also, there are several monastic schools and Sanskrit Pathshalas. In 1988, the total number of students enrolled in schools in the Kingdom was 58,000. Of these, 42,000 were enrolled in primary schools, 11,800 in junior high schools and 4,500 in high schools. Significantly, there were 21,600 females enrolled in schools, which constituted about 37% of the total enrolment. Mentionably, the number of students has increased over the past few years. In 1981, it was 36,700 and in 1988, it had reached 58,800. In 1988, there were altogether 2,208 school teachers. Of these, 1,513 were in primary schools, 447 in junior high schools and 248 in high schools.[36]

Significantly, before the introduction of non-monastic schooling in Bhutan in the 1960s, the few Bhutanese who were educated outside the kingdom studied mainly in India. Despite a vigorous government programme establishing schools throughout the country, even today a considerable number of Bhutanese go to India—especially for higher education. The Royal Government is anxious to promote a system which is in line with the developmental needs of the country, considerably stressing practical skills.

The development of the *Dzongkha* language is one of the more pronounced features of the Royal Government's education programme. Classical Tibetan was the language used in the traditional education provided by the monks. In the past, there was an immense problem of communication because of the prevalence of various dialects in various parts of the kingdom. It is because of this that the spoken language of western Bhutan was developed and refined for use among government officials throughout the country. This language came to be known and described as *Dzongkha* or the "language of dzong". Relevantly, the word dzong alludes to the monastic fortresses used as centres of administration of the main valley of the kingdom. In the beginning of the 1980s, only about 10% of the adult population of Bhutan could read and write.[37] By 1991, the percentage of literate people in Bhutan was estimated to be 12.[38]

Health

According to a report of the Royal Government of Bhutan, general health conditions of the people are affected by low nutrition intake, poor sanitation, and high prevalence of parasitic infections and contagious diseases. Efforts to establish modern medical facilities in Bhutan began in 1962. Until quite recently, institutional health facilities were concentrated in urban centres, but today the stress has shifted to the rural sector, where the majority of the people live. Basic health units (BHUs) usually serving remote districts, staffed by well-trained para-medical personnel are equipped to treat minor ailments and advise on preventive measures to avoid the spread of communicable diseases. These BHUs are supported by dispensaries. Besides, there are a number of special health programmes in Bhutan administered by the Department of Health. These include immunization, maternal and child health services, malaria eradication, leprosy and family planning. In Bhutan, some morbidity statistics are available based on patients treated by hospitals, basic health units and dispensaries. Little information is available on mortality. While a registration system exists for the reporting of births and deaths, it is recognized that there is some under coverage and problems with the identification of cause of death. Overall levels of mortality have been estimated from the Demographic Sample Surveys, but cause of death data have not yet become available. Efforts are afoot to streamline the vital registration system.[39]

In 1988, there were 28 hospitals, 69 basic health units and 46 dispensaries scattered across Bhutan. A total of 142 doctors and 674 paramedical workers service the health need of the population. This represents about 1 doctor for every 9,700 population. There were 932 hospital beds available in 1988, representing one bed per 1,480 population. The immunization programme has been accorded special priority in the administration of health services. In 1988, over 25,000 children were vaccinated for BCG, 17,000 against measles and about 21,000 against both diphtheria and poliomyelitis. The numbers were substantially lower in the previous years.[40] Malaria and tuberculosis are still widespread in Bhutan.[41]

Significantly, Bhutan joined the international community in observing World Leprosy Day on 27 January 1991. Dr. Jigme Singay, the head of the Public Health Division of the Directorate of Health Services, said that leprosy was no longer a disease to be feared in Bhutan. In fact, Bhutan, especially in the rural areas, did not have the stigma attached to the disease as in other countries. According to the National Leprosy Control Programme in the country, Bhutan was one of the first countries in the world to adopt MDT as a national policy. As a result, nearly 2,500 patients have completed the course, most of them with no sign as they ever suffered from the disease.[42]

Tourism

Until a few years ago, Bhutan's inaccessibility made foreign visitors a rare sight. To travel from the south to the central region required an arduous 7 to 10 days. The tracks were rough, and the obstacles from precipitous mountain ledges to flooded and perilous rivers, enough to daunt all but the brave and adventurous. Happily, today the same journey can be made in 6 hours by car and groups of tourists are able to visit the country. The Royal Government of Bhutan, anxious to ensure that all visitors receive the traditional Bhutanese hospitality, is expanding tourist facilities in measured, unhurried steps. Government hotels and guest houses, among them those constructed for the King's coronation in 1974, provide comfortable accommo- dation. All tour groups are accompanied by guides, young men and women specially trained, and conducted tours take visitors to many of the land's most beautiful and historic areas.[43]

The tourism industry has been an important source of hard currency to Bhutan since the kingdom was first opened to tourists in 1974. The potential of tourism in terms of foreign exchange earning is very high, though strategically the Royal Government has been following a policy of restricting tourists' number to the kingdom. In fact, Bhutan is following an undeclared policy of restricted tourism to protect the natural environment and keep the Himalayan kingdom evergreen. According to the Bhutanese Minister for Trade and Industry, Lyonpo Om Pradhan, the country allows only a limited number of foreign tourists, the earnings from which help maintain the 2 big tourist hotels, the Druk Air Services and the rest houses in district headquarter towns. In December 1990, Pradhan told correspondents that Bhutan's "policy is one of restricted tourism and we do not encourage heavy tourist inflows as it would cause pollution and effect our way of life, culture and relations".[44] Pradhan, who had also served as Bhutan's Ambassador to India during 1984-85, said only 1,500 foreign tourists were allowed to visit Bhutan in 1989.[45]

The main interesting statistics in the field of tourism relate to the characteristics of visitors and the details of existing tourist facilities. Interest centres on visitor arrivals, where they come from, when they come and the purpose of their visit. The total number of tourist arrivals in 1988 was 2,199, which is about 13% less than the previous year. The highest number of tourists recorded was 2,524 in the year 1987. The largest number of tourists came from Europe, the United States and Japan. The majority of tourists (73%) came on tour, while 27% came for trekking and mountaineering. The arrivals in the months of March, September and October accounted for well over half of all arrivals.[46]

Planning in Bhutan

Planning occupies a place of great significance and consequence in the political economy of Bhutan. In political economy, planning is the mode of thinking which emphasizes the advantages of a central planning authority to coordinate the development of the national economy, or, more loosely, of government intervention in some form (as opposed to a *lassiez faire* approach). Mentionably, in the wake of the capitalist chaos of the 1930s, the Soviet example of planning, and especially its emphasis on heavy industry, exercised considerable intellectual appeal. By the post-war period, not only had the Soviet Union, Eastern Europe, and China all adopted rigorous central planning, but the majority of the Third World countries also favoured a planned approach.

One important aspect of Bhutan's planning process could be said to be a serious effort to avoid any serious imbalance in the wellnigh traditional society. Prior to the 60s, the economic structure was stable with the ratio of land to labour being well balanced. Exposure to outside influences was negligible. Since the 60s, however, while the rural structure has not changed radically, a new modern sector has emerged, which is tightly controlled thus far. In the event, its overall economic impact has been limited.

Development planning attempts trace back to 1959 with the assistance of the Government of India. Starting from 1961, when the First 5-year Plan was formulated, Bhutan is on the verge of completing its 6th 5-year Plan in 1992. Homework for the 7th 5-year Plan has already started with all seriousness. Relevantly, to begin with a self-contained Development Secretariat was established to implement the plan. In 1971, at the time of the preparation of the Third Plan, the Planning Commission of Bhutan was established headed by His Majesty the King. In the absence of basic economic information and skilled manpower, the formulation of the Third Plan, like earlier ones, was comparatively simple. However, major developments in regard to the consolidation of the planning process took place in the 4th Plan period, when the *Dzongkhags* (districts) were involved in the developmental process.[47]

Until 1981-82, the responsibility for making Plan allocations, raising internal resources, and negotiating foreign assistance etc. lay with the Planning Commission. In 1981-82, however, a large part of the financial responsibilities of the Commission was transferred to the Ministry of Finance. The Commission was, on the other hand, invested with responsibilities for the formulation of development plans and allocation of investment resources. A substantial infrastructure for development of the economy has been built up in the first four Plans so that by the end of the Fourth Plan, the planning process had gained a good deal of comprehensiveness and sophistication. Needless to stress, these two factors enabled the economy to develop the capacity of absorbing much higher volumes of investment resources for development in the later 5-year Plans.[48]

First 5-year Plan (1961-62/1965-66)

The total outlay of the First 5-year Plan was Ngultrum(Nu.) (which is equivalent to Re. 1) 107.2 million. The highest priority was given to Public Works Department (Nu.62.9 million) and Road Transport/Aviation (Nu. 7.5 million). Health was allocated Nu. 3.1 million. While education received Nu. 9.4 million, health received Nu. 3.1 million. While power received Nu. 1.5 million, Trade and Industries received Nu. 1.1 million.[49] In a way, the First 5-year Plan was critical and crucial, the priority being transportation infrastructure to plan a communication network for opening up of the Himalayan kingdom. The outlay of 66% on this included major road network connecting India. Primarily, it was an infrastructural Plan to cater for the subsequent Plans. The major constraint—which still persists—was the shortage of manpower and technical skills.[50]

Second 5-year Plan (1966-67/1970-71)

The total outlay of the Second 5-year Plan increased to Nu. 202.2 million. As during the First 5-year Plan Public Works and Road Transport again received a high priority Nu. 70.5 million and Nu. 12.0 million respectively. Priority for education also enhanced and it received Nu. 35.7 million. This Plan also allocated Nu. 16.7 million to Information and Broadcasting. Greater significance was attached to Agriculture in comparison to the First 5-year Plan inasmuch as Nu. 21.6 million was allocated to this sector. During the Second 5-year Plan Animal Husbandry (Nu. 5.8 million) and Forestry (Nu. 6.9 million) received greater importance in comparison to the first. On the other hand, allocation to Trade and Industry (Nu. 9.1 million) was also increased. Other sectors were allocated as follows: Trade & Industries (Nu. 1.0 million), Telecommunications (Nu. 5.9 million), Health (Nu. 35.7 million), Urban Development (Nu. 1.4 million).[51]

Mentionably, the Second 5-year Plan, like the First 5-year Plan, contributed to laying the foundations of planned development in the mountain kingdom. Significant changes occurred during the First and Second 5-year Plans. The barter economy gave way to money economy, affecting a very large segment of economic activity and interaction between the inaccessible regions. During this period, a middle class emerged which began to acquire a say in the country's governance through the development process. The need of development also resulted in major changes in the administrative set-up. The linkage between economics and politics—which primarily constitutes political economy—became quite plausible in 1968, when the Cabinet system with a Council of Ministers was set up. Doing away with the earlier scheme of a Prime Minister, the Druk Gyalpo (King), assumed the role of the head of government and state. It was a significant development indeed. This brought the King directly into the process of governance, economic development and social changes.

In 1971, Bhutan joined the United Nations. It was a very significant event. It opened out Bhutan to economic aid from sources other than India. According to a knowledgeable observer: "The political and economic stance changed and serious efforts began to be made to diversify dependence—economic or political. It was a turning point in the traditional pattern of relationship between Bhutan and India".[52]

Third 5-year Plan(1971-72/1975-76)

The Third Plan not only brought in foreign aid of Rs. 15.8 million (beside India), international agencies like the UNDP and others found presence in the Himalayan kingdom for the first time, opening it out in later years to more diversified field of economic activity. In the event, the political role of Bhutan as an emerging Third World country in the contexts of South Asia and international politics became clear.[53]

The total outlay of the Third 5-year Plan was (Nu. 475.2 million) more than double than Second 5-year Plan. Health (Nu. 90.0 million) received the highest priority in this plan. Public Works Department (Nu. 84.6 million) continued to receive a serious consideration, as in the past. Priority to Agriculture (Nu. 58.3 million), too was enhanced. Allotment to other sectors was as follows: Forestry(Nu. 28.4 million), Trade and Industries (Nu. 26.2 million), Posts and Telegraph (Nu. 11.4 million), Telecommunications (Nu. 11.4 million), Information and Broadcasting (Nu. 38.1 million).[54]

Significantly, Bhutan opened itself to tourism during this period, as we have already seen. Tourism was allocated Nu. 11.4 million, side by side with the Druk Air, which was allocated Nu. 14.1 million.

Fourth 5-year Plan(1976-77/1980-81)

If the outlay of the Third 5-year Plan was more than double of the Second 5-year Plan, the outlay of the Fourth 5-year Plan was more than double of the Third Plan. The total outlay this time was Nu. 1,106.2 million. The Fourth Plan seemed to be a turning point in a number of ways. Unlike in the past, Agriculture (Nu.259.0 million) received the highest priority. Bhutan showed its inclination to move towards scientific farming. By allocating Nu. 175.0 million to Trade and Industries, the Himalyan kingdom showed its priority on that front. Greater priority was attached to Forestry (Nu. 110.3 million). On the other hand, Education (Nu. 134.6 million) received highest ever priority during this Plan. Interestingly, Tourism (Nu. 37.3 million) received less in comparison to the preceding Plan.

Allocation for other sectors were as follows: Animal Husbandry(Nu. 61.5 million), Power (Nu. 50.5 million), Public Works Department (Nu. 128.3 million), Posts and Telegraph (16.9 million), Telecommunications (Nu. 37.3 million), Information and Broadcasting (Nu. 54.6 million), Urban Development, which had been kept at a low key thus far, received Nu. 11.0 million.[55]

Significantly, the foreign aid rose to Nu.193 million during the Fourth 5-year Plan. The Fourth Plan brought about major changes in the pattern of economic perceptions. While economic growth remained the prime goal with increased emphasis on agriculture (an outlay of 29%—the highest thus far), industry, hydropower and forestry, the stress changed to multidimensional project planning fitting in a progressive image of Bhutan as an international entity forging its way to interaction with the outside world. There was a six-fold increase in overseas finance—mainly from the UN system—from 3% to 18%. In economic terms, however, the serious problems lay in mobilization of internal resources which went down from 7% envisaged to 5% of total financing.[56]

Fifth 5-year Plan (1981-82/1986-87)

The Fifth 5-year Plan, which significantly encompassed 6years, was more than four times larger than the Fourth 5-year Plan inasmuch as Nu. 4,648.3 million was earmarked for it. This plan attached highest priority to General Government inasmuch as Nu. 1,114.9 million was earmarked for this sector. Never before was any sum earmarked for this purpose. Dasho C. Dorji, then Deputy Minister, Planning Commission Secretariat, Thimphu, told me on an exclusive interview during my visit to Bhutan in October 1990 that during the Fifth 5-year Plan, the necessity of streamlining the administrative structure of the country had increased tremendously. Public Works Department once again came to claim a huge amount inasmuch as Nu. 787.5 million was earmarked for this.

Health (Nu. 519.1 million) and Agriculture (Nu. 419.4 million) remained important during the Fifth 5-year Plan. Allocation to other sectors was as follows: Food Corporation of Bhutan (Nu. 135.5 million), Forestry (Nu. 162.4 million), Power (Nu.340.5 million), Trade and Industries (Nu.323.3 million), Road Transport/Aviation (Nu. 787.5 million), Posts and Telegraph (Nu. 26.3 million), Telecommunications (Nu. 65.8 million), Tourism(Nu. 33.7 million), Druk Air (Nu. 29.1 million), Information and Broadcasting(Nu. 237.5 million), Urban Development (Nu. 187.3 million).[57]

Mentionably, the Kingdom entered a new phase in the economic and political spheres after 1981. The country took steps to extend its relationships externally on both fronts. The new move fitted into the policy of active involvement in international relations. Some of the steps taken in this phase included Trade Agreements with Bangladesh and Nepal, financial assistance from Kuwaiti Development Fund, membership of World and Asian Development Banks and setting up consulates in Singapore and South Korea. The UNDO, the FAO, the WHO and the UNESCO increased their roles substantially in Bhutan. First the SARC and then the SAARC became a major platform for the kingdom to project its regional image in the context of South Asia.

Apart from being vast in dimensions, a major thrust was introduced in formulating the Fifth 5-year Plan. It involved the people at the grass-roots level. There was sufficient and genuine stress on decentralization and participation. Significantly, there was a substantial contribution of voluntary labour to meet the large commitments and save scarce resources. With this view in mind, each district had its own plan based on expressed district priorities and projected available financial resources. In turn, each was discussed by the *Tshogdu* (National Assembly) of the kingdom. Further, these district level components were added to such projects which could come under central implementation. These comprised major projects such as large public industries, national road and power projects and higher level education.

An overall growth of 8.5% was one of the most important objectives of this plan. Areas of rapid growth were to be power, industry and tourism. Agriculture was expected to grow at the rate of 12% per annum.

Sixth 5-year Plan (1987-88/1991-92)

The Sixth 5-year Plan is more than double the size of the Fifth 5-year Plan in terms of outlay and dimensions. A total of Nu. 9,559.2 was earmarked for this Plan. General Government (Nu. 1,973.8 million) again came to be the topmost priority. Trade and Industries (Nu. 1,276.2

million) and Power (Nu.1,247.9) were other sectors that received priority over others. Public Works Department (Nu. 887.2 million) and Agriculture (Nu.880.2 million) remained other claimants of importance during this phase. Allocation to various other sectors was as follows: Food Corporation of Bhutan (Nu. 106.5 million), Animal Husbandry (Nu. 331.0 million), Forestry (Nu. 418.2 million), Geological Survey (Nu. 35.8 million), Road Transport/Aviation (Nu. 48.8 million), Posts and Telegraph (Nu. 68.1 million), Telecommunications (Nu.133.8 million), Druk Air (Nu. 391.0 million), Education (Nu. 778.8 million), Health (Nu.399.1 million), Information and Broadcasting (95.9 million), Urban Development (Nu. 248.7 million), Dzongkhags (Nu. 238.5 million).[58]

To ensure that all plans and programmes for socio-economic development of the country are clearly directed to improving the well-being of the people and the country. His Majesty the King approved the following specific objectives as a basis for the formulation of the Sixth Plan.

1. Strengthening of the Government Administration
2. Preservation and promotion of national identity
3. Mobilization of internal resources
4. Enhancement of rural incomes
5. Improvement of rural housing and resettlement
6. Consolidation and improvement of development services
7. Development of human resources
8. Promotion of people's participation
9. Promotion of national self-reliance[59]

King effects changes

Mentionably, changes of far-reaching significance and consequence were effected by King Jigme Singye Wangchuck in the Planning Commission during the 6th 5-year Plan. In June 1991, the King appointed Dasho C. Dorji, Deputy Minister, Planning Commission Secretariat, as the new Chairman of the Planning Commission. Hitherto, the Druk Gyalpo himself was the Chairman of the Planning Commission. The Planning Commission Secretariat said that His Majesty informed the Commission members of his decision to relinquish the chairmanship of the Planning Commission during a meeting held on 13 June 1991. His Majesty told the Commission that the appointment of a new Chairman would decentralize the existing system of decision-making in the Planning Commission. It would facilitate increased participation in the planning process by senior representatives from the ministries and departments.

This would, in turn, give greater responsibility and accountability to the senior members of the Royal Government and result in increased cooperation and contributions from all ministries and departments in the implementation of plans and programmes formulated by the Commission.

His Majesty expressed his full confidence in the new Chairman and the members of the Planning Commission and also the officers of the Planning Secretariat. He said that having relinquished the Chairmanship of the Commission, he would now be able to tour the dzongkhags more frequently to meet with the people and review development works throughout the country.

In an interview to *Kuensel,* Dasho C. Dorji said that he was deeply honoured by the trust and confidence reposed in him by His Majesty the King. He said that it would be his constant endeavour to ensure that the Planning Commission fulfils its role, as envisaged by His Majesty, to bring about rapid development with social justice. Dasho C. Dorji also said that the Planning Commission had achieved tremendous success under the dynamic and farsighted leadership of His Majesty the King. The national economy had achieved phenomenal growth over the past two decades. An effective nationwide network of service infrastructures, ranging from hospitals and educational institutions to metalled roads and sophisticated telecommunications systems had been established. The standard of living in rural areas had been dramatically improved with electrification, sanitation and water supply programmes penetrating deep into the interior.

Dasho C. Dorji also said that with virtually no foreign exchange reserves in 1971, the Royal Government had now built up a reserve touching US$ 85 million. The importance of creating a rupee reserve had also been stressed as most of the commodities are brought from India. Annual revenue which was Nu. 41 million in 1971 had now reached Nu. 1,000 million and the Royal Government has been able to meet 82% of its establishment costs by internal revenue in the current fiscal year. Dasho Dorji asserted further that the census revealing the correct population of the country to 6,00,000 instead of 1.3 million and the GDP growth averaging around 6% in recent years Bhutan's per capita income had now risen dramatically to $425.[60]

Seventh 5-year Plan (1992-93/1996-97)

Bhutan would launch its 7th 5-year Plan on 1 July 1992. Lyonpo C. Dorji Planning Minister, told me in an exclusive interview at his Thimphu office on 22 October 1991 that its formulation had actually been initiated two and a half years ago. He added that the Plan was based "on the valuable experiences and knowledge gained during the implementation of the current plan". He stated that these included, *inter alia*, the problems and achievements of the current plan; needs and aspirations of the people of each Dzongkhags; external and internal financial resources available for development and the general manpower capacities both within and outside the government. He also told me that as in the past, His Majesty the King had personally visited each Dzongkhag and held extensive discussions with the people on the subjects and objectives of the 7th 5-year Plan.

The Bhutanese Planning Minister told me that the main objectives of the 7th 5-year Plan were as follows:

a) Self-reliance with emphasis on Internal Resource Mobilization
b) Human Resource Development
c) Participation of the people in development through effective decentralization
d) Integrated and balanced development throughout the kingdom
e) Sustainable development with stress on environment protection
f) Development and expansion of the private sector

As for the core areas of development, C. Dorji enumerated the following:

1. Power,
2. Trade and Industry,
3. Communications,
4. Human Resource Development,
5. Health,
6. Education, and
7. Agriculture.

In fact, agriculture was included as one of the core areas at the suggestion of Druk Gyalpo Jigme Singye Wangchuck during the 70th session of the *Tshogdu.*

Of the total 6th Plan allocation of Nu. 9,559 million, recurrent expenditure amounted to Nu. 3,854 million while capital expenditure reached Nu. 5,704 million. The 7th Plan would receive a total outlay of Nu.15,000 million. Of this 57.3% (Nu.8,600 million) would be allocated for recurrent expenditure and the remaining 42.7% (Nu.6,400 million) would be devoted to capital expenditure. The total plan outlay of Nu. 15,000 million did not include the planned investment for Dungsum

Cement Plant and proposed power projects, which would amount to approximately Nu. 7,000 million. As these projects were over and above the plan outlay, this additional amount would be considered as a non-plan investment budget.[61]

In a speech in the *Tshogdu* (during its 70th session), the Planning Minister stated that Bhutan's domestic resources would only meet 30% of the total outlay of Nu. 15,000 million for the 7th Plan, excluding the additional amount of Nu.7,000 million required for the establishment of industries and new power projects. In this connection, he informed the *Tshogdu* that the Royal Government had initiated dialogue with existing and potential donors to seek financial and technical assistance on both bilateral and multilateral basis.[62]

As usual, India has helped Bhutan in a variety of ways in the formulation of the 7th 5-year Plan, even though Bhutan has been able to develop its own infrastructure in a commendable manner. An Indian delegation visited Thimphu in October 1991 to discuss Indo-Bhutan cooperation projects for the 7th Plan. The Royal Government also held talks with other donors at the Round Table Meeting in Paris in March 1992. This was an opportunity for the donors to discuss Bhutan's development strategy and requests for assistance as outlined in the 7th Plan.

An overview

To sum up the analysis of the political economy of the Himalayan kingdom of Bhutan, we may say that there is a clear-cut nexus between the politics and the economy of the country. Though the kingdom has never made any pretentions to be a socialist country, the Royal Government has always shown its predilections for the welfare of the people and concern over the plight of hoi polloi. This has palpably augured well for the all-round development of the country. We have already seen, how nature has been kind to Bhutan in terms of land-man ratio. In fact, Bhutan has exposed itself—even though unwillingly—to serious risks in terms of influx from the neighbouring countries like Nepal and India because of this ideal scenario.

But in terms of various contrivances also the Royal Government has not lagged behind. It has tried to create not only a participatory polity but also a participatory economy through the process of planning, making politics and economics join together on the plane of political economy. We have already seen how the late Druk Gyalpo Jigme Dorji Wangchuck did away with the office of Prime Minister in 1968 and himself assumed the role of the head of state. This could be said to be an attempt to facilitate what General Ziaur Rahman of Bangladesh used to describe as "politics of production". We have also seen how Druk Gyalpo Jigme Singye Wangchuck has abdicated the chairmanship of the Planning Commission to be able to tour various dzongkhags more frequently and more freely and objectively. It would, without doubt, enable him to listen to the interest articulation and interest aggregation of the Bhutanese hoi polloi.

Bhutan thus far has emphasized participation by the people as opposed to mobilization in all walks of life—including the economic. This has led to the strengthening of the process of decentralization: this has contributed to the growth of self-importance of the people. They have been allowed to feel like citizens, instead of subjects in the true sense of the word. This has stood the state structure in good stead amidst various and serious challenges.

With the comfortable per capita income (highest in South Asia), ideal land-man ratio (best in South Asia), growing foreign exchange reserve and external financial assistance pouring in, there appears no reason why Bhutan cannot make great strides on the plane of political economy. The encumbrances caused by lack of skilled and even unskilled manpower might continue for some time to come. But that should not really hamper economic development.

Notes and References

1. *The New Lexicon Webster's Dictionary of The English Language (NLWDEL):Deluxe Encyclopaedic Edition,* Lexicon Publications, Inc., New York, 1987, 777.
2. *The Concise Oxford Dictionary of Current English* (Eighth Edition), Oxford University Press, Delhi, 1990, 922.
3. *Collins Cobuild English Language Dictionary,* Collins, London and Glasgow, 1988, 1110.
4. Geoffery K. Roberts, *A Dictionary of Political Analysis,* Longman, London, 1971, 159-60.
5. Roger Scruton, *A Dictionary of Political Thought,* Pan Books in Association with the Macmillan Press, London,1982, 359.
6. Ibid.
7. Aung San Suu Kyi, *Let's Visit Bhutan,* Burke Publishing Company Limited, London, 1985, 9-10.
8. Ibid., 10-11.
9. Ibid., 11-12.
10. Ibid., 12-13.
11. Ibid., 13.
12. Ibid., 54.
13. Ibid., 55.
14. J. Denis Derbyshire and Ian Derbyshire, *Political Systems of the World,* Allied Publishers Limited, New Delhi, 1990, 579.

15. Antara Dev Sen,"The people will decide" (King Jigme Singye Wangchuck on the future of Bhutan), *Sunday,* Calcutta, 28 October 1990, 28.
16. *The Sunday Statesman,* Delhi, 10 February 1991, 6.
17. Parmanand, *Political Development In South Asia,* Sterling Publishers Private Limited, New Delhi, 1988, 50.
18. Antara Dev Sen, n. 15.
19. Kamaljeet Rattan,"Jigme Singye Wangchuck: Haste To Develop Erodes our Traditions", *India Today,* New Delhi,15 September 1989, 34.
20. Aung San Suu Kyi, n. 7, 93.
21. *Kuensel,* Thimphu, vol.5, no.41,13 October 1990,12.
22. See Parmanand, "India-Bhutan Friendship and Bhutan's Problem of National Integration", *Strategic Analysis,* New Delhi, vol. 13, no. 12, March 1991,1413.
23. Royal Government of the Kingdom of Bhutan, Thimphu, *Bhutan: Himalayan Kingdom,* 1979, 33-34.
24. Ibid., 35.
25. Central Statistical Office, Planning Commission, Royal Government of Bhutan, Thimphu, *Statistical Yearbook Of Bhutan 1989,* 54.
26. *The Statesman,* Delhi, 26 November 1990,1.
27. Ibid.
28. Ibid.
29. *Kuensel*, vol.6, no.23,15 June 1991, 12.
30. Royal Government of the Kingdom of Bhutan, n. 23, 35.
31. Central Statistical Office, Planning Commission, Royal Government of Bhutan, n.25, 47.
32. Ibid.
33. Ibid.
34. Royal Government of the Kingdom of Bhutan, n. 23, 36.
35. *Indian Express,* New Delhi, 16 March 1991, 2 and *The Statesman*, 16 March 1991, 2.
36. Central Statistical Office, Planning Commission, Royal Government of Bhutan, n.31,11.
37. Aung San Suu Kyi, n.7, 35.
38. *Manorama Year Book 1991*, Malayala Manorama, Kottaym, Kochi, Thiruvanathpuram, 1991, 227.
39. Central Statistical Office, Planning Commission, Royal Government of Bhutan, n. 31, 5.
40. Ibid.
41. *Manorama Year Book 1991*, n. 38, 231.
42. *Kuensel* vol. 6, no. 5, 2 February 1991, 2.
43. The Royal Government of the Kingdom of Bhutan, n. 23, 36.
44. *The Statesman,* 19 December 1990, 8.
45. Ibid.
46. Central Statistical Office, Planning Commission, Royal Government of Bhutan, Thimphu, n.31, 58.
47. Ibid., 78.
48. Ibid.
49. Ibid.
50. B.S. Das, "Economic Development and Social Change in Bhutan", in Urmila Phadnis, S.D. Muni and Kalim Bahadur, eds., *Domestic Conflicts in South Asia,* vol.2: *Economic and Ethnic Dimensions*, South Asian Publishers, New Delhi, 1986,89.
51. Central Statistical Office, Planning Commision, Royal Government of Bhutan, n.31,78.
52. B.S. Das, n.50, 90.

53. Ibid.
54. Central Statistical Office, Planning Commission, Royal Government of Bhutan n.31,78.
55. Ibid.
56. B.S. Das, n. 50, 91.
57. Central Statistical Office, Planning Commission, Royal Government of Bhutan, n.31,78.
58. Ibid.
59. Dasho C. Dorji, then Deputy Minister, Planning Commission, explained this to me during my interview with him in October 1990.
60. *Kuensel*, vol.6, no. 23,15 June 1991,1-2.
61. Ibid.,vol.6, no. 43, 2 November 1991, Assembly Supplement, 2.
62. Ibid.

3

The Political System

The concept of political system today occupies a place of great significance and consequence in Political Science in general and Comparative Political Analysis in particular. It is a better key to the understanding of the complex and complicated politics—which most of the time is a wheels within wheels business—of any state. It has several advantages over the analysis of legal-constitutional framework, which mostly presents the theoretical appraisal of the politics of a country, which is at times in variance with the nitty-gritty of politics thereof.

Political system's concept

Let us first understand the concept of political system itself. A political system is a combination of structures, processes and institutions which interact with each other, and, across the boundaries of the system, with the environment. It "authoritatively allocates values" for a society or attains the goals of a society and generally performs those functions which may be treated as political. Conceptually, it itself is a subsystem of the wider societal system, such as a state, the international system, a political party, a trade union or a tribe. Generally, it is regarded as an open system, involved in exchanges with its environment, and an adaptive system, capable of adaptation to changing circumstances, regulation of its own components, response to stress and, through feedback mechanisms, able to adjust its outputs to input conditions.[1]

A political system has also been defined as "those social interactions and institutions through which a society makes decisions considered binding by most members of society most of the time". The notion of a political system, indeed, represents more than just a new term. In fact, it reflects a transformation in the way in which students of politics are able to theorize about their subject-matter and pursue empirical inquiries. Not accidentally, its emergence coincided with and reinforced the introduction, through the so-called behavioural revolution, of the rigorous methods for empirical research about political phenomena.[2]

The context of Bhutan

In the context of Bhutan, then, we will do well to analyse the offices and the roles of the *Druk Gyalpo* (King) and the *Je Khenpo* (Dharma Raja), the *Lodey Tshogdey* (Royal Advisory Council), Council of Ministers, the *Tshogdu* (National Assembly), District Administration, Planning Commission, political parties and pressure groups, the bureaucracy and the Royal Civil Service Commission, the Army, the Police etc. We would also examine Bhutan's political system's place in international politics. This would help us in analysing the political nitty-gritty of Bhutan to a great extent. After all, only a multi-dimensional approach to and study of the politics of the country— which in a way is its political system—would help us in understanding and appreciating the reality.

The Druk Gyalpo (King)

The *Druk Gyalpo* or the King of Bhutan (or *Druk-yul*) occupies the place of the greatest significance in the Bhutanese political system. In fact, the Bhutanese political system could be described as the monarchical system. Before the primacy of the *Druk Gyalpo* was established in 1907, the Bhutanese political system was being described as the Shabdung political system, named after Shabdung Ngawang Namgyal, who was very largely responsible for the unification of the mountain kingdom. The Shabdung political system was marked by the concept of dual authority, one supreme in the religious matters and the other supreme in the temporal affairs. The *Je Khenpo* (Dharma Raja) looked after the religious matters; the *Druk Gyalpo* (Deb Raja) took care of the secular affairs.

Today, the core of the state in Bhutan is represented to a very great extent by the *Druk Gyalpo*. He is, in the true sense of the term, at the apex of the political system. He is the head of state as also the head of government. He reigns and rules. He enjoys both power and glory. In Bhutan, even a casual visitor or observer can discern that a sense of reverence and affection exists between the King and his people.[3] Bhutan's political system is, more or less, paternalistic. The King treats his people as citizens rather than subjects, as many tinpot autocrats or even monarchs do in their countries. In the multiethnic, multilingual and multireligious state of Bhutan, the *Druk Gyalpo* has become the greatest and the real cementing force. In any crisis situation, the whole of Bhutan, looks at the King for its resolution. It is not for nothing that Druk

Gyalpo Jigme Singye Wangchuck insists that the political system of Bhutan is quite flexible and very democratic in practice.[4] He also avers—perhaps rightly—that Bhutan's hereditary monarchy functions far more democratically than in many democratic countries of Asia.[5] Any observer of the Bhutanese political system and scene can discern that the *Druk Gyalpo* is far more accessible and more responsive to enlightened ideas than many power-holders and power-wielders elsewhere.

Any observer of the Bhutanese political system and political scene can infer that there is an obvious shift from "court to government", "from personal rule to a system that sustains itself".[6] Though at times it appears that there is so much of concentration of power in Bhutan (because all important appointments in the state are made by the *Druk Gyalpo*), in reality there is an unmistakable trend towards decentralization of power. The King is trying to involve as many Bhutanese as possible in the decision-making process, not by harping on the theme, but by shedding and abdicating his power and responsibility in various politico-economic spheres. Only recently, he has abdicated the chairmanship of the Planning Commission of Bhutan.[7] Several years ago, he had given up his power to appoint civil servants of the state by constituting the Royal Civil Service Commission.

The Je Khenpo (Chief Abbot)

Apart from the Monarchy, the core of the state in Bhutan, to some extent, is represented by the Lamas or the clergy, Bhutan being primarily a religious state. The clergy in Bhutan is headed by the *Je Khenpo* (Chief Abbot), who is equivalent in status to the King. The *Je Khenpo* is assisted in his functions by 4 *Lopons* (Masters), who are equivalent in rank to Ministers. As the status and powers of the clergy have got eroded over the years, the *Je Khenpo* has also become a mere figurehead. However, the glory (if not also power) of the office lies in the fact that the *Je Khenpo* also has his office in the same Dzong building where the *Druk Gyalpo* has his office. The *Je Khenpo* is in constant touch with the *Druk Gyalpo*.

Though the *Je Khenpo* is not the part of the political structure of the kingdom, he plays an important social and cultural role in the life of the clergy and to that extent in the life of the state. The *Druk Gyalpo* has repeatedly emphasized the need to delegate sufficient authority to the clergy in religious matters in order to restore it to its former position of respect and influence. The present *Je Khenpo* is the 69th person to occupy this office. Significantly, the *Je Khenpo* is elected by the monks of Bhutan for a tenure of 3 to 5 years. The 67th *Je Khenpo* held the office for a period of 17 years. Some have held the office even for only 1 year. Elections have always been unanimous.[8] Time was when the *Je Khenpo* was treated as the incarnation of the Shabdung and the office was not elective. The *Je Khenpo* (who is also known as Sangharaja) is generally an old man and is elected to this post because of his knowledge of Buddhist religion and philosophy. He nominates 3 persons to the *Tshogdu* (National Assembly) and 1 person to the *Lodey Tshogdey* (Royal Advisory Council).[9]

***The Lodey Tshogdey* (Royal Advisory Council)**

The *Lodey Tshogdey* is a unique Bhutanese institution. It was established in 1965. It consists of 9 members—6 representatives of the people, 2 representatives of the clergy and 1 nominee of the King. They hold office for 5 years. The main functions of the *Lodey Tshogdey* could be said to be as follows:

1. To make its advice available to the *Druk Gyalpo* and the Council of Ministers on all matters of national importance,
2. To promote the welfare of the people and the national interests of the kingdom,
3. To develop friendly and harmonious relations between the government and the people, and
4. To ensure that the laws and resolutions passed by the *Tshogdu* are faithfully implemented by the government and the people.[10]

Druk Gyalpo Jigme Singye Wangchuck further strengthened the position of this body in 1984 by including a clause in the provisions of the functioning thereof. The clause provides that "if any person, including His Majesty the King, does anything harmful to the interest of the kingdom and the people, the Royal Advisory Council without suppressing such matters and free of fear from any quarter shall bring it to the attention of His Majesty the King and, if necessary, even report to the Cabinet and the National Assembly".[11] Although the Royal Advisory Council had the authority to advise the King and to watch over the performance of the government, the *Druk Gyalpo* felt that it lacked the necessary clout to carry out its important responsibilities. As such a revised set of rules and regulations for the functions and responsibilities of the Council was formulated at the behest of the King. It was then that this new clause was added.

Quite expectedly, the *Tshogdu* strongly objected to this unique clause empowering the *Lodey Tshogdey* to report against the King. The National Assembly felt that this was a violation of traditional values and it undermined the sacred principles of loyalty and devotion to the throne. The *Druk Gyalpo*, however, insisted that this clause was of great significance and consequence and, therefore, necessary. According to him, no one can predict or guarantee the actions and sense of responsibility to the nation of future rulers.[12]

This development, to say the least, was remarkable and revealing inasmuch as the 29-year old King (in1984) showed that he was more interested in accountability and responsibility, instead of power for the sake of it. By this step he improved upon the democratic traditions set by his august father and predecessor, the Late His Majesty King Jigme Dorji Wangchuck. This episode also proved beyond doubt that the Monarch in Bhutan was and is really concerned over the variety of problems of the Bhutanese people and was prepared to make sacrifice for it. The *Druk Gyalpo* also showed that the democratic and monarchical concerns can converge, if they are genuine.

In practice, the *Lodey Tshogdey* has been given a more active role as a watchdog in overseeing the execution of government policies. Of course, there are critics, who stress the fact that as in the ultimate analysis the *Lodey Tshogdey* is the creation of the *Druk Gyalpo* himself, it cannot think of offending the latter beyond a point. What is forgotten in such observation is the fact that Bhutanese political system allows free and frank discussion and genuine political participation, not available in many Third World states. As such, it is not really difficult for such a body to offend the Monarch. But should there be offence for the sake of it? This is the most important question and on its answer hinges the real political situation in Bhutan. When the *Druk Gyalpo* emphasizes decentralization and participation both in theory and practice, can he be chosen for offence?

The *Lhengyel Tsok* (Council of Ministers)

Bhutan underwent a singnificant change in the sphere of governance and administration in 1968, when the late Druk Gyalpo Jigme Dorji Wangchuck appointed a *Lhengyel Tsok* as an administrative institution. Before the body was launched, the *Tshogdu,* had at the request of the King, approved its formation.The Council of Ministers is an important decision-making body, second only to the *Tshogdu* in importance. The Council of Ministers is presided over by the *Druk Gyalpo* and comprises ministers, deputy ministers and all Royal Advisory councillors.

By presiding over the Council of Ministers, the *Druk Gyalpo*, in fact, acts as his own Prime Minister. Significantly, Jigmie Palden Dorji and Lhendup Dorji had acted as Prime Ministers of Bhutan between 1958-64 and 1964-65 respectively. No other Bhutanese official before or since has been given either the rank or the responsibilities and functions of a Prime Minister. Normally, the King serves in this capacity.[13] According to Nagendra Singh, who had the privilege of working as the Constitutional Adviser to the Royal Government of Bhutan, Jigmie Dorji was designated as Prime Minister as a matter of courtesy only. In fact, the title originated at the time of the visit of Indian Prime Minister Jawaharlal Nehru to Bhutan in 1958 out of sheer consideration of protocol.[14]

Currently, there are 7 Ministries dealing with the following activities: Agriculture and Forestry, Communications, Finance, Foreign Affairs, Home Affairs, Social Services, and Trade, Industry and Tourism.[15]

Relevantly, the administrative secretariat of the Government is located in the capital Thimphu.

District Administration

The kingdom of Bhutan is divided into 18 districts or *dzongkhags*, each of which is under a District Administrator or *Dzondag*. Village headmen or *Gups* are elected by the people of their villages. Apart from being responsible for the day-to-day administration of the districts, the *Dzongdags* are also responsible for the implementation of development plans under the decentralized system of development administration. Under the present dispensation, administration has been decentralized and District Development Committees have been established in all 18 districts of the kingdom. The purpose is to bring about greater participation of the Bhutanese people in the nation-building process and objective.

Druk Gyalpo Jigme Singye Wangchuck has repeatedly stressed the fact that the destiny of Bhutan lies in the hands of the Bhutanese people. He has also emphasized that whatever administrative system is established must receive the support and cooperation of the people, lest they become unsuccessful and ineffective. The *Druk Gyalpo* has time and again urged upon the Bhutanese people to shoulder their responsibilities as dedicated and loyal citizens who are willing to sacrifice for the nation by placing the nation's interests above theirs. Needless to state, such an attitude and assertion is vital to the all-round development of a small country like *Druk-yul*, the land of the Thunder Dragon.

Another significant decision that the Royal Government of Bhutan took during the 5th 5-year Plan (1981-87) with a view to coordinating the development work of various districts was that it divided the kingdom into 4 zones. In a way, the division of the country into 4 zones is dictated by geophysical and agro-climatic considerations, within which regional potential can best be harnessed. The institution of 4 zonal administrations is envisaged to feel the administrative and physical problems that currently exist between the centres and the districts. Acting as a suitably congenial and accessible link between the centre and the districts, the zonal administrations are best placed to direct and oversee development initiatives in the districts towards the fulfilment of the nationally stated objectives. At the same time, the zonal administration is supposed to ensure that national objectives sufficiently account for local development circumstances and requirements. The new set-up also aims at sharing of technical expertise among the districts with a view to optimally utilizing among districts the limited number of technically competent personnel.

On the administrative plane, the delegation of responsibility to the 4 zones is likely to lessen the pressure of governance to a manageable level with each and every unit and the central ministries sufficiently attending to its fair share of governmental tasks. Perhaps, equally importantly, if not more, it is perceived that the phenomenon of zonalization of governmental activities will provide an effective framework for achieving greater equity and for enlisting increased community involvement and participation in the developmental process.

Lastly, this new innovation, based on homogeneity and complementarity is likely to bring more coordinated and integrated planning of interdistrict activities, utilizing the agri-forestry and industrial development potential of their common watersheds for accelerated production making Bhutan move towards self-reliance.[16]

Planning Commission

The importance of planning in any state is quite obvious. Development planning in Bhutan can be traced back to the year 1961, when the First 5-year Plan (1961-62 to 1965-66) was drawn up. To begin with, a self-contained Development Secretariat was set up to implement the plan. The help and guidance of India and its Planning Commission was of great significance during this period. In 1971, at the time of the preparation of the Third 5-year Plan, a Planning Commission, headed by His Majesty the King, was set up. The Commission is charged with responsibilities for the formulation of development plans and allocation of investment resources. Mentionably, a substantial infrastructure for the development of the economy had been built up in the first 4 Plans and the planning process had gained a good deal of comprehensiveness and sophistication. In fact, these two factors enabled the economy to develop the capacity of absorbing much higher volumes of investment resources for development in the subsequent 5-year Plans.

The Planning Commission is an autonomous body comprising 17 members. It deals with national planning, coordination and mobilization of resources. Its meetings are held as and when needed. However, on an average, it meets twice a year.[17]

In a development of far-reaching significance and consequence, King Jigme Singye Wangchuck, who had hitherto chaired the Planning Commission of the kingdom, appointed Dasho C. Dorji as the Chairman of the Commission in June 1991. While doing so, His Majesty asserted that the appointment of a new Chairman would decentralize the existing system of decision-making in the Planning Commission. It would, the King asserted, also facilitate increased participation in the planning process by senior representatives from the ministries and departments. This would, in turn, give greater responsibility and accountability to the senior members of the Royal Government and result in increased cooperation and contributions from all ministries and departments in the implementation of plans and programmes formulated by the Commission.[18]

The Royal Civil Service Commission and the Bureaucracy

Palpably, the building up of an efficient, dedciated and honest civil service is an enormous and challenging task that faces any developing country and Bhutan is no exception. Before 1982, civil servants in Bhutan were directly appointed by the King. In 1982, however, the King appointed a Royal Civil Service Commission, which is responsible for formulating and ensuring implementation of general policies in order to promote efficiency, loyalty and integrity among the civil servants to maintain high level of morale. It is also responsible for appointments, transfers, promotions and discipline among the civil servants.[19] Earlier HRH Ashi Sonam Chhoden Wangchuck was the Chairperson of the Royal Civil Service Commission.[20] Now the chairmanship rotates among the Ministers on the basis of seniority, each holding it for a period of 6 months. Foreign Minister Lyonpo Dawa Tsering, the seniormost minister, completed his term as the chairman of the Commission in February 1992 and was succeeded by Lyonpo T. Tobgyel, the Minister for Social Services and Communications.[20a]

The King's concept of the bureaucracy in Bhutan is "a small, efficient and effective government that is clean and not corrupt,whose members are well paid, well looked after and disciplined."[21] Bhutan's bureaucracy is relatively huge and comprised in 1981 some 20,000 Bhutanese officials. Some 40,000 Indian personnel also worked there. It involves a huge expenditure and amounted to Rs. 640 million during the 4th 5-year Plan.[22] The Royal Government had in 1981 appointed a Civil Service Commission to investigate the possibilities of reducing expenditure.[23]

A new comprehensive rule book, released by the Royal Civil Service Commission in January 1991 announced several new benefits for civil servants from 1 January. The civil servants would now enjoy more leave than in the past. Casual leave has been increased from 5 days to 10 days in 1 calendar year. Civil servants are also entitled to medical leave with full pay, if they produce the medical document certifying the illness. They will also be allowed study leave for maximum of 18 months, if they arrange their own training, but the training has to be relevant to their duties and approved by the Royal Civil Service Commission (RCSC). More importantly, fathers-to-be can now look forward to 1-day paternity leave for the first 3 children. A civil servant who has at least 30 days earned leave at credit are allowed to encash the 30 days' leave for an equivalent of 1 month's pay.[24]

Examinations: The rules and regulations for the RCSC officers selection examination have been changed. The amendments are based on feedback from within and outside the country. The views of Kanglung College students were also taken into consideration.[25]

Response to changing needs: In a foreword to the rule book, HRH Ashi Sonam Chhoden Wangchuck, stated: "The civil service had to respond to the changing needs and adapt to a diversified environment of roles, functions and responsibilities without sacrificing the values ingrained in Bhutanese society". Dasho Sonam Tobgye, the then Secretary of the RCSC, stated that the Commission had been working on these rules for the last 3 years. He further stated that the rule book contained a few additional rules as well as amendments to the rules that existed. According to him, "This has been done as an effort to streamline the procedure and improve the system." [26]

The *Tshogdu* (National Assembly)

The *Tshogdu* or the National Assembly is again a unique Bhutanese political institution. It is constituted on the principle of partylessness. Apart from Maldives, the South Asian island state, Bhutan is the only South Asian state to have a legislature based on partylessness. It comprises both elected and nominated elements. There are, in all, 154 members in the *Tshogdu*. Of them, 105 are the elected representatives of the people, 10 are the representatives of the clergy and rest 39 are the nominated representatives of the government. All the members serve for a term of 3 years. The members can be reelected or renominated, as the case may be.

Functions: The main functions of the National Assembly are to enact laws, approve senior appointments in the government and advise on all matters of national importance.

Sessions: The *Tshogdu* normally meets twice a year but it can be convened any time if an emergency arises. The Speaker of the *Tshogdu* —who is elected for a term of 3 years from amongst the members— convenes the sessions of the House. The agenda of the *Tshogdu* is compiled by its Secretariat from the proposals received from various constituencies through their respective Assembly members. The National Assembly Secretariat compiles the points submitted for discussions grouping them in different categories according to the subjects. The Speaker along with two members of the Royal Advisory Council and the Secretary of the National Assembly form the Agenda Committee to decide the final agenda, which is then submitted to His Majesty the King for his formal concurrence.[27] The average duration of *Tshogdu* session in a year is two weeks. The sessions of the *Tshogdu* are convened on the basis of the agenda and there is no fixed month or time for convening the sessions of the House.[28]

Dissolution: Like the President of India (who can dissolve the lower House of the Indian Parliament, i.e. the Lok Sabha), His Majesty the King can dissolve the House. However, it has not been dissolved since its inception in 1953.[29]

Committees: The National Assembly is a unique institution based on local tradition and culture and is suited to the genius of the Bhutanese people. As it is not based on any model of western parliamentary institution, there is no Committee of the House other than the Assembly Agenda Committee. There is no committee which has been formed to carry on specific function of the *Tshogdu*. However if need arises, the Assembly can set precedence to set up such a committee.[30] The Royal Advisory Council, already alluded to, acts as an Advisory Committee as and when the need arises. The Speaker may specify the time limit for addressing the session.[31]

Members' designations: The members of the *Tshogdu* are popularly known as "Thui-mes" or "Chhimis".[32]

Privileges: The *Tshogdu* members are entitled to receive fixed salaries and allowances with travel expenses as admissible to the 1st Class Officer in the Civil Service Cadre. In addition, a consolidated sum of Nu. 1,000 per session is paid to the members as Lecture Fee. A sum of Nu. 100 is also paid per diem as sitting fee for the period the Assembly is in session. They are, moreover, entitled to free medical benefits, while educational facilities are also provided to their children on a priority basis.[33]

Questions in the Tshogdu : Once the *Tshogdu* schedule is announced by the National Assembly Secretariat, the concerned *Chhimis* call a meeting at the *Gewog* (Block) level, where the head of each household is represented to invite points/questions from the general public. The points/questions are first deliberated at *Dzonkhag Yargey Tshogchung* (DYT), which is the District Development Committee, where issues falling under its jurisdiction are deliberated and decisions taken accordingly. The points/questions of national level importance, which are beyond the authority of the DYT are forwarded for inclusion in the agenda of the National Assembly. The members have the freedom, not only to discuss points which may have been left out from the agenda, but they are also free to raise and discuss any relevant points besides those contained in the agenda.[34]

Galleries: All interested individuals including non-Bhutanese can watch the proceedings of the House. There are two galleries for the visitors, Public Gallery and Noble Gallery. Gallery cards are issued by the National Assembly Secretariat on request.[35]

Election of Members: As we have already seen, the *Tshogdu* contains 105 elected representatives of the people, aside from other elements. These members, in order to be elected to the *Tshogdu*, must be Bhutanese citizens, must be at least 25 years' old, must not be mentally disabled or convicts and must not have served a prison sentence. The electoral system for the elected members of the *Tshogdu* is based on a limited franchise comprising village elders and heads of families. Leo E. Rose believes, however, "in Bhutan's social structure the results are broadly representative".[36] Of late, however, some people in Bhutan, especially in self imposed exile in Nepal and India, are raising questions about the representative character of the *Tshogdu*. No less a person than King Jigme Singye Wangchuck has stated:

> No. I agree with our boys in the south that the representation is not fair. When my father established the National Assembly in 54 *(sic)*, no one had any idea about it and nobody wanted it. So when he forced

its creation, the seat representation was done on an ad hoc basis. We had no census. It definitely needs to be changed in accordance with demographic distribution in the districts.[37]

B.S. Das also opines that the "representation is lopsided without incorporation of the new class".[38] One hopes that some corrective measures are adopted sooner than later to make the *Tshogdu* more representative in character. In terms of the ratio of elected members, as of now, they constitute 78% of the total. This obviously augurs well.

Origin: Having discussed so many aspects and dimensions of the *modus operandi* and *modus vivendi* of the *Tshogdu*, it is time and place to delve into the origin of this unique Bhutanese institution. In any case, its origin in itself is interesting. The *Tshogdu* was established by the third Druk Gyalpo Jigme Dorji Wangchuck in 1953. Dasho Rigzin Dorji is of the opinion that the initiative to establish the *Tshogdu* emanated from the throne, as King Jigme Dorji Wangchuck wanted "to develop political consciousness among the people and give them the greater say in the running of the country".[39] Leo E. Rose is of the opinion that "Jigme Dorji's primary innovation was the establishment of the *Tshogdu* (National Assembly) in 1953, thus introducing the concept of representative government in the Wangchuck system".[40]

However, there are people who tend to see a nexus between the establishment of a political party, called the Bhutan State Congress, at Patgaon in Assam in November 1952. This political party was formed under the political leadership of 3 Bhutanese Nepali—D.B. Gurung, D.B. Chhetri and G.P. Sharma. The main objective of the party was to change the discriminatory policies of the Bhutanese government against the Nepali Bhutanese *vis-a-vis* other ethnic groups in Bhutan.[41] Of course, not much was heard of the party after the establishment of the *Tshogdu* and the leaders of the Bhutan State Congress were allowed to come back to Bhutan and participate in the political activities of the state. But the establishment of the *Tshogdu* seems to be linked to the party-formation phenomenon. Thereafter the Nepali Bhutanese were sought to be incorporated in the kingdom's political, bureaucratic, military and police lives.

But there can be no two opinions about King Jigme Dorji Wangchuck's honest and enlightened objective of making the polity more participatory. In the context of 1953, it would appear to be a revolutionary move, even if viewed in the scenario of the whole of the South Asian region, where democracy had taken some concrete shape only in India and Sri Lanka (then Ceylon). Though Ram Rahul is of the opinion that "actually by establishing the *Tshogdu* he gave new life to an old institution of the Bhutanese tribes"[42], there is no doubt that the decision was immensely democratic and praiseworthy.

The King and the Tshogdu: Perhaps, one of the most important aspects of the structure and functions of the *Tshogdu* is its relation- ship with the *Druk Gyalpo*. We have already seen that the *Druk Gyalpo* can dissolve the *Tshogdu* even though it has never been done so since its inception in 1953. Though it is not mandatory for the *Durk Gyalpo* to sit in all the sessions of the *Tshogdu*, the present *Durk Gyalpo* attends most of the sessions of the House. His Majesty the King offers his views as and when he wishes, or when his views are requested from the House. All Cabinet Ministers are appointed by the *Druk Gyalpo* but the National Assembly can object to it if the appointment is not to its satisfaction.[43]

Many believe that the King's sitting through the National Assembly debates and his interventions whenever necessary is in contravention of the Westminster model.[44] But what is forgotten in such an observation and attitude is the fact that neither the Bhutanese are enamoured of the Westminster model nor does the presence of the Monarch in the *Tshogdu* affect the freedom and frankness of debates in the House. It is a fact of immense significance and consequence. More revealing is the fact that the *Druk Gyalpo* can be and even is criticized in the *Tshogdu* for his acts of omission and commission. During my tour of Bhutan in October 1990 I gathered from a number of *Thui-mes* and Ministers that the criticism is always in sophisticated language and His Majesty has not taken any offence. Herein lies the crux and the democratic temperament of the Monarch is revealed. It is also significant to note at this point that the King does not enjoy veto powers and decisions are taken through consensus. In the background of all this, King Jigme Singye Wangchuck's assertion that although "we have a hereditary monarchy, the way we function is more democratic than in any other country in the region"[45] is not off the mark.

In the late King's reign, the Monarchy needed a three-yearly vote of confidence by the *Tshogdu*. The requirement was done away with in 1972, though King Jigme Singye Wangchuck is of the opinion that the reason for the abolition are no longer valid. In an interview to an Indian editor he said in July 1983 that "the King has less work and less direct responsibility than 10 or 15 years ago".[46] Relevantly, the system of seeking vote of confidence was introduced by the late His Majesty Jigme Dorji Wangchuck in 1968. It was also in 1968 that the then King surrendered his veto power on the decisions of the *Tshogdu*. Thus, without the approval of the King, the decisions of the *Tshogdu* were to be treated as final. The King, however, retained the power to address the *Tshogdu* and refer back to it any resolution about which he had "serious misgivings". He also recommended to the *Tshogdu* that all appointments of ministers be decided by it. But even more radical and indeed unprecedented in monarchical polities was Jigme Dorji Wangchuck's recommendation to the *Tshogdu* is 1968 that all government officials including the King be obliged to resign from office, if a vote of no-confidence was passed in them in the Assembly.[47]

Level of debates and discussions in the Tshogdu: In the last lap of our discussion of various aspects of the *Tshogdu*, let us now turn to the levels of the debates and discussions in the House. According to some analysts of the Bhutanese political scene, the debates in the *Tshogdu* are far more forthright than before and the members of the *Tshogdu* argue with gusto.[48] However, B.S. Das is of the opinion that the *Tshogdu* "does not encourage public debates on economic or political issues, which cannot remain suppressed for very long".[49] On the basis of my interviews with some members of the *Tshogdu* as also some *Lyonpos* (Ministers) during my visits to *Druk-yul* in October 1990 and October 1991 and my watching of the proceedings, I feel inclined to believe that the debates and discussions in the *Tshogdu* are quite free and frank and all kinds of issues are debated without any hindrance and hesitation. The *Tshogdu* is not a decorative piece of the Bhutanese political system. Its debates and recommendations are always taken seriously. Whether it is the *Driglam Namzha* (etiquette), which generated so much controversy in 1990 or Bhutan's relations with the People's Republic of China, everything is discussed in detail in the *Tshogdu*. It augurs well for the existing political system and democracy in Bhutan.

The Judiciary

Bhutan's legal code—both civil and criminal—is based on what was laid down by Shabdung Ngawang Namgyal (the first Shabdung).Though a number of modifications have been effected in recent years, the substance and spirit of the traditional Buddhist precepts have been preserved.[50] All the laws of the kingdom are codified. Minor offences are judged and arbitrated by the village headmen. Above them, there are District Courts, having both original and appellate jurisdiction. The next higher court is the High Court, located in the capital, Thimphu. The final appeal is made to the *Druk Gyalpo*, who, then, delegates to the Royal

Advisory Council to investigate and ensure that the courts have dispensed justice in accordance with the kingdom's laws.

Significantly, the present judicial system was separated from the executive and legislative branches in 1968. It was in that year that the *Thrimkhong Gongma* (High Court) was convened and at the local level District Courts, which are located one each at the District headquarters of each district such as Paro, Punakha, Ha,Wangdiphodrang etc. Then come the basic units of administration in the country, namely the villages.

The *Thrimkhong Gongma (High Court)*: The highest court of Bhutan (not the highest court of appeal) is named *Thrimkhong Gongma* ("Thrim" means law or justice and "Khong" means home). Thus *Thrimkhong* means "the House of Justice". The High Court comprises 5 Judges, of whom 3 are nominated by the Royal Government of Bhutan, 1 by the monk body and the other by the *Tshogdu*. Eventually, all the judges are appointed to the *Thrimkhong Gongma* by the King but nominations by respective bodies are of essence. Significantly, the Home Minister of the Royal Government plays a vital role in the working of the judicial administrative machinery which could be said to be falling under his charge. Apart from appointing the District Magistrates, he also inquires about the eminence of the local judges, frames his recommendations and consults the Cabinet before sub- mitting the final list of recommendation to the *Druk Gyalpo*. Usually, the *Druk Gyalpo* approves the list submitted by the Home Minister.

All the judges of the *Thrimkhong Gongma* enjoy equal powers and authority. The person who functions as the Chief Justice is supposed to be the most experienced and seniormost among them. The Home Minister, while recommending names to the *Druk Gyalpo*, ensures that the judges are from various regions of the country. In fact, all the judges of the High Court cannot be from the same region.

District Courts: We have already seen that the next to the *Thrimkhong Gongma* in hierarchy is the District Courts. Each District Court has 1 judge who is assisted by a Sub-Divisional Officer, called *Ramjam.*

The Gappa: At the lowest rung of the judicial system is the village. The *Gappa* (or Village Headman) is the official at the village level. He is assisted by a person called *Chipon* who is both an assistant and a messenger. The *Gappa* has the power and authority to take decisions in the day-to-day administrative and legal matters. He is, however, free to take the advice of the *Chhimi* (the representative of the village in the *Tshogdu*). Serious cases—like those of murder—are, however outside the purview of the *Gappa*, whose function, then gets restricted to the reporting of the matter to the district authorities. Significantly, the decision-making process by the *Gappa* involves the recording of evidence by examining witnesses if any is coming forth.

The Jambis: The *Jambis* are like legal counsels who are appointed by the opposing parties to argue their cases. They are well conversant with the law and relevant facts of the dispute.They are like ordinary villages but are considered to be more experienced in terms of argument and negotiations. The *Jambi* usually works on cash considerations. It is interesting to note that ultimately it is the losing party which has to pay the *Jambis* of both the parties to the dispute.

Bah-geinja: Bah-geinja is a written statement made and signed by both the parties and their respective *Jambis* under stamp of the court with court fee paid at prescribed rates, contending their case and undertaking to suffer such penalty as may be mentioned in the *Bah-geinja* itself in case the contention of one of parties is proved wrong. This arrangement is usual when there are no witnesses forthcoming or where the parties have no confidence in the witnesses. If the stand taken by one party was thereafter found to be false or not maintainable, the punishment could take the form of compensation and or fine whether in cash or kind or it could be even restitution of property. This step, however, is generally reserved for the higher courts at the district level and when the plea of *Bah-geinja* is raised the *Gappa* usually reports the case to the District Court where the final award is made.[51]

The aforesaid discussion and analysis make it clear that Bhutan has made sufficient attempt to decentralize the process of rule-adjudication. Sufficient attempts also seem perceptible in the direction of making justice easy and worth affording in terms of money. By making efforts to fill the *Thrimkhong Gongma* by judges from all regions, a significant contribution has been made in the direction of national integration, something which is needed in today's Bhutan.

Political Parties and Pressure Groups: Political parties and pressure groups occupy a place of prime significance in any political system which is based on competitive pluralism and decentralization of power. Political parties and pressure groups do perform significant functions of interest articulation and interest aggregation in any political system. A political party is an organized group, made up of members who subscribe to some common set of values or policies, which has as its fundamental aim the attainment of political power and public office generally by constitutional means, in order to implement these policies. On the other hand, a pressure group is an organized group which has as one of its purposes the exercise of influence (or 'pressure') on political institutions, for the purpose of securing favourable decisions or preventing unfavourable decisions.[52]

Bhutan so far does not have the experience of the functioning of a political party within its territory. But this does not mean that the Bhutanese have never formed any political party. We have already seen how a group of Nepali Bhutanese formed a political party, called Bhutan State Congress in November 1952 in India. Of course, the Bhutan State Congress became non-existent soon thereafter. There was a time in the early sixties, when a shadowy group calling itself the Bhutan National Congress unfurled its flag at Jalpaiguri (India) and looked to the southern Bhutanese for support.[53] Nothing was heard of this organization, too, thereafter. This, in fact, reveals how contented and satisfied the Bhutanese people, by and large, are with their existing political system.

But the groups of frustrated Bhutanese and now even non-Bhutanese (who went to Bhutan to improve their livelihood) have once again come out with a political party, called the Bhutan People's Party (BPP). R.K. Budhathoki, President of the BPP said in an interview to an Indian Fortnightly:

> We organized on June 2, 1990 the Bhutan People' Party, as a political platform was needed to intensify our pro-democracy agitation. On September 19, 1990, the Government killed 327 people at a rally organized by pro-democracy activists. Many were injured in the police firing. The BPP became targets of the Government's attacks.[54]

Though many Bhutanese and outside observers do not believe in the charges levelled against the Bhutanese political system from time to time, there are people, including the *Druk Gyalpo*, who believe that the Bhutanese Nepali have several genuine grievances. The BPP has mostly, rather exclusively, ethnic Nepalese as members and supporters. Worse, many follow this party out of fear and terror perpetrated by the BPP in southern Bhutan. The Party, thus, far, has been functioning mainly from Nepal and India in exile. The Royal Government of Bhutan accepts the existence of the party but insists—and rightly so— that the party exists only in Nepal and India. On the other hand, the Royal Government of Bhutan has never insisted on the indispensability of partylessness in any fashion, a theme which was most vigorously harped on in Nepal till April 1990 (when the multiparty constitutional monarchy was established in the kingdom). Of course, the relationship between the BPP and the

Bhutanese political system is yet to be decided. Another political party called the Bhutan National Democratic Party (BNDP) surfaced in New Delhi on 5 February 1992.

As for the pressure groups in Bhutan, a large number of human rights' groups have mushroomed of late. They, too, like the BPP and the BNDP are functioning outside the kingdom only. They include: the United Liberation People's Front, People's Forum for Human Rights and the Students' Union of Bhutan, supported by organizations like the Asian Students' Association and the Asia-Pacific Students' Association.[55] These pressure groups, too, indulge in the politics of agitation and violence from time to time against the Bhutanese political system. Like the fate of the BPP and BNDP, the fate of the human rights' groups is also to be watched. Like the BPP and the BNDP, the various human rights' groups have only Nepali Bhutanese as their leaders, followers and supporters. The intensity of their activity keeps fluctuating.

The Army and the Police

The strength of the Bhutanese army is 5,000 and that of the Bhutanese police is about 1,800.[56] Time was when the army found itself surrounded by a controversy when the then Prime Minister, Jigmie Palden Dorji, was assassinated in April 1964. In fact, no less a person than Chabda Namgyal, Chief of the Army of Bhutan, who was also distantly related to the then King, Jigme Dorji Wangchuck, was found guilty of the assassination of the Prime Minister. True, death penalty was given to him in 1964 itself,[57] but what became revealing was the fact that all was not well with the army. At one point of time in 1964, even the King appeared apprehensive of the Army's loyalty.[58] As of now the Bhutanese army appears to be disciplined and without political ambition. This augurs well for any crisis situation in Bhutan.

Another significant aspect of the Bhutanese army is that in 1962, the then Prime Minister, Jigmie Palden Dorji, placed the Bhutanese army at India's disposal.[59]

As for the Bhutanese Police, it is considered to be a disciplined force, but its overenthusiasm in executing the decree on dress contributed to the creation of a crisis situation in the kingdom. In 1989, the Royal Government ordered that all Bhutanese men (irrespective of their ethnic affiliation) must wear *ghos* and all Bhutanese women (irrespective of their ethnicity) must wear *kiras* at government offices and on formal occasions. The Bhutanese Police was given the authority to fine Nu. 100 those who violated the law. As an incentive, the policeman executing the law was to be given Nu.50 out of the total. This made them work overenthusiatically and at times they fined those people who did not deserve to be fined. The fallout of this was that a large section of the Bhutanese Nepali protested against it and it led to some kind of the problem of national integration. In fact the execution was diluted subsequently but the damage was done.

The Constitution

A constitution has been defined as a fundamental statement of laws governing the citizen's political rights, the political institutions, their functions and their relationships, within a particular political community. In most cases, it is in written form, though the United Kingdom is said to possess an "unwritten" constitution.[60]

Bhutan, like Britain, could be said to possess an "unwritten" constitution, but like Britain most of its laws, as we have already seen, are codified. Of course, Bhutan dose not have a constiutional text comprising various articles, as most of the countries in South Asia, like Bangladesh, India, Maldives, Nepal, Pakistan and Sri Lanka have. However, the essence of constitutionalism is the existence of a limited government rather than an unlimited and arbitrary government. We have already seen how various checks and balances have been devised in the Bhutanese political system to preempt authoritarianism and arbitrariness. The constitutional system of any state is, to a very great extant, the indicator of its political system. Seen on this plane, we find that there is a palpable trend in the Bhutanese political system towards participation and decentralization.

The Media

The media—print as well as electronic—occupies a place of great significance in any political system. In Bhutan, one does not come across multiplicity of newspapers, as in several other countries. This may be due to a low rate of literacy and a different kind of political consciousness. But the *Kuensel* (Bhutan's national newspaper) meaning "clarity" is published every Saturday in 3 languages—Dzongkha, English and Nepali. It is, by and large, a credible newspaper and has no tendency to suppress the news—even if unpleasant. Published from Thimphu, it gives sufficient news about the happenings in various parts of Bhutan as also abroad. The weekly duration of its publication makes some people wait rather eagerly for several days after going through one issue. Its editor is young and energetic Kinley Dorji.

On the front of the electronic media, Bhutan Broadcasting Service broadcasts its programmes from 5 p.m. to 9 p.m. on weekdays and from

10 a.m. to 4 p.m. on Sundays. It broadcasts 10-minute news bulletins in 4 languages—Dzongkha, Sarchopka, Nepali and English— every evening. Besides, it plays music in all these languages. Also, it makes relevant public service announcements every evening.

Bhutan in global politics

Once Bhutan decided to abandon its centuries' old isolation in regional and international politics in the 1950s, it obtained the membership of various international organizations and established diplomatic relations with some countries. More importantly, it entered into bilateral talks with the People's Republic of China—of course, without establishing ambassadorial-diplomatic relations to demarcate its borders with the Autonomous Region of Tibet. The trend, in fact, became more pronounced after Jawaharlal Nehru became the first head of government to visit this mountain kingdom in 1958, undergoing great travails.

Bhutan joined the Colombo Plan in 1962. It became a member of the Universal Postal Union in 1969. In 1970, a Department of Foreign Affairs was formed and in 1972 it was accorded ministerial status. Bhutan was made a member of the United Nations' Organization in 1971 by a unanimous decision of its General Assembly and opened the permanent Mission of the kingdom of Bhutan at the UN in Yew York. In the same year, Bhutan also joined the Group of 77 and in December that year became the second of the world governments to recognize Bangladesh. Bangladesh is the only country, apart from India, with which Bhutan has established (1979) diplomatic-ambassadorial relations. Again, in 1971 itself, the Royal Bhutan Mission was established in New Delhi, which was subsequently designated as the Royal Bhutanese Embassy (8 August 1978). In 1972, Bhutan joined the ECAFE (now called ESCAP). In 1973, Bhutan joined the Non-Aligned Movement. In 1979 an office of the UNDP Resident Representative was established in Thimphu. In 1985, it joined the South Asian Association for Regional Cooperation (SAARC) along with all other South Asian states. In fact, Bhutan had been involved in this movement from the outset and was also a member of the SARC (South Asian Regional Cooperation) from the beginning. Bhutan has lately established diplomatic relations with Nepal as well, the Bhutanese Ambassador in India being accredited to that country, too.

Bhutan, thus, has become an international personality in the true sense of the term and there is no question of looking backward on this front. Bhutan has been receiving development assistance from friendly countries like Australia, Switzerland, Japan, the UK, Singapore, New Zealand and Austria.[61]

Summing-up

There is, thus, little doubt about the fact that the political system of Bhutan has thus far given a good account of itself. It has very largely succeeded in facing various challenges emanating from various quarters in the country. It has shown that it is truly capable of conflict resolution in the real sense of the term. It has, indeed, taken sufficient care of the political processes and functions of interest articulation and interest aggregation. This becomes all the more creditable in view of Bhutan's being a multiethnic, multilingual and multireligious state.

True, the Bhutanese have a monarchical form of government and from outside it may appear to be an absolute monarchy, but when one delves into the details of the political system, it becomes quite clear how much stress has been and is being laid on decentralization of political powers not only in theory but also in practice.

Participation, coupled with decentralization, have become the hallmark of the Bhutanese political system. It is in this context that the *Druk Gyalpo*, Jigme Singye Wangchuck, often insists that though Bhutan has a hereditary monarchy, the way it functions is much more democratic than many other political systems. The observation of the King is not off the mark.

We have already seen how the *Druk Gyalpo* has abdicated the chairmanship of the Planning Commission of the kingdom recently. We have also seen how in 1984 he got a clause added to the rules and regulations of the *Lodey Tshogdey* (Royal Advisory Council) making the monarch an object of criticism. And the *Druk Gyalpo* did so, despite serious objection to this step in various quarters in Bhutan. This goes to show how dedicated and enlightened is the Monarchy in *Druk-yul*. Over the years various other political institutions like the *Tshogdu*, the Council of Ministers and the *Lodey Tshogdey* have also been allowed to assert themselves. All this however does not mean that there are no dissenters in the Bhutanese political system. There are many Bhutanese who remain unreconciled to their political system. The *Durk Gyalpo* not only concedes the fact that some in Bhutan have been wronged but is also ready to talk to them to redress their grievances. Therein lies the crux.

This, if anything, shows that notwithstanding the non-existence of multiparty competitive pluralism in Bhutan, the system does not lack in responsiveness in any manner. It has, under the active and enlightened leadership of its King, always risen to the occasion in crisis situations.

There is, as of now, no reason to apprehend that it would lose or dilute its responsiveness in future.

Notes and References

1. Geoffrey K. Roberts, *A Dictionary of Political Analysis*, Longman, London, 1971, 167P.
2. See David Easton, in *The Blackwell Encyclopaedia of Political Institutions*, Basil Blackwell Ltd., Oxford, 1987, 478-80.
3. See K.P. Bhanumathy,"Bhutan: Some Impressions", *Mainstream*, New Delhi, 18 August 1990, 25-26.
4. Druk Gyalpo Jigme Singye Wangchuck told me so in an exclusive interview at the Tashichho Dzong, Thimphu, on 13 October 1990.
5. Ibid.
6. Sunanda K. Datta-Ray,"Flight of Dragon-II: Challenge of Settlement With China", *The Statesman*, Delhi, 28 April 1984,6.
7. *Kuensel* (Bhutan's National Newspaper), Thimphu, vol.6, no.23,15 June 1991,1-2.
8. Dasho Rigzin Dorji, Secretary, Special Commission for Cultural Affairs, Royal Government of Bhutan, told me in an exclusive personal interview at Thimphu on 14 October 1990.
9. Ibid.
10. Dasho Rigzin Dorji, *A Brief Religious, Cultural And Secular History of Bhutan*, The Asia Society Galleries, New York, 1989,13.
11. Ibid.
12. Ibid.
13. See Leo E. Rose,"Bhutan" in Francis Robinson, ed., *The Cambridge Encyclopaedia of India,Pakistan, Bangladesh, Sri Lanka, Nepal, Bhutan And The Maldives*, Cambridge University Press, Cambridge, 1989, 231-2.
14. Nagendra Singh, *Bhutan: A Kingdom In The Himalayas*, Thomson Press India Limited, New Delhi, 1978,122.
15. Dasho Rigzin Dorji, n.10,13.
16. Ibid.,14-5.
17. Dasho C. Dorji, then Deputy Minister Planning Commission (now Chairman, Planning Commission) told me in an exclusive interview at Thimphu on 12 October 1990.
18. See *Kuensel*,vol.6, no.23,15 June 1991,1-2.
19. Dasho Rigzin Dorji, n.10,15. Also See Kapileshwar Labh, "Monarchical System of Bhutan: Challenges of Modernization", in Urmila Phadnis, S.D. Muni and Kalim Bahadur, eds., *Domestic Conflicts In South Asia: vol.2: Economic and Ethnic Dimensions*, South Asian Publishers, New Delhi, 1986,193.
20. *Kuensel*, Vo1.6, no.1, 5 January 1991,4.

20a. Ibid.,vol.7, no.8, 29 February 1992,1.

21. Sunanda K. Datta-Ray, n. 6.
22. Sunanda K. Datta-Ray,"Return Of Dragon-III: Economic Progress Without Hurrying", *The Statesman*, 20 July 1981,6.
23. Ibid.
24. *Kuensel*, vol.6, no.1, 5 January 1991, 2.
25. Ibid.
26. Ibid.
27. All this information is based on the response sent by the Honourable Speaker of the *Tshogdu* to my Questionnaire presented to him.
28. Ibid.

29. Ibid.
30. Ibid.
31. Ibid.
32. Ibid.
33. Ibid.
34. Ibid.
35. Ibid.
36. Leo E. Rose, n.13, 232.
37. See Anatara Dev Sen, "The people will decide: King Jigme Singye Wangchuck on the future of Bhutan", *Sunday*, Calcutta, 28 October 1990, 28.
38. B.S. Das,"Economic Development and Social Changes in Bhutan", in Urmila Phadnis, S.D. Muni and Kalim Bahadur, eds., n. 19,88.
39. Dasho Rigzin Dorji, n.10.
40. Leo E. Rose, n. 13, 231.
41. Leo E. Rose, *The Politics Of Bhutan*, Ithaca, London, 1977, 111.
42. Ram Rahul, *The Himalaya as a Frontier*, Vikas Publishing House Pvt. Ltd., New Delhi, 1978, 92.
43. This information is based on the response to my questionnaire submitted to the Honourable Speaker of the *Tshogdu*.
44. Sunanda K. Datta-Ray, n.22.
45. "On Record", *The Statesman*, 8 September 1984, 6.
46. Sunanda K. Datta-Ray,"Druk Past & Present-II: Strategies For Survival", *The Statesman*, 11 July 1983, 6.
47. Ram Rahul, *Royal Bhutan*, Motilal Banarsidass, Delhi, 1983, 42-43.
48. Sunanda K. Datta-Ray, n.6 and K. P. Bhanumathy, n. 3.
49. B.S.Das, n. 38.
50. The Royal Government of the Kingdom of Bhutan, *Bhutan: Himalayan Kingdom*, Thimphu, 1979, 32.
51. See Nagendra Singh, n.14,135-48.
52. See Geoffrey K. Roberts, n. 1,P 145-6 and 173-4.
53. Sunanda K. Datta-Ray, n. 46.
54. M. Vinayak,"Unrest in Bhutan: The voice of a people uprooted," *Frontline*, Madras, 27 April 1991,110.
55. Sunanda K. Datta-Ray,"The Phoney Crisis: Propaganda War Against Bhutan", *The Sunday Statesman*, Delhi, 2 September 1990, 6.
56. King Jigme Singye Wangchuck told me in an exclusive interview at Thimphu on 13 October 1990.
57. Nari Rustomji, *Bhutan: The Dragon Kingdom In Crisis*, Oxford University Press, Delhi,1978, 54-66.
58. Ibid
59. Sunanda K. Datta-Ray,"Return of the Dragon-I: Bhutan Prepares To Talk To China", *The Statesman*, 17 July 1981, 6.
60. Geoffrey K. Roberts, n.1,49C.
61. See The Royal Government of the Kingdom of Bhutan, n. 50, 30 and Dasho Rigzin Dorji, n. 10,15.

4

Monarchy And Monarchs

We have seen how important and pivotal has been the role of the monarchy in Bhutan's political, social, economic and religious spheres. In fact, the core of the kingdom's political system, to a very great extent, is represented by the institution of monarchy. As such, it rightly deserves an independent chapter.

At the outset, let us be clear about the words "monarchy" and "monarch" in order to understand their various manifestations in the context of the Himalayan kingdom. Monarchy has been defined as "a form of government with a monarch at the head" as also "a state with this".[1] It has also been described as "a state ruled by monarch, rule by a monarch".[2] It has, moreover been explained as "a system in which a monarch reigns over a country and in which the next monarch will be another member of the same family".[3]

Roger Scruton has rather dealt with the concept in a greater detail. Dwelling upon the concept of monarchy, he observed the following:

> Literally, rule by one. As now understood, however, the form of government in which the head of state holds office, usually with the title of King or Queen, either for life or until voluntary renunciation (by 'abdication'). Monarchies are of two fundamental kinds: absolute monarchy and limited monarchy (of which the modern constitutional monarchy is a variant). In the latter, the person who reigns does not necessarily rule, in the strict sense of controlling the outcome of executive decisions, but may perhaps exert no more than a merely ceremonial, or perhaps partly regulative function. The absolute monarchy is obsolete in one sense: that is, those who hold absolute power for life nowadays rearely do so as a matter of law, and tend to dignify themselves not with the title of King or Queen, but with that

of Chairman (when the government is through the machinery of a party) or President. The distinction is a nice one. It is not that the title of King is hearditary, while that of Chairman is not. There have been elected kings (as in Poland), and hereditary 'lord protectors' (Richard Cromwell) : there might easily be hereditary party chairmen.

Commenting on the reasons for praise or cirtcism of hereditary monarchy, Scruton observes:

> Hereditary monarchy is often praised, on the ground that it enables the Head of State to achieve office without having to scramble for it, and on the ground that it implants an idea of continuity and legitimacy at the heart of popular sentiments towards the state. It is criticized, like all applications of hereditray principles, on the ground that it is arbitrary—i.e., there is no relation between the office filled and qualifications of the person destined to fill it.[4]

Analysing the origin and power of the institution of Monarchy, the noted philosopher, Bertrand Russell, has written that:

> The origin of kings, like that of priests, is pre-historic, and the early stages in the evolution of kingship can only be conjectured from what still exists among the most backward savages. When the institution is fully developed, but has not yet begun to decline, the king is a man who leads his tribe or nation in war, who decides when to make war and when to make peace; often, though not always, he makes the laws and controls the administration of justice. His title to the throne is usually in a greater or lesser degree hereditary. He is, moreover, a sacred person; if not himself a god, he is at least the Lord's anointed.[5]

Dwelling upon the increase of power of the kings, Russell has observed that:

> It is clear that war must have played a great part in increasing the power of kings, since in war the need of unified command is obvious. To make the monarchy hereditary it is the easiest way of avoiding the evils of a disputed succession; even if the king has power of appointing his successor, he is pretty sure to choose one of his family. But dynasties do not last for ever, and every royal family begins with a usurper or foreign conqueror. Usually religion legitimizes the new family by means of some traditional ceremony. Priestly power profits by these occasions, since it comes to be an essential support of the royal prestige. "No Bishop, no King", said Charles I, and the

> analogue of this maxim has been true in all ages in which kings have existed. The position of king appears to ambitious people such a desirable one that only powerful religious sanctions will make them renounce the hope of acquiring it themselves.[6]

It is also significant to note that kings appealed to 'divine right', and sought, as far as possible to make their power traditional and quasi-religious. They were partially successful in this. The execution of Charles I, for instance, was felt to be an impiety, not merely an ordinary crime. In France, St Louis was erected into a legendary figure, some of whose piety descended as a cloak even to Louis XV, who was still "the most Christian King". Having created a new Court aristocracy, monarchs tended to prefer it to the bourgeoisie.[7]

Palpably, as an institution or as a political system, monarchy is both ancient and religious. It is also obvious that without constitutional checks, this institution can create havoc. The conflict between the concepts of absolute monarchy and constitutional monarchy is going on in several parts of the world, especially wherever the institution exists. Of course, the degrees and forms of the debates vary. But in many a Third World state monarchy has somehow become most accepted institution within the political system. The reasons for this are not far to seek. Other political institutions having more or even same kind of political legitimacy and credibility have not emerged. Also, in most of the cases, where monarchies do exist, the kings have become great unifying forces within the political systems. Hence their importance. On the other hand, political culture of these states are also responsible for sustaining this institution within their political systems. The very fact that the desirability of the restablishment of monarchy—no matter in whatever form—is discussed in countries like Afghanistan and Iran from time to time by various segments of their populace makes it patent that the institution remains important and also relevant. That the British are not thinking of any alternative to this institution, despite the beheading of one king and banishment of another, also makes it amply clear how important and relevant this institution is to them. The recent happenings in Cambodia also focus on the institution's importance.

Of course, while discussing the institution of monarchy, much clarity has been achieved about the word "monarch" or "king". But we will do well to devote some more space to this word exclusively. A "monarch" has been defined as "a sovereign with the title of king, queen, emperor, empress, or the equivalent", "a supreme ruler", "a powerful or pre-eminent person".[8] He has also been described as "a person ruling, usually by hereditary rights and for his life time, over a kingdom or people, and invested either with absolute or constitutional power", "the chief person of this kind or class".[9] Also, a "monarch is a king, queen, or other royal person who reigns over a country or an empire".[10]

In other words, the post or office of a monarch is based on hereditary principles. Generally, the eldest son of the reigning or ruling (or both) king succeeds him to the throne upon his death or abdication. In case the king has no son, the rule of succession to the throne is determined by the due process of law. Such problems and their solutions vary from country to country. As such, there are no fixed solutions. What, however, is certain in such an eventuality is that such a successor is often a close relative of the preceding monarch. Generally, conventions and practices to deal with such situations are so common and well-known in various monarchical systems that rarely ever has a crisis situation appeared. In fact, this in itself is considered as a very strong point in support of the institution of monarchy or the monarchical political system.

Origin of the Monarchical System in Bhutan

The origin and establishment of the monarchical system in the Himalayan kingdom of Bhutan indeed constitutes a very significant chapter of its political history. It has perhaps one of the most recent origins inasmuch as it was established as late as 1907. Equally significant, if not also more, was the fact that the monarchy in Bhutan was established as an elected institution. Of course, subsequently it became hereditary and continues to be so. Before the establishment of the monarchical system in 1907, the kingdom was under a system which can be appropriately called the Shabdung system, named after Shabdung Ngawang Namgyal.

It was in 1637 (some believe it to be 1639) that Lama Shabdung Ngawang Namgyal became the supreme sprititual head of the kingdom of Bhutan. He was mainly responsible for the unification of Bhutan in the true sense of the term. It is also worth mentioning here that from 1637 (when Lama Shabdung Namgyal established his hold) to 1907 (when monarchy was established), Bhutan conducted its internal and external affairs independenly of Tibet, China and Britain.[11] Relevantly, Shabdung Ngawang Namgyal was the first lawgiver of Bhutan and he ruled in accordance with the Buddhist laws. For the protection of the peasantry, he passed laws forbidding the levy of anything beyond voluntary contribution. He successfully suppressed banditry in the kingdom. Namgyal also paid special attention to irrigation and bridge-building. He encouraged commerce and handicrafts in Bhutan. In the event, he was held in the highest esteem by the Bhutanese.

Mentionably, 3 separate manifestations of Shabdung Ngawang Namgyal were recognized. They were *Kutul* (body mainfestation), *Sungtul* (speech manifestation) and *Thugtul* (mind manifestation). The *modus operandi* of descovery of his rebirth as well as his installation was similar to that of the Dalai Lama and other high lamas of Tibet. The successive manifestations continued to rule the country actually or nominally till the monarchy was established in 1907.[12] Relevantly, the Shabdung system was inherently unstable. The Shabdungs, like the Dalai Lama, being reincarnates, led to long gaps in succession. During the 250 years of theocracy, thus, there were only 7 Shabdungs, leading to long periods of struggle and turmoil. There used to be serious struggle for power among the interim rulers like the *Druk Desi* (the secular head), the *Penlops* (governors) and the *Dzongpens* (regional heads).[13]

1903 proved to be a dividing line in this development. In 1903, both the Shabdung Lama and Desi Yanglob Sangye Dorji (1883-1903) died. As a result, both the spiritual and temporal authorities of Druk-yul were vested in Chhole Tulku Yishi Ngodub, the then *Je Khenpo* of Bhutan. 1907 was to prove another turning point. In that year Chhole Tulku died. On 17 December 1907 the high lamas and key chiefs of Bhutan acclaimed Ugyen Wangchuck, the then Tongsa Penlop and the most powerful chief among the contenders for the office of the Durk Desi, as the *Druk Gyalpo* (King) of Bhutan, or the hereditary ruler of the kingdom. For some years, a few chiefs owing allegiance to the then Paro Penlop, Dawa Paljor—who was also Ugyen Wangchuck's erstwhile adversary—remained practically independent. However, in 1918, Dawa Paljor died and in that very year the *Druk Gyalpo* ensured the loyalty of all chiefs to himself.[14] Indeed, it was a great achievement as far as the consolidation of the Bhutanese political system was concerned.

Significantly, in the Shabdung political system, the concept of dual authority—one supreme in the religious matters and the other supreme in the temporal matters—prevailed. Whereas the Dharma Raja exercised authority over religious matters, the Deb Raja looked after secular matters. While the former was chosen through the reincarnation process, the latter was elected by a council of lamas. However, the division of authority could not prevent the rise of civil strife in the kingdom. The Deb Raja, who was elected by a council of Lamas, became merely a nominee of the most powerful of Penlops in the 19th century. This period witnessed a number of civil wars. The kingdom was wellnigh divided among semi-independent chiefs. It was under these circumstances that monarchy came to be established in 1907.[15] Needless to stress, the institution of monarchy was badly needed at that point of time to save Bhutan from chaos and disintegration.

How important a place religion occupied in Bhutan even after the establishment of monarchy in 1907 is palpable from the fact that the present royal family of Bhutan traces its ancestory from Lama Pemalingpa or Peling for short (1450-1521) of central Bhutan.[16]

A couple of more facts need to be mentioned here in the context of the origin of monarchy in Bhutan. First, the British imperial and colonial masters of India had throughout the 18th and 19th centuries sought for a strong central authority in Bhutan. This desire had become more pronounced after 1865, when a treaty between India and Bhutan was signed. The British had always disliked the idea of having to deal directly with the powerful chiefs over the head of the central Bhutanese authority. The British, therefore, not only fully supported the installation of Ugyen Wangchuck as the first *Druk Gyalpo* of *Druk-yul*, but also decided to address him as His Highness the Maharaja of Bhutan.[17] Secondly, the institution of monarchy became the first such institution of national importance and, therefore, it could command the loyalty of all segments of the Bhutanese society.[18] In a way, it converted the society into the state. It ushered in a new era in the kingdom's history and marked the beginning of the process of modernization. no matter whatever its pace at that particular point of time.

Druk Gyalpo Ugyen Wangchuck (1907-1926)

Druk Gyalpo Ugyen Wangchuck, who had the privilege and distinction of becoming the first King of Bhutan in 1907, had on several occasions in the past shown his political clouts, guts and maturity. For instance, towards the end of 1884, Ugyen Wangchuck (then Tongsa Penlop) and Tshewang Norbu (then Paro Penlop) revolted against Desi Kawa Zangpo (1882-83) for withholding their shares of the British subsidy. The *Desi* was supported by Phuntshog Dorji and Alo Dorji, *Dzongpons* of Punakha and Thimphu respectively. In the battle of Changlimithang (May 1885), immediately below Thimphu and on the right of the Wang river, Phuntsog Dorji was killed and Alo Dorji was defeated. This established the supremacy of Ugyen Wangchuck so firmly and unequivocally that no important civil or internecine strife occurred in Bhutan thereafter.[19] Moreover, Emperor Kuang-hsu (1875-1908) had conferred on Ugyen Wangchuck (in his capacity as the Tongsa Penlop) the title of the Chief of Bhutan, as Bhutan had remained neutral during the Anglo-Tibetan War of 1888-89.[20] This, once again, proved Ugyen Wangchuck's diplomatic maturity. In fact, this episode made the British more cautious and they viewed with great concern this increase in the Manchu interest in Bhutan.

Besides, Ugyen Wangchuck had impressed the British during its military expedition to Tibet in 1903-04. In his capacity as the Tongsa Penlop, Ugyen Wangchuck allowed western Bhutan to be surveyed for the road up to Amo Chhu. Ugyen Wangchuck along with Lama Kunzang, head of the Da Tshang (monastic college) of Punakha and Thimphu (who was also related to the former), accompanied the British expeditionary force to Lhasa. Because of the great respect commanded by these Bhutanese leaders), Colonel Francis Younghusband, leader of the British expedition, succeeded in getting the convention signed by the high lamas and officials of the Government of Tibet on 7 September 1904.[21] Obviously impressed by the gesture and influence of Ugyen Wangchuck, the British Government in India conferred in 1905 on the former the title of the Knight Commander of the Indian Empire (KCIE).[22]

J.C.White, the political agent to Bhutan, functioning to enforce the well-defined policy of the Government of India, had realized that Ugyen Wangchuck was the most important and most strong personality in Bhutan. It is because of this that the British also wished to see him occupy the throne of Druk-yul with a view to obviating the problem of dealing with so many people. It is now widely held that the British had played a significant place in getting Ugyen Wangchuck elected as the Druk Gyalpo of Bhutan in 1907. But even without any external help, Ugyen Wangchuck would have established himself as the monarch of Bhutan sooner or later.[23] He had, in fact, always risen to the occasion and proved his mettle. In fact, by being elected as monarch, he had shown that he had succeeded well in a competitive political process. He gave a good account of himself subsequently as well.

Modernization: At the turn of the 20th century, Bhutan entered a new phase of modernization. Its problems and relations with the neighbouring countries hastened its modernization. The post-1904 developments in Tibet were rather ominous for Bhutan. No sooner had the troops of Chao Erh-feng occupied Lhasa on 12 February 1910 and compelled the 13th Dalai Lama to seek refuge in India than the Manchu government laid claim to Bhutan along with Nepal and Sikkim. After his two visits to India (to Calcutta in 1905 and to Delhi in 1911), Ugyen Wangchuck realized the importance of education in his own country. He decided to introduce modern education in Bhutan and move his country towards modernization. In 1914, he set up a school at Ha in, Western Bhutan. He also established another school at Bumthang in Central Bhutan. During 1924-29, he sent about 15 Bhutanese students, who had passed Matriculation examination, for training in different technical institutions in India.

Moving his country on the path of modernization, Ugyen Wangchuck also attempted to develop his country's economy. He took a great step in this direction in 1914, when he appointed J.C.White, ex-political officer in Sikkim, as agent empowering him to enter into agreement with capitalists desirous of making investment in Bhutan. White drew up schemes for the exploitation of mineral and timber resources of his country. However, the scheme for development of the natural resources of Bhutan came to naught, as appointment of White as the country's agent was cancelled following differences over White's remuneration, which he estimated at Rs.45,000 per annum. Lack of capital was, in any case, a big stumbling block in the way of introducing programmes of modernization. Bhutan needed foreign economic resources and none was forthcoming at that point of time. Pace of modernization, therefore, had to be quite slow.[24]

Foreign Affairs: The activities of the Ugyen Wangchuck regime in foreign affairs were also quite significant. The Government of India revised the Treaty of 1865 on 8 January 1910 in view of China's effort to bring Bhutan within its sphere of influence. There were several important features of the 1910 Treaty signed at Punakha. First, the British pledged never to interfere in the internal affairs of Bhutan and Bhutan declared its readiness to abide by the advice of the Governmant of India in regard to its external affairs. Secondly, the Government of India also increased the annual subsidy to Bhutan from Rs. 50,000 to Rs. 1,00,000. This treaty was a turning point in the history of modern Bhutan inasmuch as it placed Bhutan on the same footing as Sikkim as far as the management and conduct of its foreign relations were concerned.

A significant question arises here. Why did Ugyen Wangchuck cast his lot with the British? There were, of course, several reasons for that. First, the success of the British against the Tibetans in the summer of 1904 had left a strong imprint in his mind. Secondly, Druk Gyalpo Ugyen Wangchuck wanted protection against Manchu expansionism in Bhutan. Thirdly, a shrewd politician as he was, Ugyen Wangchuck realized the impossibility of Bhutan's existance as a separate political entity without the British pleasure. Fourthly, Ugyen Wangchuck was impressed by various progresses made during the British rule in India.

He visited Delhi in 1911 for the Darbar of King George V, formerly His Royal Highness the Prince of Wales. Ugyen Wangchuck had first met him in Calcutta in 1906.

How did the British view the status of Bhutan during the reign of Druk Gyalpo Ugyen Wangchuck? In 1924, the Secretary of State for India defined Bhutan's political status as "an autonomous state under British suzerainty" but not as "an Indian princely state", even though its transition to that status could have easily been affected then with the concurrence of both the parties.[25]

In foreign affairs, Bhutan faced a serious problem with China, when the latter tried to bring it under its influence. We have already seen how China occupied Lhasa on 12 February 1910 and compelled the 13th Dalai Lama to seek refuge in India. More ominously, the Manchu government laid claim to Bhutan along with Nepal and Sikkim. However, because of his diplomatic skill, which had helped him in establishing good relations with the Government in New Delhi, Ugyen Wangchuck succeeded in overcoming this crisis. Bhutan succeeded in maintaining and retaining its independent political identity.

Despite showing his diplomatic skill and maintaining his country's independence, Ugyen Wangchuck could not take his country further on the path of modernization. The traditional isolationist policy of Bhutan made him abandon the experiment in modern education in Bhutan. Nor could Bhutan make much stride in the economic field because of the lack of capital and support from other quarters. However, the importance of Ugyen Wangchuck in Bhutan's history lies in the fact that he was the main initiator of a political system in the country which continues to this day in a reformed and beneficial form. His contribution to Bhutan's political life will be remembered for ever.

Druk Gyalpo Jigme Wangchuck (1926-52)

Druk Gyalpo Ugyen Wangchuck, the first king of the Wangchuck dynasty in Bhutan, passed away on 21 August 1926. He was succeeded to the throne by his eldest son, Jigme Wangchuck (b. 1906). His formal coronation was held on 14 March 1927. In his reply to the speech of Colonel F.M.Bailey, Political Officer in Sikkim and leader of the British party, the young Maharaja expressed his loyalty to the British connection. Revealingly, Jigme Wangchuck spoke in Hindi on that occasion. It was palpably a great compliment to India in then existing political circumstances. He promised to continue the policy of his father *vis-a-vis* the British rule.[26]

The second Druk Gyalpo, Jigme Wangchuck, consolidated his authority over the entire kingdom. Significantly, during his rule, the authority of the Penlop was assumed by the King himself and the office of the Penlop remained but an honorary title.[27] In a way, the office of the Penlop was eclipsed.

Modernization: Jigme Wangchuck continued the process of modernization set in motion by his illustrious father and predecessor. He also opened new schools and sent Bhutanese students to different cities in India for technical training. In 1933, he sent about 15 Bhutanese youngmen to India for military training. However, the politico-economic and social spheres of the country remained by and large unchanged.[28]

Foreign Affairs: King Jigme Wangchuck accompanied by the Queen paid his first visit to India in December 1934. The Royal couple visited the gun and shell factory at Cossipore (Calcutta) and inspected each and every department of the factory. They showed special interest in the various processes of manufacture. The Druk Gyalpo also visited the Statesman House during his tour and acquainted himself with the mode of production of the newspaper.[29]

During the visit of the British Cabinet Mission to India in 1946, the Government of Bhutan presented a memorandum. While confirming its special ties with India, it affirmed its separate identity from the other princely states in India. On its part, the Cabinet Mission made no commitment beyond reaffirming Bhutan's political status in line with the minute of the Secretary of State for India in 1924. When the British withdrew from India on 15 August 1947, Bhutan's status in relation to new India became a matter of conjecture. At that time, Bhutan was autonomous and not a part of India. Relevantly, it was more free of British control than Sikkim, but it was less free from British control than Nepal. In the event, the Himalayan kingdom's relations with new India began in a climate of suspicion and misunderstanding. Ram Rahul writes:

> Owing the certain extraneous reasons the Bhutanese authorities felt that the new India would be imperialistic towards their country. They, therefore, thought of forging a federation of Sikkim and Bhutan in association with Tibet as a counter-weight to India. Towards the end of 1948,. a Bhutanese delegation visited India to discuss Bhutanese relations. The Government of India assured Bhutan that it would respect Bhutan's autonomy if it maintained the same relationship with Independent India as with British India.[30]

To end the existing and growing confusion, Druk Gyalpo Jigme Wangchuck decided to renew Bhutanese connections with the post-colonial and post-imperialist India by signing a Treaty called "India-

Bhutan Treaty of Friendship, 1949" in Darjeeling on 8 August 1949. Bhutan agreed to be guided by India's advice in regard to the country's external affairs. On its part, India pledged not to interfere in the internal affairs of Bhutan. (Article 2). India undertook to guide not to control Bhutan's external affairs. Moreover, India agreed to pay Bhutan an annual subsidy of Rs. 5,00,000. (Article 3). It was in place of "the compensation granted to the Government of Bhutan under Article IV of the treaty of Sinchula and enhanced by the treaty of the eighth day of January 1910 and the temporary subsidy of Rs.1 lakh per annum granted in 1942". Besides, India consented to return to Bhutan, within a year from the signature of the treaty, the 32-square mile territory known as Dewangiri. The Bhutanese government renamed it Deothang. It now forms the southernmost tip of Bhutan. Other articles of the 1949 Treaty relate to free import by Bhutan—with the approval of the Government of India—from or through India, arms, ammunition and machinery required for the development and progress of Bhutan. (Article 6). Free trade and commerce between the territories of the Government of India and the Government of Bhutan was also agreed upon.(Article 5). Both the Governments also agreed to give equal justice to the subjects of others in their territories.(Article 7).

The Treaty of 1949, which still remains in existence, provided a broad famework of relationship between the two neighbours disproportionate in sizes and different in political status, aims and objectives. It was something that was very badly needed at that point of time. King Jigme Wangchuck's contribution on this front will be remembered for ever. The Indo-Bhutan Treaty was the result of negotiation in which Bhutan found that it was to her advantage to get the aid of free India in guiding her external relations once it was clearly and unequivocally established that Bhutan was no part of India. As the Bhutanese delegation had pointed out that it did not like the use of the title of "Maharaja" (which was uniformally borne by the rulers of Indian states), the 1949 Treaty is careful enough to recognize the title of the "Druk Gyalpo". Besides, whereas the instruments of accession and the merger agreements signed by the Government of India with Indian rulers were all solemnized by the signature of the ruler himself and not by his representative, the Treaty of 1949 does not bear the signature of the Druk Gyalpo himself, but of his representatives who had full powers to sign on behalf of the Government of the Druk Gyalpo of Bhutan. Again, significantly, like any other treaty negotiated with a full sovereign power, instruments of ratification were exchanged at the highest level, namely C. Rajagopalachari,

Governor General of India, who ratified the treaty on behalf of India on the one side and Jigme Wangchuck, the Druk Gyalpo of Bhutan, on the other side.[31]

It would be no exaggeration to suggest that the second Druk Gyalpo of the Wangchuck dynasty, Jigme Wangchuck, tried to modernize Bhutan in a number of ways, while being careful and cautious in doing so with a view to preserving the identity and culture of the country by keeping it away from outside influence.[32] Needless to stress, by moving with care and caution, he consolidated the political system which his father had established and elevated the position of Bhutan as a political entity by signing a treaty with India. Circumstances at home and around were such as did not call for going radically in any direction. Jigme Wangchuck played his part well. He did what was needed.

Druk Gyalpo Jigme Dorji Wangchuck (1952-72)

Druk Gyalpo Jigme Dorji Wangchuck was the third person from the Wangchuck dyanasty to ascend the throne of the kingdom of Bhutan. He was the product of a different political socialization process in comparison to his father and immediate predecessor, Jigme Wangchuck, and grandfather and first Wangchuck king, Ugyen Wangchuck. He came to occupy the throne (27 October 1952) at a time when South Asia had witnessed and was still witnessing significant political changes. India had become independent, of course, after a division into two states. The British colonial masters had also withdrawn from Sri Lanka (then Ceylon) in February 1948. The only other Himalayan state in South Asia, Nepal, had also perforce given up its political isolation and after the overthrow of the Ranarchy (the system of hereditary prime ministership) in February 1951, the country was moving towards a responsible and accountable government along with the subsystem of constitutional monarchy. Political parties, including the most popular Nepali Congress, were being accepted as the agents of modernization. In the vicinity of Bhutan, while Sikkim (an autonomous state between India and China) was still free and untouched by political turmoils, Tibet had been taken over by China in 1950. The take-over of Tibet could not have left the Bhutanese elite in peace in any sense of the term. The importance of Tibet and Sikkim at that time also lay in the fact that apart from Bhutan these were the only 2 other states in the world based on Mahayana Buddhism.

Under those circumstances prevailing in the region, Druk Gyalpo Jigme Dorji Wangchuck rose to the occasion and gave a good account of himself by effecting significant and substantial changes and reforms in every walk of Bhutan's life.

Political Reforms: On the political plane, King Jigme Dorji Wangchuck effected a change of great significance and consequence by establishing the *Tshogdu* (National Assembly). By establishing this institution, the Druk Gyalpo, in fact, introduced the concept of representative government into Wangchuck system.[33] When it was established in 1953, it aimed at involving different sections of the people in the decision-making process of the kingdom. Intitially, there were about 130 members—10 government officials, 10 lamas and 110 representatives of the people. In the 1960s, the membership was increased to 150 with the addition of 20 more members from the government services. The *Tshogdu* members have been guaranteed complete freedom of speech. Thay can discuss and pass resolutions on any subject. Under the 1953 royal order, the decisions of the *Tshogdu* have to be passed by a two-thirds majority to be assented by the King before it becomes a law.

In the 1960s, Druk Gyalpo Jigme Dorji Wangchuck took further steps in the direction of political reforms and in that context he also vested the *Tshogdu* with soverign authority. In 1968, he surrendered his veto power on the decisions of the *Tshogdu*. The decisions of that body were thereafter to be regarded as final without the approval of the King. However, the Druk Gyalpo retained the power to address the *Tshogdu* and refer back to it any resolution about which he had "serious misgivings". He also recommended to the *Tshogdu* that all appointments of ministers "be decided by the National Assembly". But what was a more radical and quite unprecedented step in the history of monarchies all over the world was the Druk Gyalpo's recommendation to the *Tshogdu* in 1968 that all government officials, including the King, be obliged to resign from office if they receive a no-confidence vote in the Assembly.[34]

King Jigme Dorji Wangchuck established the *Lodey Tshogdey* (Royal Advisory Council) in 1965 to advise him on the development implementation programmes and on other matters of national importance. The *Lodey Tshogdey* had 8 members—5 representatives of the people, 2 representatives of the monastic order and 1 nominee of the King. Subsequently, the number of people's representatives was increased to 6 and now it comprises 9 members in all. Continuing his political reforms, King Jigme Dorji Wangchuck appointed 3 Ministers in 1968 and constituted what may be regarded as the first Council of Ministers in Bhutan. Till 1964, there existed the office of Prime Minister in Bhutan. In that year Prime Minister Jigmie Palden Dorji was assassinated and the office remained vacant thereafter. By not appointing anyone to that office even in 1968, the King showed that he would like to function as his own Prime Minister.

The Druk Gyalpo was keenly aware of the importance of the rule of law. He took a great step in the direction of judicial reform by separating the judiciary from the executive and by establishing a High Court at Thimphu. Being essentially modern in his outlook and actuated also by the great religion which the Buddha taught, he abolished capital punishment in Bhutan.[35]

These steps of King Jigme Dorji Wangchuck were obviously aimed at converting a hereditary monarchy into a constitutional monarchy. He moved Bhutan towards democratization, decentralization, participation and modernization in every sense of the term. It was a grand exercise in political development. It is palpable that he was quite alive and alert to what was happening in the South Asian region outside Bhutan. He did not wish Bhutan to be left behind completely in the race. Of course, he had to take into account the socio-political consciousness of the Bhutanese, by and large, as well. As such, he moved with care and caution and did it very well. The official bulletin of the Royal Government of Bhutan, the *Kuensel*, wrote something revealing in its issue of 15 June 1969. Referring to the proceedings of the *Tshogdu* held between 9 and 31 May 1969, the *Kuensel* wrote:

> Although Bhutan has so far achieved stability and prosperity under a system of hereditary monarchy vested with absolute powers, the present ruler felt that in keeping with the changed circumstances prevailing in the world at present, a system of constitutional monarchy would be the most desirable form of Government for the country. It was suggested to the Tshogdu by the present ruler that we should develop a system of Government in which the King would continue to rule only as long as he enjoyed popular support. His Majesty the King, therefore, proposed that if the people did not want a particular ruler, he could be removed by a two-thirds of majority of votes of the Tshogdu members. The throne would be occupied by the next in order of succession of the Wangchuck dynasty. After a prolonged debate the proposal was carried by an overwhelming majority.
>
> The incumbent ruler also proposed that the *Tshogdu* should vote on the issue of a King's continuance as a matter of routine after a fixed period of time. After debate it was decided by the Tshogdu that the routine vote on whether the ruling King should continue or not should be taken by secret ballot every three years. This routine voting on whether the King enjoys the confidence of the people or not is in addition to the right of the Tshogdu to move a motion of no

confidence against a ruler at any Assembly session. The Tshogdu also decided to initiate this procedure of routine voting by taking a vote of confidence on the present ruler. *Vote was taken by secret ballot and it was found that 135 members were in favour of the present King's continuance, two were against and one abstained from voting.* (emphasis mine).[36]

Economic Reforms: King Jigme Dorji Wangchuck effected significant reforms in the economic sphere as well. In 1956, the Druk Gyalpo introduced land reforms aimed at ensuring the security of tenure and enabled the country to change over from a barter to a money economy. He placed ceilings on large land-holdings.[37] More importantly, he surrendered a considerable portion of his own private lands to the government.[38] Needless to state, his reforms in the economic field were commendable.

Social Reforms: The steps taken by King Jigme Dorji Wangchuck in the direction of social reforms were no less significant and commendable. He abolished serfdom and took steps to improve the position of women in Bhutanese society.[39] He was quite conscious of the problem of societal disintegration which arises, *inter alia,* because of conflicts among various ethnic groups in any society.Knowing as he did the pluralistic reality of Bhutanese society after he ascended the throne in 1952, serious efforts were made to integrate the Nepalese in the state in and societal structures in the true sense of the term. This aspect was not stressed or even taken seriously earlier. They were given representation in the *Tshogdu*, when it was established in 1953. They were recruited in the army and the police. They were also selected for various civil service posts in the kingdom. Thus, the King made serious efforts to bring the Nepalese to the mainstream of the country's national life.

Cultural Consolidation: While effecting various significant reforms in various spheres of the Kingdom's life, the King was not oblivious of the necessity of preserving the country's cultural heritage. The country witnessed a renaissance of its art and culture under his patronage. Numerous schools were established to promote painting, dancing, singing and sculpture. A school of language was set up at Thimphu to teach the *Dzongkha* language. The Druk Gyalpo took care to see that regular books were published in the language of the soil. Besides, a national museum was founded at Paro.[40]

Advancement Towards Secularism: Aware and conscious as the *Druk Gyalpo* was of all-round change and reforms in the particular time frame, he even attempted at advancing his country in the direction of secularism to some extent. That obviously was a revealing step in the given socio-religious framework of the mountain kingdom. Writing in 1974, Gisela Bonn and Giselher Wirsing observed that the late Monarch had reduced the subsidies to the state monasteries substantially. "Instead of one-fourth of the state budget, the monks have received only five per cent from the treasury in the last few years." They opined that even the private monasteries had only scanty means at their disposal.[41] In the then socio-politico-religious milieu of Bhutan this step cannot be called anything short of radical.

Building-up the Army : King Jigme Dorji Wangchuck also made serious attempts to build an army for *Druk-yul*. It was, in fact, a difficult and challenging task. Prior to the mid-1950s, *Druk-yul* did not have a regular military force. Of course, the royalty maintained a small palace guard but it was not a trained force. The *Dzongpen* (district officer) of every district maintained a small militia, more or less, on the line of a police force to maintain law and order at the local level. In 1955, the King took up the task of establishing an army as a regular military force. However, by 1964, the size of the country's army grew to about 9,000-strong. In 1961, 2 years after the flight of the Dalai Lama from Tibet to India, King Jigme Dorji Wangchuck called military instructors from India to his country. The tension between India and China concerning the Himalayan region had increased. The only chance to keep his neutrality, the *Druk Gyalpo* saw was in strengthening his Royal Bhutanese Army, which he had called up in the mid-50s. Since the Sino-Indian conflict, Bhutan earmarks half of its budget for defence.[42] A significant dimension related to the Royal Bhutanese Army is that in 1962, the then Prime Minister, Jigmie Palden Dorji, placed it at India's disposal.[43]

However, the building-up of the army proved to be a tortuous task inasmuch as it, *inter alia,* led to the assassination of Prime Minister Jigmie Palden Dorji on 5 April 1964. The then Chief of the Royal Bhutanese Army was said to be indirectly involved in the conspiracy to eleminate Dorji. It was widely believed that the old elements in the Royal Bhutanese Army were not happy with the preponderance of new elements there and they considered Jigmie Dorji responsible for this state of affairs. Hence his assassination. For quite some time it appeared that indiscipline had gripped the army. However, this toothing trouble appears to be over today.

Foreign Affairs: We have already seen how Jigme Dorji Wangchuck came to occupy the throne of Bhutan at a time when things were changing rapidly and fundamentally in the whole of South Asia. Obviously,

Bhutan could not have remained secluded any more. One of the tasks to be performed by the *Druk Gyalpo* became the conduct of foreign affairs with care and caution. He had to do a tightrope walking indeed. And he came out with flying colours.

Needless to state, the relations between India and Bhutan were put to a great strain after the Sino-Indian War of 1962. China had, indeed, been trying to treat Bhutan as an independent personality beyond the framework of the Treaty of 1949 signed between India and Bhutan, even during the era of Sino-Indian friendship. The Chinese attempted to send gifts to the Druk Gyalpo in 1953. In 1955, the Chinese officials in Lhasa started issuing visas directly to the Bhutanese citizens oblivious of the spirit of the 1949 Treaty. In 1959, China forcibly occupied Bhutanese enclaves in Tibet. Consequently, Bhutan withdrew its representative in Lhasa and its officer in Western Tibet, and sealed its frontier with Tibet.[44]

Relevantly, the Druk Gyalpo in his capacity as the Crown Prince had visited the United Kingdom in January 1950. This was the first ever visit of the Bhutanese King or Prince to that country. Jigmie Palden Dorji—who subsequently became the Prime Minister of the country in 1958—and Da Tsap Namgyal had accompanied him there.[45]

Druk Gyalpo Jigme Dorji Wangchuck visited India in the summer of 1954. He received a grand welcome during his tour of the huge South Aisan neighbour. King Jigme Dorji Wangchuck visited India again in February 1960, especially for discussing Bhutan's defence and economic development. A great friend of India—who could speak chaste and fluent Hindi—he was given a warm welcome, wherever he went. Prior to the King's visit of 1960, a Bhutanese delegation, led by Prime Minister Jigmie Palden Dorji, had visited New Delhi on 18 September 1959 for discussing with the Government of India development needs of Bhutan. Accordingly, India gave a sum of Rs. 150 million as aid to Bhutan for taking up road projects there.[46]

Jigme Dorji Wangchuck toured India officially on the eve of his kingdom's admission to the United Nations between 6 and 12 April 1971. This visit was, to a great extent, a turning point in the relationship between the two countries. Speculations were rife, before the visit of the King to India, both in India and abroad, that the 1949 Treaty would require changes in view of Bhutan's admission to the UN. The King set such speculations at rest by averring that Bhutan's advent in international affairs would be gradual, and as a friend and partner of India. He expressed his satisfaction with the 1949 Treaty and ruled out any revision thereof.

India was no less warm in its friendship towards Bhutan. Prime Minister Jawaharlal Nehru visited Bhutan in September 1958 undergoing an arduous journey. He visited that country via the Chumbi Valley of Tibet. On 23 September 1953, in a public address in Paro, he pooh-poohed any pressure on Bhutan which might impair its independence. Speaking in the Lok Sabha on 28 August 1959, Nehru stressed that the protection of the frontiers and territorial integrity of Bhutan was the responsibility of the Government of India. In other words, India committed itself to the security and integrity of Bhutan, despite the absence of any clause relating to Bhutan's defence and secuity in the 1949 Treaty.

In 1970, President V.V. Giri of India was specially invited by King Jigme Dorji Wangchuck on a state visit to Bhutan. He reached Thimphu by helicopter which landed on the new heliport of Bhutan's capital. Nagendra Singh, India's Political Officer in Bhutan accompanied the President on this state visit. The visit was marked by great cordiality on both sides. It was during this state visit that India's wish to sponsor Bhutan as a new member of the United Nations was given a concrete shape.[47]

It was during the reign of King Jigme Dorji Wangchuck that the Governments of India and Bhutan decided by mutual agreement to appoint a Special Officer of India in Bhutan in 1968. This was an important event in the history of *Druk-yul* because for the first time it had permitted a Resident Representative of another country on its soil. This signified the first remarkable step towards Bhutan's abandonment of its isolationism. This step had been necessitated by the growing political, economic and cultural relations between the two countries. The function of the Political Officer was primarily the coordination, expedition and facilitation of the implementation of various India-aided projects in Bhutan. He was also expected to act as a Liaison Officer of the Government of India with the Government of Bhutan on all matters of mutual interest.[48]

A significant outcome of King Jigme Dorji's visit to New Delhi in April 1971 relating to the relations between India and Bhutan was the decision to elevate the representation of both countries in each other's capital to full diplomatic level. A Bhutanese Ambassador was appointed to India in May 1971 and in July the same year an Indian Ambassador was welcomed in Bhutan. Lyonpo Pema Wangchuck presented his credentials as the first Ambassador of Bhutan to the President of India on 17 May 1971. Likewise, B.S. Das presented his credentials as India's first Ambassador to Bhutan to the Druk Gyalpo of Bhutan on 15 July 1971.[49]

Needless to say, King Jigme Dorji made great strides in his country's foreign affairs. Inevitably, Bhutan could not have maintained its seclusion and isolation in the 1950s. But there was no guarantee of its not going awry in trying to find its place in the comity of nations. We have already seen how China was trying to deal with Bhutan to the chagrin of India from the outset. The King could give a good account of himself in adverse circumstances. That he befriended India without offending China speaks volumes for his diplomatic skill and maturity.

Facing Coups and Assassination Attempts: While King Jigme Dorji was taking significant—perhaps epoch-making—steps, elements hostile to all this were trying to remove him from the political scene physically. After the assassination of Prime Minister Jigmie Palden Dorji in April 1964, rumours were abroad that conspirators were trying to annihilate the King as well. At the time of the Prime Minister's assassination the King was abroad.[50] A group of dissident officials, led by Ugyen Tangi attempted a coup d'etat on 16 December 1964 but their attempt was foiled.[51] According to Ram Rahul, Lhendup Dorji, brother of the assassinated Prime Minister, Jigmie Dorji, was also involed in the coup. After the coup failed, the conspirators fled to Nepal and were given asylum there. Except for Lhendup Dorji, most of those participating in the 1964 coup attempt returned to Bhutan from Nepal and received the pardon of King Jigme Dorji.[52] However, many in Bhutan, including Lyonpo Dawa Tsering, do not believe that Lhendup Dorji was involved in the coup.

An attempt on the life of King Jigme Dorji was made on the night of 31 July 1965, when he was on a visit to the sacred Kyichhu Monastery near Paro. Some miscreants, acting at the instigation of some reactionary elements, fired at him. However, the Druk Gyalpo escaped unhurt. Obviously, it was an attempt to thwart the movement of the country towards democratization, modernization and decentralization.

An overall Assessment of His Personality: No analysis of the attempts of democratization, modernization and internationalization of *Druk-yul*, the Land of the Thunder Dragon, would be complete without an assessment of the personality and contribution of Druk Gyalpo Jigme Dorji Wangchuck. The Druk Gyalpo was a Bhutanese to the core in his upbringing, education and culture, albeit he received education in India as well as in England and broadened his outlook by contact with the rest of the world. He knew and could speak fluently Hindi, English and Nepali. He knew a little bit of French as well. He maintained a very rich library and was a voracious reader. With a view to showing respect to the Bhutanese culture, he emphasized for himself the title of "His Majesty the Druk

Gyalpo" instead of "His Highness the Maharaja". Thus, he carried forward what was recognized even by India in the Treaty of 1949. This step of the King was welcomed by all concerned.

There was hardly a sphere in Bhutan's life—political, social economic, cultural and what not—which did not attract the attention of King Jigme Dorji Wangchuck and where reforms were not effected. We have already seen how he effected reforms in economic and social spheres, apart from the political sphere, in the 1950s. In view of this the remark of Kapileshwar Labh that apart "from establishing the National Assembly no other step was taken towards introducing reforms in the country in the 1950s"[53] does not seem tenable.

A significant question arises here. Did King Jigme Dorji Wangchuck execute these reforms because he was a true reformer or he was forced by the existing circumstances to execute them? It is not difficult to answer this question. It is true that a number of reforms were called for. It is true that the whole political scenario in South Asia was in a flux. It is true that there was an obvious movement towards democratization. It is true that Bhutan could not have shut its eyes to all this. But it is equally true that political consciousness in Bhutan was far less in comparison to various other countries and therefore the King—if he would have so desired—postponed these reforms for some more time. Moreover, political power has its own capacity and capability to prevent such reforms—for some time, even if not for all time to come. In Bhutan's neighbourhood, in Nepal, the Ranas had been oblivious of all kinds of reforms and yet they continued to enjoy power for quite some time in the 1940s. Likewise in the 1960s, 70s, 80s and 90s, the Kings in Nepal bothered little about relevant reforms and yet they continued to enjoy power for a long time. Of course, the incumbent King in 1990 eventually came to grief and lost his real power. King Jigme Dorji Wangchuck by effecting relevant reforms only proved that he could visualize things in advance. This is the chief quality of a true statesman and reformer, which he was in the true sense of the terms.

Druk Gyalpo Jigme Singye Wangchuck (1972—)

Druk Gyalpo Jigme Singye Wangchuck is the fourth King of the Wangchuck dynasty in Bhutan. He succeeded his august father and enlightened predecessor, Jigme Dorji Wangchuck (who died on 21 July 1972 in Kenya), to the throne on 24 July 1972 at an auspicious occasion, as decreed by the Buddhist monks in the Kingdom. He was formally crowned on 2 June 1974 at another auspicious hour, as decreed by the

Kingdom's monks. At the time of the assumption of the throne consequent upon the death of his illustrious father, King Jigme Singye Wangchuck was only 17 and thus he achieved the distinction of being the youngest monarch in the world. Present on the historic occasion of the enthronement of the young King in June 1974 were representatives of the 5 permanent members of the UN Security Council, the President of the Republic of India, the President of the Republic of Bangladesh, HRH Prince Dhirendra Bir Bikram Shah of Nepal (as the representative of His Majesty the King of Nepal) and His Majesty Palden Thondup, the then Chogyal of Sikkim.[54]

His Majesty King Jigme Singye Wangchuck was born at Dechenchholing Palace in Thimphu on 11 November 1955 corresponding to the Wood Sheep Year of the Bhutanese Calendar. He is the only son of the Late Majesty. His Majesty King Jigme Singye Wangchuck received his early education from private tutors, after which he studied in India and then in England. Because of the deteriorating health of his father, Crown Prince Jigme Singye Wangchuck returned to Bhutan in 1970 and continued his education at the specially established Ugyen Wangchuck Academy at Paro. Here he renewed his acquaintance with Bhutan's rich spiritual and cultural heritage.[55]

Married to 4 Queens (all sisters). His Majesty has 8 children. In accordance with the tradition which enjoins that the King must marry into the highest spiritual family of the country, he was married in 1980. However, a formal marriage ceremony with all the customary royal rituals was solemnized in 1988. It so happened that the auspicious occasion to solemnize the ceremony according to the Mahyana Buddhist traditions occurred only in 1988. Mentionably, the Druk Gyalpo is a teetotaller and a voracious reader.

Training in statecraft: Druk Gyalpo Jigme Singye Wangchuck was installed as the Crown Prince of Bhutan on 15 May 1972 by the then King, Jigme Dorji Wangchuck, at a spectacular ceremony at Thimphu. King Jigme Dorji Wangchuck even taught the Crown Prince the almost forgotten ritual of the ceremony. The Crown Prince was actively associated by his father in the business of the government. In fact, he was associated with all matters of national and international import as the Crown Prince since 1972. He participated in the meetings of the *Lhengye Shungtshog* (State Council), the highest policy making body—which is composed of the Council of Ministers and the Royal Advisory Council. In 1972, he was also appointed the first Chairman of the Kingdom's Planning Commission. During the same year, the *Tshogdu* recommended that the

Crown Prince be appointed as the Penlop of Tongsa. His Majesty the Late King accepted this proposal and on 15 May 1972 Crown Prince Jigme Singye Wangchuck was installed as the Penlop of Tongsa.[56] The office of the Penlop of Tongsa occupies a place of tremendous significance in Bhutan's history. It was from this office that Ugyen Wangchuck graduated to the office of the Druk Gyalpo in 1907 to become the first Wangchuck King of the Kingdom.

Modesty as the hallmark: It would be no exaggeration to say that modesty is the hallmark of the present Bhutanese monarch. In fact, it has been so ever since he assumed the throne of the Kingdom. In his first ever address to the *Tshogdu* as the *Druk Gyalpo* on 10 September 1972, he said:

> Although I myself do not possess wide experience in Government work, I shall be able to consult with the Royal Advisory Council and with the *Lhengye Shuntshog*. In addition to this, it will be convenient to refer important matters of state to the bi-annual meetings of the Assembly. Speaking for myself, I have an earnest desire to serve our beloved country and its people as best as I can. I also hope that all of you, the monks of the state monsteries, the government servants and the public will assist me as well as you assisted my late father.[57]

Speaking about the Council of Regents (an institution provided for in Bhutan's political system in case the King was less than 21 years of age), the Druk Gyalpo said on the same occasion:

> With regard to the question of regency, in Clause No. 7 of an agreement drawn up by this Assembly, there is a provision for the appointment of a Council of Regents by this Assembly until I reach 21 years of age. It will be very useful, therefore, if you can pass a resolution as to who should be appointed to this Council of Regency.[58]

In the first Royal Proclamation to the people of Bhutan after the death of King Jigme Dorji Wangchuck, Druk Gyalpo Jigme Singye Wangchuck said:

> It now falls upon me to join the line of dynastic succession to the therone, although I feel quite unworthy of undertaking this task. However, since all of you have strong loyalty for me and have placed great hopes in me, for my part, I hope to serve my kingdom and its people to the best of my ability and with all my heart and soul for as long as possible.[59]

Needless to say, in all these statements there are palpable and praiseworthy elements of modesty. Rarely can one find such utterances emerging on the part of any ruling monarch in the world. All these statements would appear to be real examples of political modesty, when one thinks that these statements were being made by a King who was still 17—a time when people are more ambitious and less modest, more power-conscious and less prudent. In an exclusive interview to me on 13 October 1990, Druk Gyalpo Jigme Singye Wangchuck averred: "I have always maintained that future of Bhutan must always lie in the hands of Bhutanese people".

While the King has been showing from the beginning that he is a people's King in the true sense of the phrase, the representatives of the people of Bhutan have also been reposing their faith in him from the outset. Although Bhutan's Constitution provides for the appointment of a 4-member Council of Regents in the eventuality of the Crown Prince ascending the throne before attaining the age of 21, the *Tshogdu* unanimously decided that a Regency Council was not necessary. Expressing their full faith and confidence in the Crown Prince, they vested in him all powers and prerogatives of the King. The *Tshogdu* also decided to abolish the system of vote of confidence in the Druk Gyalpo every 3 years in view of the complete confidence and the overwhelming loyalty of the people to the new King. It may be recalled that the system of vote of confidence had been proposed by His Majesty the late King and approved by the *Tshogdu* in 1969. The unanimous decision effecting the abolition of this system is a clear indication of the fact that within a very short span of time the fourth Wangchuck Druk Gyalpo had proved the qualities of leadership and had made the Bhutanese repose their faith in him overwhelmingly.

It is indeed relevant and significant to note that all the love, affection, regard and faith were being shown to the new *Druk Gyalpo* of *Druk-yul*, the land of the Thunder Dragon, at a time when the institution of monarchy was being challenged in Bhutan's neighbourhood, like Nepal and Sikkim. It palpably proved that the enlightened monarchy, as opposed to autocratic or authoritarian monarchy, had penetrated into the hearts and minds of the prople of Bhutan. It was, indeed, a great achievement.

It is also worth mentioning here that Bhutan was not faced with any serious problem—political, economic or social—when the fourth Druk Gyalpo ascended the throne. It helped him to concentrate on the problems and objectives of Bhutan's development in a more relaxed and objective atmosphere. It augured well for Bhutan at that point of time.

Articulating the Objectives: Druk Gyalpo Jigme Singye Wangchuck took the earliest opportunity to articulate the objectives of his rule in the sphere of domestic as well as international politics. In the sphere of domesatic politics, the Druk Gyalpo stressed the achievement of the following objectives in his various addresses to the *Tshogdu* and the people.

1. Achievement of economic self-reliance and welfare of the rural masses;
2. Creating essential infrastructure in all aspects of life;
3. Development of human resources as the highest priority;
4. Modernization and development of the country and maintenance of balance between development, modern values and cultural heritage;
5. Attempt at an effective social integration programme and creation of a singular harmonious society; and
6. Achievement of the willing participation of the people of Bhutan in various development programmes.

From the outset, His Majesty King Jigme Singye Wangchuck has shown that he is in every sense of the term an enlighened King. He has a deep understanding of and sympathy for the common man. Under his farsighted and able guidance, the entire economic development policies, plans and programmes have been redefined and directed towards the needs of the rural masses. The *Druk Gyalpo* has defined the achievement of economic self-reliance as the main objective of "our development programme". He has, indeed, repeatedly emphasized that definite efforts must be made to ensure "equal distribution of the benefits of our development programme among all segments of our society".

Clearly, such objectives cannot be achieved without the essential infrastructure. Hence under the guidance of the *Druk Gyalpo* the basic thrust of the 5-year Plans thus far has been "towards the establishment of basic infrastructural facilities". More importantly, the development of human resources is being given the highest priority. In fact, every effort is being made to ensure that the process of Bhutan's development will not result "in a widening of the gap between our programmes and manpower capabilities". Many schools and training institutions have been recently started in order to avert this common problem among developing nations.

While Bhutan avails itself of assistance from various countries, including India, and organizations, in meeting its needs for expertise and finacial resources, the *Druk Gyalpo* has cautioned several times that "our very goal of self-reliance would be defeated should we become too dependent on foreign assistance". He has exhorted the people to face the realities of "our problems of economic development and show our determination and endevour in overcoming these problems with our own efforts and resources to the extent possible".

Needless to stress, the process of modernization is often painful. Care, therefore, needs to be taken to see that Bhutan's development programme must inevitably bring in modern values which do not conflict with those of the people, thus, creating social instability and disorienting people's attitude and behaviour. His Majesty the King has, therefore, adopted as a salient feature of his modernization policy the need to retain *Druk-yul's* cultural and religious heritage, while at the same time ensuring that no conflict between the old and new values would jeopardize Bhutan's process of economic development.[60]

Another reckonable feature of the *Druk Gyalpo's* polity is the direction towards an effective social integration programme. Bhutan, it is true, is a multiethnic, multilingual, multireligious and multicultural society. The King has from the outset felt the need to build a lasting and integrated society in the small country. As early as 1 January 1974, in a speech delivered at Sibsoo in southern Bhutan, which is predominated by the ethnic Nepalese in terms of population, the Druk Gyalpo exhorted the Nepalese never to regard themselves as aliens. King Jigme Singye Wangchuck said:

> You, the citizens of Southern Bhutan must never regard yourselves as aliens, because you and your forebears also, were born and raised in Bhutan and as such, all of you are Bhutanese. Regarding yourselves thus, you must look to the betterment and progress of Bhutan. All of us must remain united as one people and as one nation, and forge ahead together.[61]

On the occasion of the National Day celebration at Gaylegphug (in Southern Bhutan) on 17 December 1978—which was done for the first time in that region—King Jigme Singye Wangchuck said:

> I have often heard that some of our Southern Bhutanese people do not consider themselves as true Bhutanese. Those of you, who think this cannot be true Bhunanese because our people of Southern Bhutan are

> not people of Nepal nor are you Indians from Kalimpong and Darjeeling. But there is a great difference and that difference is because you are all people of the Pelden Drukpa. All of us are like one family.[62]

More importantly, the Druk Gyalpo tried to acquaint himself with the real problems of the Southern Bhutanese on that occasion and promised to solve them as one family. He said:

> From tomorrow onwards we will be holding developmental meetings and I will be meeting your representatives and mandals. I would like you to know that as far as the development of Southern Bhutan is concerned in the field of Animal Husbandry, Agriculture, Schools, Hospitals, Cash Crops and overall development, I will myself personally look after them. It is our desire to start such development work which will be useful, beneficial and necessary to the people. As far as your individual problems and difficulties are concerned I want you to know that they will also be looked into personally by me and I will try to solve them as in one family.[63]

Needless to stress, the future of a country of Bhutan's size and stature is something that hinges on the unity of the people. In fact, Bhutan's national goal cannot be achieved without the continued effort of the people as one united family. National integration and unity, of course, cannot be steamrollered or superimposed but psychological and developmental devices are a must. It needs to be emphasized that King Jigme Singye Wangchuck has been making efforts in that direction from the beginning. It is through these efforts only and exclusively that a singular and harmonious society can be created. It is with this objective in mind that His Majesty has continuously stressed the importance of integrating the people of Bhutan. He has repeatedly called upon the government and the people to make sincere efforts towards his integration programme. With this objective in mind the Education Department brings and educates together the children from the East, West, North and South in schools all over the country so that the feeling of brotherhood and belonging to one large family may be injected into their minds and hearts.

Political reforms and innovations: Druk Gyalpo Jigme Singye Wangchuck has been quite alive to timely and relevant politico-socio-economic reforms. He has taken the earliest opportunity to effect a reform, if warranted by a particular situation. Several instances may be cited in this context.

Before 1982, Bhutan did not have a Public Service Commission to recruit civil servants for various jobs. The King himself used to appoint people to various posts and they were responsible to him. Their transfers, promotions etc. were dealt with by the King himself. When the King realized that the recruitment of civil servants was becoming more complicated and cumbersome a process, he appointed a Royal Civil Service Commission to recruit personnel for various civil service posts. Now this body is functioning well and the King is relieved of this burden to that extent.

Likewise, when the Planning Commission was established in Bhutan, King Jigme Singye Wangchuck acted as its chairman. He continued to hold this post till recently. However, in a change of far-reaching significance and consequence, the Druk Gyalpo abdicated the chairmanship of the Planning Commission and appointed Dasho C. Dorji, Deputy Minister, Planning Commission Secretariat, as the new Chairman of the Planning Commission. His Majesty informed the Commission members of his decision to abdicate its chairmanship during a meeting held on 13 June 1991. His Majesty stressed that the appointment of a new chairman would decentralize the existing system of decision-making in the Planning Commission. He also emphasized that it would facilitate increased participation in the planning process by senior representatives from the ministries and departments. This would, in turn, give greater responsibility and accountability to the senior members of the Royal Government and result in increased cooperation and contribution from all ministries and departments in the implementation of plans and programmes formulated by the Commission, it was averred. Expressing his full confidence in the new chairman and the members of the Planning Commission and also the officers of the Planning Secretariat, the *Druk Gyalpo* stated that having abdicated the Commission chairmanship, he would be able to tour the *dzongkhags* more frequently to meet with the people and review development works throughout the country.[64]

More important than his act of abdicating the Planning Commission chairmanship was a step he took in 1984 making him more responsible and accountable in the political system—which a few power-holders or power-wielders will like to do. In 1984,His Majesty King Jigme Singye Wangchuck further strengthened the position of the Royal Advisory Council. Although the Council had the authority to advise the King and to watch over the performance of the government, His Majesty felt that it lacked the necessary clout to carry out the important responsibilities. A revised set of rules and regulations for the functions and responsibilities of the Royal Advisory Council was, therefore, formulated on the instruction of His Majesty the King. The most significant addition was the inclusion of a clause stating that "if any person, including His Majesty the King, does anything harmful to the interest of the Kingdom and the people, the Royal Advisory Council without suppressing such matters and free from fear from any quarter shall bring it to the attention of His Majesty the King and, if necessary, even report to the Cabinet and the National Assembly".

The *Tshogdu* strongly objected to this clause empowering the Royal Advisory Council to report against the *Druk Gyalpo*. The *Tshogdu* considered it to be a violation of traditional values that undermined the sacred principles of loyalty and devotion to the throne. On his part, the *Druk Gyalpo* insisted that this clause was of great importance and was very necessary. He stressed that no one could predict or guarantee the actions and sense of responsibility to the nation of the future rulers.[65]

These three incidents would sufficiently prove that King Jigme Singye Wangchuck is a democratic king. If his father had tried to convert the hereditary monarchy into a constitutional one, his own contribution has been no less or insignificant. It is quite heartening, especially so if one sees this happening in reverse direction in other parts of the world. For instance, in Bhutan's neighbourhood, in Nepal, the monarchy went on assuming tremendous powers in the 1960s, 1970s and 1980s, without ever becoming responsible and accountable. In the context of Nepal, one discerned the concept of decentralization being stressed to the hilt, without, of course, being explained how and whether did it result in the diminution of the powers of the King. In the case of Bhutan, quite hearteningly, one does not find this kind of confusion in existence. This could be said to be auguring well both for democracy and monarchy.

Relations with the Tshogdu: Relations between the head of state—and in this case head of government as well—and the national legislature, to a great extent, indicate the state of democracy in any particular country. Ever since the *Tshogdu* came into existence in 1953, it has been taken seriously by the Kings. King Jigme Dorji Wangchuck, the father and the predecessor of the present monarch, went on assigning more and more powers and functions to the *Tshogdu*. He went to the extent of empowering the *Tshogdu* to pass a vote of no-confidence in the monarch and three-year renewal of confidence in him. No hereditary monarch in the world or even a protector like Oliver Cromwell or Richard Cromwell did ever go to the extent of diminishing his powers and privileges in this manner. True, after King Jigme Singye Wangchuck ascended the throne, the *Tshogdu* removed the provision of 3-year passage of confidence in the *Druk Gyalpo*, but the King, on his part, has never shown any disrespect to the former. In fact, the King, Jigme Singye Wangchuck, said in 1983 that the reason for the abolition of the 3-yearly vote of confidence was no longer valid as "the King has less work and less direct responsibility than 10 or 15 years ago".[66]

Today His Majesty King Jigme Singye Wangchuck sits through the sessions of the *Tshogdu* on a high gilded throne, taking notes and even occasionally intervening in the debate in violation of Westminster's most sacred principles. But, as the Bhutanese explain, they do not need blindly to obey alien conventions. As a matter of fact, their parliamentary institutions are developing in cooperation and not in opposition to the throne.[67] All Cabinet decisions need only the *Tshogdu's* approval and there is no such thing as a royal veto.[68] But that does not in any sense mean that the institution of the monarchy is on the wane. The system, if anything, is "paternalistic".[69]

The debates in the *Tshogdu* are more forthright than before. Members of the *Tshogdu* discuss policy matters and argue with gusto. Decisions are taken through consensus.[70] During my visit to *Druk-yul* in October 1990, I discovered to my utter surprise that the *Druk Gyalpo* has been criticized from time to time in the *Tshogdu*. Of course, I was told that the criticism has always been in proper and dignified language. But the very fact that criticism of the Monarch is allowed in the *Tshogdu* speaks well for the future of the monarchy in Bhutan. Wherever monarchy has been considered above all kinds of criticisms and the monarch has participated in active politics, the very existence of this institution has been challenged and threatened. What happened in Iran and recently in Nepal are, if anything, an eye-opener. In Bhutan, one comes across an ideal balance. While the *Druk Gyalpo* is allowing more and more participation of the people in the decision-making process, including that in the *Tshogdu*, he does not consider himself above criticism.

Modus operandi and modus vivendi: There is little doubt about the fact that the King and the Queens of *Druk-yul* see themselves as the people's rulers in their land. They are, in fact, following the rules and customs which the people and the royal family have followed for over 1,300 years—a period in which *Druk-yul* had never been subjected to colonial rule.[71] King Jigme Singye Wangchuck could be said, without exaggeration, to be the most accessible king in the world. The Bhutanese always see in him a ray of hope, whenever they are in any serious trouble. Every citizen of Bhutan has a right of access to the *Druk Gyalpo*.

During my tours of Bhutan, I discovered that the King usually meets the people individually without the presence of any official lest people are diffident in articulating their grievances before him. This is something which lacks at most of the high offices whether it be the office of a king or of an ordinary minister. Most high officials of the world, including the kings and ministers, would do well to emulate this *modus operandi* and *modus vivendi* of Druk Gyalpo Jigme Singye Wangchuck.

Druk Gyalpo Jigme Singye Wangchuck tries to receive all petitions of his people in Tashichho Dzong, where long streams of ragged villagers wait with their petitions. Each is received in audience and given a patient hearing and asked to come back and report on the execution of the *Druk Gyalpo's* orders. Revealingly, little ceremony surrounds the dragon throne.[72] On the other hand, the King is on regular tours of all 18 districts where he receives petitions from the aggrieved citizens. I was told by a prominent Minister in Bhutan that the *Druk Gyalpo's* caravan stops, whenever it is so signalled by any aggrieved person or a group of persons. Rarely does one hear such a thing happening even in the case of a democratically elected minister or even prime minister.

Druk Gyalpo Jigme Singye Wangchuck also tries to mix up as well as and as deeply as with his people while playing football and volleyball with them. He trudges the golf links by himself, followed at some distance by deferential ADCs. This augurs well not only for the institution of monarchy in *Druk-yul* but also for the development of a balanced and lasting relationship between the people and their enlightened ruler.

Someone has rightly observed:

> The system is undoubtedly a monarchy. But before we assume that its negative connotations are always true we must note that Bhutan has also a dedicated and hard-working King, who, after almost two decades of efforts, has been able to improve greatly the living conditions of the people. International organizations like the U.N. are beginning to consider Bhutan a model for the developing countries of the Third World. Is it not reasonable to believe that the ends of a democracy have been or are being achieved?[73]

Bhutan of his dreams: In an interview to an Indian author, King Jigme Singye Wangchuck elaborated on the Bhutan of his dreams. The King asserted:

> It has been my constant endeavour to build Bhutan into a country that retains the best aspects of its rich traditional and cultural heritage

> while at the same time achieving economic growth and social progress. It is my fervent wish and prayer to be able to leave behind the legacy of a strong, prosperous and cohesive nation with a secure future for all the Bhutanese people.[74]

Talking about his priorities, the *Druk Gyalpo* told the same author:

> One of my important priorities is to create a system of government that is small, compact and efficient, a system that is not dependent on individuals but will function smoothly on its own inbuilt merits. Raising the per capita income and improving the quality of life of the rural population, which comprises about 90 per cent of the total population. It is one of our more important national goals. At the same time, another important national objective is to promote social unity and harmony through the strengthening of our national identity.[75]

Only an enlightened ruler can think in this manner. The *Druk Gyalpo's modus operandi* ever since he assumed the throne shows that he really means what he avers.

The problem of national integration : We have seen by now how the last two Wangchuck Kings the late King Jigme Dorji Wangchuck and the present King Jigme Singye Wangchuck tried their best to integrate the Bhutanese society ensuring proper participation of the people and proper distribution of values. They did seriously try to work in the directions of state-building (What has been described as the problems of penetration and integration) and nation-building (what has been described as the problems of loyalty and commitment).[76] However, the present *Druk Gyalpo's* regime is facing the most serious problem on this front. Thanks to the illegal and unchecked immigration of the Nepalese from Nepal and India with a view to finding a better livelihood in Bhutan, the southern part of *Druk-yul* has become a hunting ground for *ngolops* (anti-nationals).

The problem was accentuated when King Jigme Singye Wangchuck introduced the principles of *Driglam Namzha* (etiquette) and made it mandatory for the Bhutanese of all hues to wear *ghos* (in the case of men) and *kiras* (in the case of women). Before it was introduced, the representatives of southern Bhutan in the *Tshogdu* had urged upon the King to introduce *Driglam Namzha* and dress norms. In fact, during the various visits of the King to sourthern Bhutan also, he was urged upon to introduce these norms and rules in the Kingdom.

However, this decision of the Royal Government of Bhutan created a golden or godsend opportunity for many non-nationals, anti-nationals and some innocent Bhutanese. They started levelling charges of discrimination on the part of the incumbent government of Bhutan, *vis-a-vis* the Nepalese of southern Bhutan. They also alleged that the Drukpa culture was being imposed on them by the royal regime at Thimphu. A number of political outfits—including 2 political parties called the Bhutan People's Party and the Bhutan National Democratic Party have come into being with the purpose of articulating and aggregating the demands of the Nepalese in Bhutan. They have, among other things, demanded constitutional monarchy and multiparty pluralistic democracy. Very many of them have found supporters among the various political elements, including the Nepali Congress and the Nepal Communist Party (United Marxist-Leninist) in Nepal and to some extent in India as well.

On his part, King Jigme Singye Wangchuck, again unlike other dictatorial rulers, has risen to the occasion and has stated several times that the problem of Southern Bhutanese are serious one and needs to be solved soon. In fact, he has agreed to a dialogue. But can any government agree to deal with non-nationals to solve the problems of its country and its people? Therein lies the crux. On the other hand, the non-nationals and anti-nationals have indulged extensively in terrorism, killing and maiming a large number of Bhutanese Nepalese, who do not wish to toe their line. Many Bhutanese Nepalese have been kidnapped by these anti-nationals and non-nationals. Though the government has relaxed the execution of the norms of the dress and has acted with utter restraint in dealing with terrorism, the leadership of the ethnic Nepalese have done nothing to show that they believe in peaceful socio-politico-economic reforms, which in any case is a continuous phenomenon and from which the present King has never wavered.

Foreign Affairs: In foreign affairs also, King Jigme Singye Wangchuck has been quite active. In fact, during his tenure, *Druk-yul* has seen more and more of its internationalization. Bhutan had joined the United Nations during the reign of the late Majesty King Jigme Dorji Wangchuck. It joined the Non-Aligned Movement (1973) during the reign of the present *Druk Gyalpo*. Bhutan became a member of the South Asian Association For Regional Cooperation (SAARC) (1985) from its very inception. In fact, Bhutan hosted the meetings of the Standing Committee of the Foreign Secretaries and Council of Ministers (comprising Foreign Ministers) in Thimphu in May 1985. Besides, Bhutan established diplomatic and residential ambassadorial relations with Bangladesh in March 1979. In addition, Bhutan opened office of the Resident Representative of the

United Nations Development Programme (UNDP) in May 1979. All this showed Bhutan moving in the direction of internationalization.

It is no exaggeration to suggest that good relations with India has been the bedrock of Bhutan's foreign policy. It has been so not merely because of the provisions of Treaty of Friendship between India and Bhutan (1949) but also because of practical reasons in this region. It is not for nothing, then, that Bhutan is viewed as India's closest friend in this region—or perhaps in the whole world. India cannot claim to have the same clear-cut understanding with any other country, as it is having with *Druk-yul*. In his first ever address to the *Tshogdu* on 10 September 1972, Druk Gyalpo Jigme Singye Wangchuck stated: "I would like to say that I hope very much that our relations with the Government of India which has been so greatly assisting us up to the present, will grow even stronger".[77] Of course, the relations between the two have grown stronger and stronger, notwithstanding some aberrations during the existence of the Charan Singh Ministry in New Delhi.

This aberration was created because of the wrong handling of relations between the two countries by the then Indian Minister for External Affairs. Commenting on the state of the India-Bhutan relations at the present juncture, Druk Gyalpo Jigme Singye Wangchuck told me in an exclusive interview at Tashichho Dzong at Thimphu on 13 October 1990 that "Indo-Bhutan relations had never been closer and better than now". Obviously, this relationship has been more than tested in the context of the spread of terrorism in Bhutan and India's attitude to this problem. India has not only not uttered a word of interference but has also made it clear that it would not allow its land to be used by the terrorists or Nepali Bhutanese for political purposes. This augurs well for the relationship between the two countries.

King Jigme Singye Wangchuck told me in an exclusive interview on 13 October 1990 at Thimphu that there are 4 pillars of Bhutan's domestic and foreign policies:

1. Ensuring peace and stability in Bhutan,
2. Providing bright and prosperous future for the Bhutanese people,
3. Ensuring a balance between development, tradition and culture of Bhutan while taking the country on the path of prosperity, and
4. Strengthening Indo-Bhutan relations.

Thus, it is apparent that relations with India form part of Bhutan's thinking even in normal times. One finds that India, too, has been quite cautious—more often than not—while dealing with Bhutan. It has tried to see that nothing is done to hurt the sentiments of the friendly Bhutanese people overall. Though there were talks of Bhutan's demand for the revision or updating of the Treaty of 1949, during the prime ministership of Charan Singh, Bhutan soon changed its thinking and in February 1980, King Jigme Singye Wangchuck stated that there was no need to discuss the provisions of the Indo-Bhutanese Treaty of Friendship of 1949.[78]

Bhutan is one country in this region which has always refrained from using the China card against India which many other countries, including Nepal, Pakistan, Bangladesh, and Sri Lanka, have done from time to time. In fact, Bhutan has not even established diplomatic relations with the People's Republic of China, despite several temptations. Mentionably, I discovered during my visit to Bhutan in October 1990 that the decision-makers seemed determined not to establish diplomatic ties with their northern giant Asian neighbour. Bhutan's decision of not establishing diplomatic relations with China despite several rounds of talks between the two to demarcate their borders, if anything, is of great signficance and consequence.

There were reports in a section of the Indian Press in 1985 that Dhaka was trying to persuade Thimphu to review its pact (of 1949) with New Delhi. Bangladesh was reported to have suggested to Bhutan to seek a revision of the India-Bhutan Treaty with a view to excluding its security from the purview of India. Diplomatic sources in Calcutta reported that Humayun Rashid Chowdhury, Adviser to President Ershad on Foreign Affairs, and Farukh Ahmed Chowdhury, Foreign Secretary of Bangladesh, during their stay in Thimphu in May 1985 stressed the necessity for Bhutan to seek a revision of the Treaty in order to take security out of its purview.[79] Subsequent events proved beyond doubt that Bhutan refused to fall in any such trap. In fact, no third country—howsoever powerful and mighty it may be—has been able to spoil relations between India and Bhutan. Therein lies the test of firendship. And therein lies the test of the diplomatic skill of Druk Gyalpo Jigme Singye Wangchuck.

Notwithstanding Bhutan's deep and traditional relations with India, the former has expressed itself strongly on various issues from time to time. This should, in no case, be seen as the adoption of antithetical posture *vis-a-vis* India. Speaking in Calcutta on 14 September 1980, Bhutan's Foreign Minister Dawa Tsering stated that Bhutan was opposed to the presence of Soviet troops in Afghanistan. Speaking to newspersons, the Minister said: "We are opposed to the presence of foreign troops in any country. Such presence increases tension and brings big power rivalry to our doorstep".[80]

In 1985, Bhutan became a signatory to the Nuclear Non-Proliferation Treaty (NPT), which has been opposed to by India vehemently. On the other hand, Bhutan has gone along with Pakistan in the United Nations declaring South Asia as a nuclear-free zone.[81] Many cynics may see in this Bhutan's desire to act against the stated policy of India. What, however, matters is whether the steps of Bhutan are worth criticizing in principle.

It is worth mentioning that Bhutan has been participating quite actively in various activities of the SAARC and has given a good account of itself. Speaking at the first SAARC Summit in Dhaka on 7 December 1985, Druk Gyalpo Jigme Singye Wangchuck said something which was quite remarkable and revealing as far as frankness was concerned. He said:

> Mr. Chairman, it may neither be possible nor desirable to limit discussions in our meetings to issues of a non-political nature, for the political climate of our region will undoubtedly cast a long shadow over our deliberations. In the geopolitical realities of our region, it would be unrealistic to ignore the primacy of the political factor, as, in the final analysis, it will be the political environment of the region which will determine the shape and scope of regional cooperation in South Asia.[82]

An overview

To sum up, one can say on the basis of the discussion and analysis in the foregoing pages that the institution of monarchy and the 4 Wangchuck monarchs have contributed significantly to the all-round development of the Kingdom of Bhutan. In fact, the very establishment of the institution of (elective which subsequently got converted into hereditary) monarchy in 1907 implied the country's unification in the true sense of the term. It also implied the end of the duality—or at times even multiplicity—of centres of power in *Druk-yul*. It facilitated the British government in India to deal with *Druk-yul* in a more proper and beneficial manner even for the benefit of Bhutan and the Bhutanese.

It is obvious from the discussion and analysis on the foregoing pages in the chapter that the Kings of Bhutan have always risen to the occasion. They have done what was needed at particular points of time. For instance, Druk Gyalpo Ugyen Wangchuck, the first King of the Wangchuck dynasty, came to occupy the Kingdom's throne at a particular point of time when unity and integrity of it coupled with the abolition of various competing and confusing centres of power was the crying need of the hour. That he dealt with the situation with utmost adroitness and perseverance is obvious. In fact, much before he was elected the Druk Gyalpo of Druk-yul on 17 December 1907 by the Lamas and the general people of the Bhutanese society, he had showed his administrative and diplomatic skills in dealing with various internal and external agencies. He was modern-minded but he knew the meaning of modernization in the context of the then Bhutan. He maintained a delicate balance, which, if anything was demanded by the circumstances. It was in his regime that the famous Treaty of 1910—which was an improvement on the Sinchula Treaty of 1865—was signed. This Treaty very appropriately institutionalized relations between India and Bhutan.

The second Druk Gyalpo, Jigme Wangchuck, ascended the throne at a time when Bhutan was not faced with many problems. Quite conscious of it, he took steps to consolidate Bhutan along with some steps of modernization—again, strictly in the context of existing circumstances. By visiting India, he tried to befriend it to the greatest possible extent. He knew that the withdrawal of the British colonial masters from the colonized parts of South Asia would create a new political environment and it was essential for Bhutan to adjust to it. It was in this context that the Treaty of Friendship Between India and Bhutan (1949) was signed during his reign. The significance of this Treaty lies in the fact that it still provides the guiding principles of relations between India and Bhutan to a very great extent—in spirit, if not also entirely in letter. Though there arose an occasion, as we saw, when there were talks of revising and updating the Treaty, the very fact that it has survived speaks volumes for its durability and desirability.

The third Druk Gyalpo, Jigme Dorji Wangchuck, came to occupy the throne when the scene in South Asia had completely changed. India and Sri Lanka had become free from the colonial yoke, the former after a division into two. Nepal had freed itself from the clutches of the Ranas (1951) and had started moving in the direction of multiparty democracy and constitutional monarchy. On the other hand, China had emerged as a strong communist country after the revolution of 1949 and had taken over Tibet, obviously to the chagrin of Bhutan. Tibet was, like Bhutan, a Mahayana Buddhist state. King Jigme Dorji Wangchuck realized with alacrity that the situation outside Bhutan called for Druk-yul's socio-politico-economic modernization, of course, with care and caution.

Jigme Dorji Wangchuck, as we saw, took various steps in reforming the existing political system and tried to convert Bhutan into an international personality.

In doing these things, the King faced various challenges from the vested interest in Bhutan. His Prime Minister was assassinated in 1964 and two attempts were made to assassinate the King himself. The King, however, survived both these attempts. And he continued to move on the path of democratization, modernization and decentralization till he breathed his last. He knew that like his two predecessors, he could not maintain socio-politico-economic status quo and, therefore, moved towards enlightened reforms, which brought encomiums from many quarters. He is known as the King who established constitutional monarchy in Bhutan in the true sense of the term. It was King Jigme Dorji Wangchuck who devised various checks and brakes against any authoritarian step by the King. One does not come across any such attempt on the part of any reigning and ruling monarch anywhere in the world.

King Jigme Singye Wangchuck, the forth and present King of the Wangchuck dynasty came to occupy the throne at a time when Bhutan was not faced with any serious problem. There was peace and tranquility and thanks to Bhutan's internationalization, the Himalyan kingdom was receiving plenty of ecnomic aid for its all-round development. The King realized, to some extent, that the southern Bhutanese, or the Nepalese, were not feeling very much entrenched in the country's politico-administrative system and, therefore, during his various tours of southern Bhutan, he exhorted the ethnic Nepalese to feel as much the part of Bhutan as eastern and western Bhutanese. In fact, the King tried his level best to solve the individual problems of the ethnic Nepalese of Bhutan. He allotted a reckonable portion of his land to the ethnic Nepalese for their economic development. However, when *Driglam Namzha* (etiquette) and dress prescriptions came to be enforced, some Nepalese found a godsend opportunity to rebel against the Bhutanese political system.

The rebellion got impetus because of the support it received from a large number of non-nationals and anti-nationals in Bhutan. True, some innocent Bhutanese were also brainwashed and were made to believe that a millenium was to descend on Bhutan sooner rather than later. This did create an embarrassing scenario for the young, energetic and enlightened Druk Gyalpo who has always considered Bhutan's interests and welfare to be his own. In various interviews, including the ones given to me, the Druk Gyalpo has stressed that the wants to solve the genuine problems of the southern Bhutanese but what is lacking completely is the atmosphere of dialogue. What, in fact, is palpable in southern Bhutan is the environment of terrorism and violence. It is rather intriguing that all this is happening in a political system which was noted for its capacity of grievance-redressal. Palpably, there is much more to it then meets the eye.

On the international plane, several new things happened during the regime of the present monarch. Bhutan continued to maintain friendly and cordial relations with India, notwithstanding some small differences. The talks about Bhutan's desire to get the Treaty of Peace and Friendship revised and updated proved to be very shortlived and Bhutan has expressed satisfaction with the working of the Treaty. In fact, the *Druk Gyalpo*, Jigme Singye Wangchuck, told me in an exclusive interview on 13 October 1990 at Thimphu that he saw the relations between Bhutan and India as something which should be emulated by other South Asian states while shaping their relations with India.

On the other hand, Bhutan established diplomatic and residential ambassadorial relations with Bangladesh. Though Bhutan has no diplomatic relations with the People's Republic of China, it has held several rounds of talks with the latter with a view to demarcating the boundary between the two. Though India is not involved in these talks, there is no difference between India and Bhutan.

Bhutan has been quite active during the regime of the Druk Gyalpo, Jigme Singye Wangchuck, on the front of the South Asian Association for Regional Cooperation (SAARC) and the Druk Gyalpo has been the only head of state who has thus far attended all the 6 SAARC summits. It adds to his credit.

Notes and References

1. *The Concise Oxford Dictionary Of Current English (COD)*, Oxford University Press, Delhi, 1990, 765.
2. *The New Lexicon Webster's Dictionary of The English Language (NLWDEL)*, Lexicon Publications Inc., New York, 1987, 644.
3. *Collins Cobuild English Language Dictionary (CCELD)*, Collins, London, 1988, 932.
4. Roger Scruton, *A Dictionary Of Political Thought*, Pan Books in association with the Macmillan Press, London, 1983, 303-04.
5. Bertrand Russell, *Power: A New Social Analysis*, George Allen & Unwin Limited, London, 1946, 75.
6. Ibid., 76-7.
7. Ibid., 81.
8. *COD*, n.1.
9. *NLWDEL*, n.2.
10. *CCELD*, n.3.
11. Ram Rahul, *The Himalaya as a Frontier*, Vikas Publishing House Pvt Ltd. New Delhi, 1978, 89.

12. Ibid., 78-9.
13. B.S. Das, "Economic Development and Social Changes in Bhutan", in Urmila Phadnis, S.D. Muni and Kalim Bahadur, eds., *Domestic Conflicts In South Asia:* vol.2: *Economic and Ethnic Dimensions,* South Asian Publishers, New Delhi, 1986, 83.
14. Ram Rahul, n. 11, 88.
15. See Kapileshwar Labh, "Monarchical System of Bhutan: Challenges of Modernization", in Urmila Phadnis, S.D. Muni and Kalim Bahadur, eds., n.13,183.
16. See Ram Rahul, n.11, 76.
17. See Ibid.,89.
18. See Kapileshwar Labh, n.15, 184.
19. Ram Rahul, n.11, 87.
20. Ibid.,88.
21. Ibid.
22. See Nagendra Singh, *Bhutan: A Kingdom In the Himalayas,* Thomson Press India Limited, New Delhi, 1978, 101.
23. See Ibid., 94.
24. Kapileshwar Labh, n.15, 184-5.
25. Ram Rahul, n.11, 90.
26. See Ibid.
27. Leo E. Rose, *The Politics of Bhutan,* Cornell University Press, Ithaca, 1977, 37.
28. Kapileshwar Labh, n.15, 185.
29. Ram Rahul, n.11, 91.
30. Ibid.
31. Nagenera Singh, n.22, 103.
32. See R.N. Anil, "The Kings of Bhutan", *The Hindustan Times,* New Delhi, 21 February 1985, 9.
33. Leo E. Rose, "Bhutan", in Francis Robinson, ed., *The Cambridge Encyclopaedia of India, Pakistan, Bangladesh, Sri Lanka, Nepal, Bhutan and The Maldives,* Cambridge University Press, Cambridge, 1989, 231.
34. Ram Rahul, *Royal Bhutan,* Motilal Banarsidass, Delhi, 1983, 42-3.
35. Nagendra Singh, n.22, 109-10.
36. Cited in Ibid., 110-11.
37. Ibid., 109.
38. Ram Rahul, n.11, 92.
39. Nagendra Singh, n.22, 109.
40. See Ibid.
41. Gisela Bonn and Giselher Wirsing, *India And The Subcontinent: An Introduction To India, Pakistan, Bangladesh, Nepal, Sikkim and Bhutan,* Oxford and IBH Publishing Corporation, New Delhi, 1974, 105.
42. Ibid. 107.
43. Sunanda K. Datta-Ray, "Return Of The Dragon-I: Bhutan Prepares To Talk To China", *The Statesman,* Delhi, 17 July 1981, 6.
44. Ram Rahul, n.11, 93.
45. Ibid., 92.
46. Ibid.
47. Nagendra Singh, n.22, 112.
48. Ibid., 111-2.
49. Ibid.,112.
50. For a detailed and analytical account see Nari Rustomji, *Bhutan: The Dragon Kingdom In Crisis,* Oxford University Press, Delhi, 1978.

51. Ram Rahul, n.34, 41.
52. Ram Rahul, n.11, 93.
53. See Kapileshwar Labh, n.15, 186.
54. Druk Gyalpo Jigme Singye Wangchuck told me in an exclusive interview at Tashichho Dzong, Thimphu, on 13 October 1990.
55. Ibid.
56. Ibid.
57. See The Department of Information, Ministry of Development, *Our Beloved King*, Royal Government of Bhutan Press, Thimphu, 1979,11.
58. Ibid.
59. Ibid., 9.
60. See Ibid., 6-7.
61. Ibid., 13.
62. Ibid., 25.
63. Ibid., 25-6.
64. *Kuensel* (Bhutan's national newspaper), Thimphu, vol.6, no. 25, 15 June 1991, 1-2.
65. Dasho Rigzin Dorji, *A Brief, Religious, Cultural and Secular History of Bhutan*, The Asia Society Galleries, New York, 1989,13.
66. Sunanda K. Datta-Ray, "Druk Past & Present-II: Strategy For Survival", *The Statesman*, 11 July 1983, 6.
67. Sunanda K. Datta-Ray, "Return Of The Dragon-III: Economic Progress Without Hurrying", Ibid., 20 July 1981, 6.
68. Sunanda K. Datta-Ray, "Flight Of The Dragon-II: Challenge Of Settlement With China", Ibid., 28 April 1984, 6.
69. Ibid.
70. K.P. Bhanumathy, "Bhutan: Some Impressions", *Mainstream*, New Delhi, 18 August 1990, 25.
71. Narendra Kumar, "Uneasy Lies The Head. . .", *The Sunday Statesman Miscellany*, 14 July 1991, 4.
72. Sunanda K. Datta-Ray, n.68.
73. Karma Chophel, "Democrats' Terror In Bhutan", *The Statesman*, 15 January 1991, 6.
74. Narendra Kumar, n.71.
75. Ibid., 5.
76. See Gabriel A. Almond and G. Bingham Powell, Jr., *Comparative Politics: A Developmental Approach*, Amerind Publishing Co. Pvt. Ltd., New Delhi, 1975, 16-41.
77. Department of Information, Ministry of Development, n.57, 11.
78. *Indian Express*, New Delhi, 26 February 1980, 7.
79. *The Hindustan Times*, New Delhi, 17 May 1985,10.
80. *The Times of India*, New Delhi, 15 September 1980,10.
81. Prakash Nanda, "Foreign Afairs: Is Bhutan Likely to do a Nepal on India", Ibid., 11 May 1989, Agenda 3.
82. Royal Government of Bhutan, Ministry of Foreign Affairs, SAARC Division, *Major Statements Made By Bhutanese Delegations On SAARC:1980-1991*, Thimphu, 1991,60.

5

Contrived Problems of State-building and Nation-building

The small and beautiful mountain kingdom of Bhutan or Druk-yul confronts today the contrived but serious problems of state-building and nation-building. The problem of state-building generally arises out of a threat to the survival of the political system from the international environment. It may also arise out of a threat to the political system from the society in the form of revolutionary pressure challenging the stability or the survival of the political system. Besides, it may arise from the development among the political elite of new goals such as national expansion or the creation of an extravagant court life. State-building takes place when the political elite creates new structures and organizations designed to "penetrate" the society in order to regulate and increase the extractive capabilities of the political system, with the creation of a centralized and penetrative civil service related to the increase in these capabilities and with the formation of attitudes of obedience and compliance in the population which are associated with the emergence of such a bureaucracy.

The problem of nation-building refers to the problem of loyalty and commitment. This problem, in fact, stresses the cultural aspect of the political development. It refers to the process whereby people transfer their commitment and loyalty from smaller tribes, villages, or pretty principalities to the larger central political system.[1]

On the front of state-building, one finds that Bhutan's political system is being challenged by a group of people who have been hitherto enjoying all fruits and values emanating from it. They have now started treating the political system as something that does not belong to them. Likewise, on the front of nation-building, they seem to have withdrawn their loyalty and commitment to the central authority and are giving the same to a group of people who are indulging in the acts of terrorism and anti-nationalism.

Not only peace has become a thing of the past in a substantial part of the small kingdom, some well-meaning people do not feel very optimistic about the maintenance of the state structure in the present form in the whole of Bhutan. Should there be a change in the state structure in the Himalayan kingdom—as is feared by some—it will not only give rise to more turbulent situation in this area but will also create serious problems on the front of security even for the core state, India, which has thus far been Bhutan's true friend in need. And should Bhutan be dismembered in any manner, it would also encourage economic migrants and refugees of one variety—i.e., the Nepalese—to work on creating more provinces in India by means of fraud and force. This is something which needs to be nipped in the bud. What happened in Sikkim in terms of demographic invasion should always serve as an eye-opener not only to India but also to all Bhutan watchers. Bhutan's foreign minister, Lyonpo Dawa Tsering, has very aptly pointed to this problem by stating that Bhutan was today the only country in the world whose very survival as a nation was threatened by a flood of illegal immigrants.[2]

Bhutan's ethnic groups

In order to dive deep into the problem of ethnicity which has become a serious challenge to the processes of state-building and nation-building in Bhutan, it would be in order to have an understanding of the word "ethnic" and then of various ethnic groups in the Himalayan kingdom. The word "ethnic" has been defined by *The Concise Oxford Dictionary Of Current English, inter alia,* as ". . .a social group having common national or cultural tradition . . .denoting origin by birth or descent rather than nationality. . .relating to race or culture. . ."[3]

The New Lexicon Webster's Dictionary of the English Language has defined the word as "of relating to a people whose unity rests on racial, linguistic, religious or cultural ties. . .deriving from or belonging to such racial etc. ties of a people or country. . ."[4]

Thus, these two famous dictionaries make it clear that the word "ethnic" denotes commonality and unity of a group of people which is based on racial, linguistic or cultural ties. It is also obvious by the explanations given in these dictionaries that origin by birth or descent, as different from origin by nationality, is of essence in determining somebody's ethnic salience.

Like various other South Asian states, Bhutan, too shows multiplicity on the plane of ethnicity. This is so despite the fact that in terms of population Bhutan is the second least populated state in this region, being next only to Maldvies. 3 main ethnic groups called the Sharchops, the Ngalops and the Nepalese constitute the population of Bhutan. The Sharchops were the earliest inhabitants mainly residing in eastern Bhutan. The Sharchops' origin can be traced to the tribes of north-east India and north Burma. The Ngalops were the migrants from Tibet and they brought Buddhism with them to the mountain kingdom. The Nepalese, mostly Hindus, came much later in the late 19th and early 20th century to work as labourers in the inhospitable climate of southern Bhutan. According to one account, the influx of Nepali immigrants had not commenced during the important period of Bhutan's history. A handful of Nepali migrants had begun trickling into the western foothills of Bhutan only towards the end of the 19th century from Darjeeling, Kalimpong and Sikkim. The flow of the Nepali migrants into southern Bhutan's foothills only picked up in the first half of this century. "British documents have confirmed that the flow of the Nepali migrants had not gone beyond Gaylegphug in the 1930s".[5]

Each of these ethnic groups had its distinctive cultural and religious identity. The Ngalops and the Sharchops, however, got integrated with each other. The Ngalops became the rulers subduing the Sharchops and integrating them through conversion to Buddhism and inter-marriages. The Nepalese population was confined to the south and the members of this group have since the beginning been officially described as "southerners" or "Lhotshampas". Initially, the Nepalese were confined to the south not being permitted to migrate or own property in the upper regions. Though this policy was subsequently relaxed, the Nepalese by and large were not keen on moving to other parts of Bhutan. The reason for this may have been their desire to maintain close proximity with their ethnic brethren in other parts of South Asia, outside Bhutan, including the areas in India and Nepal, where the ethnic Nepalese preponderate. Needless to state, the political consciousness of the ethnic Nepalese is generally higher than various other ethnic groups. This is borne out by what happened in Sikkim and Darjeeling. In fact, the political aspirations of this segment of population does not seem to have been even substantially fulfilled, despite the privileges that they enjoy. To that extent the integration of the Nepalese in Bhutan remains incomplete.

Relevantly, the country's geographical zones generally cover the ethnic distribution. The Sharchops live mostly in eastern Bhutan; the Ngalops mostly reside in the west and central Bhutan; the Nepalese, as we saw, live mostly and predominantly in southern Bhutan, which is contiguous to the Nepali-dominated areas of India and Nepal.

Relevantly, one could discern a clear division of the country on ethnic lines in the geographical and historical contexts. Notwithstanding the rigid power apex, each ethnic group was, overall left to itself in its socio-cultural-economic context. The economy of the state was such as did not permit much interactions between various regions and ethnic groups. This obviously contributed to the confinement of the ethnic groups to their traditional way of life. However, in matters relating to monastic order the entire Buddhist community was under a rigid control exercised by the ruling group of the Drukpas.[6]

However, this situation, could not have continued *ad infinitum* because of changes in the regional and international, more particularly in the former, environments. The Bhutanese protected and confined in this environment were suddenly faced with a new situation when China occupied Tibet and thereby became a powerful neighbour of Bhutan. Bhutan was now left with no alternative but to open out to the outside world for its security. The factors that contributed to this situation were: happenings in Tibet, China's claim on Bhutan's territory and the fear of communism. Needless to state, the Drukpa dominance and traditional culture could only be maintained and retained through the policy of seclusion and there was a transparent tendency to avoid foreign contacts or presence. Perhaps, one could say with a great degree of certainty that Bhutan would have preferred to remain in splendid isolation, had the events of 1959 and the Sino-Indian war of 1962 not occurred and a threat to its traditional way of life not felt. It might, of course, have made some minor changes in its economic perceptions.

Be that as it may, it is time and place to have some idea of ethnic break-up in the multi-ethnic society of the tiny state. The people of Tibetan origin, called Ngalops, are overall concentrated in the west and constitute about 28% of the population. The country's ruling elite hails from this group. *Dzongkha*, a Tibetan dialect, which has developed a distinct Bhutanese features of its own over the past few centuries, is the language of this group of people.This language has now become the official language of Bhutan. Moreover, these people follow the Drukpa school of Mahayana Buddhism, which distinguishes them from Tibetan and other brands of Buddhism. Significantly, the kingdom's Drukpa identity is also its national identity.

The people of the ethnic group called Sharchops live in the northern and eastern parts of Bhutan.They are the original inhabitants of the country and belong to the Indo-Mongoloid family.They are akin to the inhabitants of the north-eastern states of India. They account for about 44% of the kingdom's population and speak about the 11 different dialects of non-Tibetan origin.They have their own dress, food habits and festivals. However, far from posing any threat worth the name to the Royal Bhutanese Government, they have been wellnigh completely integrated with the Drukpa cultural pattern.

The third ethnic group is the one that has not integrated itself even substantially on the psychological plane with the state structure in Bhutan, thereby creating the problems of nation-building and state-building in the kingdom. This ethnic group is that of the Nepalese,who have nevertheless been taking all advantages of the service state in Bhutan. Most of the Nepali settlers of southern Bhutan came here during the late 19th and early 20th century. There are reasons to suspect that the influx of the Nepalese in Bhutan is still continuing.[7] Predictably, the size of the ethnic Nepalese has been a matter of serious controversy. Writing in 1978, Nari Rustomji, who had the privilege of serving as the Adviser to the then King of Bhutan in the 1960s, states that the "Nepalese immigrants now constitute over a quarter of the population".[8] Dwelling upon the problem of the Nepalese influx in Bhutan, Rustomji writes:

> The Bhutanese have seen how, in neighbouring Sikkim, the original inhabitants have been gradually outnumbered by Nepalese immigrants, and are determined to stop the process in their own country before it assumes unmanageable proportions. The Nepalese are a polygamous race and household of three or four wives and a dozen to fifteen children is not an uncommon phenomenon. The Bhutanese have therefore just reason for apprehension that, unless restrictions are set on further settlement, the Nepalese will in course of time emerge, as in Sikkim, as the majority community and seek to exert political and cultural dominance over their erstwhile hosts.[9]

Nari Rustomji was, of course, one of the few Indian authors who could envisage the problem as early as 1978. But F.M. Bailey, a Political Officer in Bhutan, appreciated the danger in 1928. He wrote:

> A possible source of difficulty for Bhutan, and one to which His Highness is quite alive, is the settlement of large number of Nepalese in the lower valleys. . . In the eighties of last century some Nepalese settlers came and they are now estimated at 50,000. His Highness is considering the prohibition of Nepalese settlers beyond certain boundaries as is done in Sikkim.[10]

Focusing again on the percentage of the Nepalese in Bhutan, Bhutan's foreign minister, Lyonpo Dawa Tsering, is on record that one third of the kingdom's 6,00,000 population is that of Nepalese origin.[11] This seems rather more accommodative on the part of the ruling elite in Bhutan. Nepalese and some motivated people even in India seem never tired of exaggerating the figures of the ethnic Nepalese in Bhutan. According to Kapileshwar Labh, an expert on Bhutanese politics, "while some ethnic Nepalese claim that they account for 25 to 28 per cent of the population, the kingdom's official estimates indicate that they constitute 15 to 20 per cent of the population".[12] But even Labh has tried to underrate the figures quoted by the Nepalese of Bhutan. In fact, what is worrying Thimphu the most is that many of the ethnic Nepalese of Bhutan have begun to believe "the propoganda of the Pan-Nepal concept that the Bhutanese of Nepalese origin comprised more than half the population of Bhutan".[13]

A propaganda booklet of the Nepalese of Bhutan, aimed at creating confusion among themselves and also in the outside world, for instance, *inter alia,* says:

> Rather than adopt the Drukpa customs and dress we Gurkhas must insist that we are the majority, they the Drukpa minority must accept our customs and traditions. If this is not acceptable to them then we must fight for our rights like the Tamils of Sri Lanka and like them we must call upon the support of our brothers and sisters in Nepal and India in our liberation struggle against the despot Drukpa king and his corrupted Drukpa government. We Gurkhas must all unite together and create another Gurkha state in Bhutan and extend the borders of Gurkha states along the Himalayas which has always been the rightful home of our people.[14]

Apart from the motive of the ethnic Nepalese or a segment thereof, the aforesaid passage is relevant inasmuch as it talks about the majority status of the ethnic Nepalese in Bhutan. This is how the disinformation campaign is carried out inside and outside the kingdom. However, a curious aspect of the disinformation campaign is the fact that even some Indian presspersons are veering round the view. For instance, an Indian journalist wrote in June 1991:

> Of the 2.46 million *(sic)* population spread over an area of 1,24,186 square km *(sic)* in the lap of the mighty Himalayas, Nepalis constitute 64%. If the number of unregistered Nepalis is added, then the percentage would go up to nearly 75% of the total population.[15]

Obviously, nothing can be further from the truth. Palpably, the imaginative capacity of some people have gone beyond limits.

Disproportionate increase in population

We have already seen how has Nari Rustomji viewed the family structure and the *modus operandi* of the Nepalese in terms of population.We have also seen how even in 1928, the then King had expressed his fear of the growth of the Nepali population in Bhutan.The rate of population growth of the southerners is estimated to be about 2.8%, as against less than 2% of the rest.[16] This imbalance is a serious cause of concern. Bhutan Foreign Minister Lyonpo Dawa Tsering said recently in an interview that what was certainly true was that the population of some districts like Samchi in the south, which was the most accessible part of southern Bhutan for the Nepalese migrants, had doubled in 10 years. The survey of Samchi district revealed that the total illegal landholding there was 47,235 acres, which was more than the total landholding in Tashigang, Bhutan's largest district.[17]

Apart from the Nepalese predilection for large families, the illegal exodus of the Nepalese to Bhutan to get more and more economic privileges there is also responsible for the tremendous growth of population in the southern region. It is common knowledge that because of the plenty of land available in Bhutan and its high fertility, many Nepalese invite their relatives from Sikkim, Darjeeling and Nepal to come and settle in the mountain kingdom. In fact, even when the initial census process was on in 1988, it was discovered that some 15,000 Nepalese could not prove that they or their forefathers had been living in Bhutan before 1958. Significantly, the census authorities had adopted 1958 as the cut-off year because it was believed that most of the non-nationals had come to Bhutan after 1958.[18] In a candid and exclusive interview in his Tashichho Dzong (the Royal Government's headquarters) on 23 October 1991 Bhutan Foreign Minister Lyonpo Dawa Tsering told me that Bhutan was today the only country in the world whose very survival as a nation was threatened by a flood of illegal immigrants who were of the same ethnic salience and as an assertive minority were bent on increasing their demographic size.

True, the imbalance is a serious cause for concern, but the government cannot force family planning in one region on the basis of ethnicity. "Yet, to retain the supremacy of the ruling community, it needs to offer incentives for higher rate of growth of the Drukpa population on one hand and control rate of the southerners to maintain a balance on the other".[19] The tragicomedy in the situation is that while Bhutan is facing ethnic invasion both in terms of enlargement of families by the Nepalese and unbridled exodus by them from across the border, it is one of the very few countries, if not perhaps the only one, where it needs a larger population for its economic growth. This dilemma is much more serious than it appears at the first sight. Perhaps for decades together Bhutan would have to make serious efforts to solve this dilemma. If it lacks manpower, its economy, which has made great strides, would suffer a setback. If it allows unchecked exodus of non- Bhutanese, its security would suffer immensely.

Government's attempts to integrate and incorporate the Nepalese into the national mainstream

It is true that until the 1950s, the Bhutanese government made no serious attempt to integrate the Nepalese into the country's political system. But it must also be said here that till that time the state structure itself had shown no inclination towards a movement in the direction of political modernization, even in the limited sense of the term. The state structure, if anything, was too simplistic to worry about these things.

But as soon as Bhutan started moving on the path of modernization, even in a limited sense of the term, it initiated incorporating the Nepalese in the national mainstream. As soon as King Jigme Dorji Wangchuck, the third Wangchuck King, ascended the throne in 1952, the attitudinal change of the government *vis-a-vis* the ethnic Nepalese was transparently visible. Since then the Bhutanese authorities have been making efforts to integrate them into the country's political system. The Nepalese were given representation in the *Tshogdu* (National Assembly), when it was established in 1953. Of course, there are observers and analysts who believe that the institution of the *Tshogdu* was created to satisfy the aspirations of the Nepalese on the political front. But it was not a matter of small significance and consequence that an all-powerful king sought to convert the monarchy into constitutional monarchy, when he did not face any serious challenge to his own power and authority.

Apart from being given representation in the *Tshogdu,* the ethnic Nepalese in Bhutan were recruited in the police, the army and the civil service on the basis of equality.They were posted in the capital, Thimphu, and other important places in the country. King Jigme Dorji Wangchuck also excelled in speaking Nepali and was very fond of talking to the ethnic Nepalese in their own mother tongue.

Attempts at incorporating and integrating the Nepalese into country's socio-politico-economic mainstream has continued unabated during the regime of King Jigme Singye Wangchuck, who ascended the throne in

July 1972, consequent upon the death of his father and predecessor, King Jigme Dorji Wangchuck. In December 1973, he undertook a tour of southern Bhutan and exhorted the Bhutanese of Nepali extraction not to regard themselves as "aliens" and called upon them that they "must remain united as one people, one nation and forge ahead together".[20]

Likewise speaking on the occasion of the National Day celebration at Gaylegphug (in southern Bhutan) on 17 December 1978, King Jigme Singye Wangchuck encouraged the ethnic Nepalese to join the national mainstream.The King stated:

> I have often heard that some of our Southern Bhutanese people do not consider themselves as true Bhutanese. Those of you, who think this cannot be true Bhutanese because our people of Southern Bhutan are not people of Nepal nor are you Indians from Kalimpong and Darjeeling. But there is a great difference and that difference is because you are all people of Pelden Drukpa. All of us are like one family.[21]

Referring to the execution of the development programme in Southern Bhutan and his own commitment to going into the individual problems of the ethnic Nepalese, Druk Gyalpo Jigme Singye Wangchuck averred:

> From tomorrow onwards we will be holding developmental meetings and I will be meeting your representatives and mandals. I would like you to know that as far as the development of Southern Bhutan is concerned in the field of Animal husbandry, Agriculture, Schools, Hospitals, Cash Crops and overall development, I will myself personally look after them. It is our desire to start such development work which will be useful, beneficial and necessary to the people. As far as your individual problems and difficulties are concerned I want you to know that they will also be looked into personally by me and I will try to solve them as in one family.[22]

Obviously, the King's observations in these lines are instructive. It will be almost impossible to trace any King personally so committed to the casuse of any segment of society and so involved in redressing the grievances of the people, if any. One reason for this could be his youthfulness and energy. But equally, if not more important, is his enlightenment and commitment to the cause of national integration and national development.

It was because of the enlightened leadership of King Jigme Singye Wangchuck that the National Council for Social and Cultural Promotion was set up in 1980, the objectives of which are broadly as follows:

(i) Organization and promotion of social, cultural and educational activities to inculcate a feeling of national community transcending regional loyalties. (ii) Establishing programmes/schemes for the youth to instil a sense of national indentity and dedicated service to the King and the country. (iii) Initiating plans/programmes to emphasize social, cultural and spiritual aspects of life to integrate youth with the national development programmes at the rural levels.

Obviously, the three objectives point to national integration, a national consciousness and national identity. These also indicate that modernization has created an imbalance in the old social order. "In such a situation, the sharing of economic power and the interaction between the State and the new class or the interaction between the various ethnic groups becomes critical".[23] Needless to state, this kind of exercise puts the monarchy to real test. But the present monarch has always been prepared to subject himself to such tests. It is altogether a different matter that vested interests among the Nepalese have from time to time sought to negate such enlightened efforts of the king.

Likewise, a Committee for Integration, headed by no less a person than the King's own sister was created with a view to integrating various ser-gments of the society on the psychological plane. The constitution of such a committee goes to show that the ruling elite has been concious of bringing into the national mainstream that segment or those segments of people who have not felt psychologically integrated in the country's socio-politico-economic structure.

The task of national integration has never been easy in any society, much less so in a developing society. But personal example offers an inspiring lead. The Druk Gyalpo receives and bestows vermilion tilaks every Dussehara, which is celebrated as national festival. Not only does the King participate enthusiatically in these programmes, even the Crown Prince is being groomed to participate in the Dussehara and Tikka ceremonies every year.

Quite significantly, in 1982, the *Druk Gyalpo* happily "welcomed the marriage of one of his attractive young sisters, Princess Pem Lhaden Wangchuck, to the son of a Hindu Nepalese landowner in Samchi,"[24] who had been to school with His Majesty in Paro before attending the university in the United States. True, the marriage did not last long. But an example worth emulating was set by the royal household itself. It goes to prove that the question of national integration is not something which is used as rhetoric by the ruling elite in Bhutan. Genuine importance is attached to it in practice by the royal family itself.

Writing in 1983, Sunanda K. Datta-Ray, a well-known analyst and commentator on the politics of this region, stated:

> Within the frame of an equal citizenship, the King has set in motion a vigorous programme to make Drukpa and Nepalese feel part of a common nation while fostering their individual cultural legacies. Dasho Meghraj Gurung, Director of the National Council for Social and Cultural Promotion, describes the school exchanges, cultural festivals, books, talks, films, youth camps and system of cumpulsory social service through which the Royal Government is trying to invest young people not with pride in the Drukpa ethos but also with a sense of interdependence. Far more Nepalese are to be seen now in Thimphu than even six or seven years ago; Durkpa officials are as common in the south; a number of districts in the north and east have Southern Bhutanese dzondags; and as at the coronation languid Nepalese dances featured prominently in the archery competition.[25]

Needless to state, it shows that the Royal Government has been quite conscious of integrating the Nepalese in the mainstream of national life from the outset. Even today no cultural programme in any part of Bhutan is considered complete without Nepalese dances and other items. No foreign tourists, including Indians, can miss this fact anywhere in Bhutan, including Thimphu. One could easily see the magnanimity of the Drukpas *vis-a-vis* the Nepalese when the former speak in fluent Nepali.

Speaking to an Indian journalist in 1991, Druk Gyalpo Jigme Singye Wangchuck talked about Bhutan of his dream in the following words:

> We do not want a weak, divided and fragmented society but wish to create a strong, united and cohesive nation with a distinctive national identity.Some of the other challenges we face are how to achieve economic progress, social justice, to ensure rapid development and yet conserve our environmental and natural resource base.[26]

Talking about the problem of nation-building to the same correspondant, Druk Gyalpo Jigme Singye Wangchuck stated:

> We are facing many challenges in the process of nation building. As you know, after following a policy of isolationism for several centuries, we are taking a leap from the Middle Ages to the 20th century.What countries have achieved in many centuries we are trying to achieve in a few decades. The main challenge before us

today is how to create one nation and one people out of the many ethnic and religious groups in the kingdom.[26a]

Clearly, various statements of the Druk Gyalpo and various acts of the Royal Government of Bhutan have been aimed at effecting national unity and integration in the country, which, if anything, is the crying need of the hour. One cannot say that various statements of the King in the direction of creating a psychological background were designed to serve any rhetorical purpose. Nor can one say that various steps taken on the front of national integration was a part of show-politics, for much had emerged from such statements and acts.

Developmental activities in Southern Bhutan

How serious and concerned the young *Druk Gyalpo,* Jigme Singye Wangchuck, is about the developmental projects and activities in Southern Bhutan is illustrated by the fact that during the 70th session of the *Tshogdu* (October 1991), he sought for himself the authority to undertake developmental activities in that part which had been shattered by the terrorists of Nepali origin. Not only this, the King stated that he would offer to abdicate if he failed in solving the current problem created by a segment of the ethnic Nepalese.

Clearly, it is difficult to find any example of a reigning and ruling monarch offering to abdicate for such a purpose. This aside, facts speak for themselves, if one tries to scan the data on the developmental plane, especially in Southern Bhutan, even casually. Indeed, Southern Bhutan has been given preferential treatment in all developmental programmes and allotted with relatively large budgetary allocations than other parts of the country. This is transparent from the fact that there are more educational and health facilities in 5 southern districts as compared to the other districts of the kingdom. The employment ratio in government service is higher for the Lhotshampas in terms of their population in the kingdom. The rural population in Southern Bhutan also enjoy much higher income because of a far larger land holdings and lucrative cash crop earnings.The average land holding per household in southern Bhutan is 8 acres, as compared to 2 acres in northern Bhutan.[27]

Between 1978 and 1989, His Majesty the King granted over 2,645 acres of land to 997 landless households in southern Bhutan. Very few northern Bhutanese were given the same benefits. The Royal Government also arranged for special loan facility of Nu. 87.13 lakhs to be extended exclusively to those people in southern Bhutan whose orange gardens and cardamom fields were so heavily mortgaged to Indian money-lenders that it was wellnigh impossible for them to reclaim their land without governmental assistance. This enabled 203 farmers in southern Bhutan to reassert full control and effective ownership over their cash crop fields and gardens.[28]

The data about the location of various schools, educational institutions and hospitals in southern Bhutan also speak for themselves. Out of 195 schools and educational institutions in the 18 *dzongkhags* (districts) of the country, 79 are located in 5 *dzongkhags* of southern Bhutan. Out of 24 hospitals in the country (including 5 leprosy hospitals and 3 Royal Bhutan Army hospitals), 8 full-fledged general hospitals are located in southern Bhutan.[29]

The developmental activities and projects undertaken by the Royal Bhutan Government in southern Bhutan, thus, make a mockery of the charge that the southerns are discriminated against by the government at Thimphu. What in fact is bewildering is that the process of national integration remains far from complete, despite these developmental activities of the government at Thimphu. It is baffling that the processes of nation-making and state-making in the modern sense of the term are far from complete, thanks to the determination of disgruntlement on the part of an assertive and vocal as also politicized linguistic minority. Obviously, there is much more to the whole contrived problem than meets the eye. The tragicomedy, on the whole, seems that more the mountain kingdom has moved towards the concept and goal of a service and welfare state, the more serious have the problems of national integration, nation-building and state building become.

The Lhotshampas' incorporation in the military-bureaucratic structure

Not only has the Royal Government been very serious and particular about the developmental activities in southern Bhutan, it has, indeed done everything possible to incorporate the Lhotshampas in the bureaucracy the police and the militry of the state.The Royal Bhutan Civil Service Commission has always had a uniform policy for all Bhutanese citizens, and, as such, had provided opportunities to the Lhotshampas in the fields of training, appointments and promotions in the civil service.As a result of this policy 5,383 of 12,023 civil servants in Bhutan were Lhotshampas.[30] Mentionably, during the last 6 years, 127 out of 213 students sent to India alone for further studies were southern Bhutanese.[31]

In other words, the percentage of the ethnic Nepalese in the civil service is 44.75: they account for 59.62% in the sphere of getting scholarships from the government of Bhutan on the basis of data during the last 6 years. These figures again make transparent the fact that the non-accommodation of the ethnic Nepalese in the state structure is not the cause of the phoney crisis prevalent in Bhutan.

That the Royal Government of Bhutan never discriminated against the southern Bhutanese is also borne out by the fact that they have been incorporated in the Royal Bhutanese Army and Police. "The representation of the southern Bhutanese in the police is about 22% and in the army about 25%. In fact, many of the Nepalese occupy senior posts in the army, the police and the civil service and they are fully involved in all aspects of policy formulation and decision making."[32]

By incorporating the ethnic Nepalese in the most important arms of the state—like the civil service,the police and the army—the Royal Bhutanese Government has from the outset reposed its trust in that segment of society. The government had also encouraged inter-marriages between northern and southern Bhutanese with cash incentives of Nu. 10,000. However, this programme did not succeed much, thanks to the reservations or non-enthusiasm of the people about it.

Interest articulation and organization formation by the Nepalese

Though technically Bhutan has never banned political parties, as had been done by many South Asian states like Nepal and Pakistan, political parties have not existed in most of the times of Bhutan's history. But political parties formed by Bhutanese with various objectives have surfaced from time to time. Two facts appear quite discernible on this front. All political parties, no matter whatever their life-span, have been set up by the ethnic Nepalese in Bhutan. Secondly, all such political parties have been formed and operated outside Bhutan. These two facts appear instructive. It easily becomes clear that at least some segments of Nepalese are determined not to reconcile themselves with the state structure or the existing political framework. But the very fact that no political party has ever received the support of the Drukpa segment of Bhutanese society drives the lesson home that the Nepalese are much more politically ambitious than the former. It also becomes clear that not very sure of local support, the ethnic Nepalese, who set up political parties from time to time, try to thrive on international support and sympathy. Political parties *per se* are no panacea for all socio-economic problems anywhere on earth. Nor are they to be viewed as paranoic. They have been, in fact, accepted in most of the democratic countries of the world. In South Asia, no political parties exist in Maldives, either theoretically or practically. In Nepal political parties had remained banned for more than 29 years in the post-1960 phase and for a longer period in the pre-1951 phase, even though political parties existed in practice in quite a pronounced manner in the post-1960 phase and at the underground level in the pre-1951 phase. But what has been happening in Bhutan in the name of political parties from time to time leaves much to be desired.

As for the formation and existence of political parties in Bhutan, one could divide the history of party formation into two phases:1) the pre-1990 phase and 2) the post-1990 phase.

In the pre-1990 phase, one comes across the phenomena of the formation of two political parties by the Bhutanese. Let us take up here for discussion the formation of political parties in the pre-1990 phase.

The Bhutan State Congress: By the early 1950s, the ethnic Nepalese in Bhutan began to organize themselves to protest in what they described as the discriminatory policy of the government in Thimphu. The Bhutan State Congress was formed in November 1952 under the political leadership of D.B. Gurung, D.B. Chhetri and G.P. Sharma.[33] This party was formed at Patgaon in Assam. The main goal of the party was to change the discriminatory policies of the Bhutanese government against the ethnic Nepalese.[34]

Nothing was heard of this party after the formation of the *Tshogdu* and ensuring representation of the Bhutanese people, including the ethnic Nepalese therein, in 1953 by the then King, Jigme Dorji Wangchuck.

Bhutan National Congress: The Bhutan National Congress was another political party whose name was heard in the pre-1990 phase. Sometime in the sixties, a "shadowy group" called the Bhutan National Congress unfurled its flag in Jalpaiguri and looked to the Southern Bhutanese for support.[35] Not much is known about the aims and objectives of this party but this, too, was believably led by the ethnic Nepalese. Like the Bhutan State Congress, nothing was heard of this party, too, subsequently.

We would take up for discussion the formation of other political parties and organizations after taking into account some steps taken by the Royal Government of Bhutan what might be called the streamlining of the state structure in Bhutan.

Some recent steps taken by the government

Some steps taken by the Royal Government of Bhutan in the recent years apparently with a view to streamlining the administrative process of the state and fostering unity among the various segments of the kingdom's people seem to have alienated a substantial segment of Nepalese further and farther. It may not be incorrect to say that though these steps were of symbolic significance and also were needed to bring more discipline in the country, the troublemakers among the Nepalese got a godsend opportunity. Very many of the troublemakers are either non-citizens or those who have been involved in corruption an embezzlement charges. Some innocent Nepalese also joined them. Some also joined being convinced of the need of protest.

Let us now discuss some of the steps taken by the Royal Bhutanese Government.

Census: The Royal Government of Bhutan initiated the process of census in 1988 with a view to correcting the discrepencies of the earlier exercise. Believably, the earlier census records had listed many non-nationals as nationals and many bona fide nationals as outsiders. Allegedly, many of those who are currently participating in the movement launched against the government in Thimphu had illegally registered outsiders as members of their households, while others like Gopal Sharma were themselves not bona fide nationals.[36]

In fact, even when the process of census initiated in 1988 was on, it was discovered that some 15,000 Nepalese could not prove that they or their forefathers had been living in Bhutan before 1958. Significantly, the census authorities had adopted 1958 as the cut-off year because it was believed that most of the non-nationals had come to Bhutan after 1958. It is noteworthy that despite the detection of a large number of non-Bhutanese living in Bhutan the government did not banish them. If the citizens were given red cards, the non-citizens were given green cards and they were entitled to all facilities except franchise. The non-citizens were described, rather more liberally, as "residents". In fact, they were given the facility of being naturalised.[37]

Instead of appreciating the magnanimity of the Royal Government in accommodating the Nepalese segment of society by not evicting even the non-nationals, allegations were made that the census was conducted to evict as many southern Bhutanese as possible. The census would also have brought the figures of the Nepali-speaking people in Bhutan in a proper perspective. This was something which was certainly not to their liking. They made every possible effort to stall the census process. When many Nepalese took to arms, census records and census officials became their easy targets.

Commenting on the problems of census and citizenship, a commentator has observed:

One of the King's main concerns is to tackle, peacefully and efficiently and justly the problem of 'citizenship', an aftermath of the Nationality Act of Bhutan of 1958 which was drafted by Sardar D.K. Sen. Trouble, in fact, started after the 1988 census in Bhutan from the people of Nepalese origin which is estimated at about 25 per cent of Bhutan's population. Following the 1958 Act there were two Citizenship Acts enforced in 1977 and 1985. A decision was taken by the National Assembly in 1989 that all those foreigners who had married Bhutanese were given a permanent residence card, like the U.S. Green Card, valid initially for 10 years and automatically extended for another 10 years, giving them all rights during this period, except for voting and seeking scholarship for studies abroad.[38]

Overall, the census process created a serious tension among the Nepalese. But the question is: How long could have the government avoided census?

Driglam Namzha: Like the process of census, the introduction of *Driglam Namzha* also became a matter of serious controversy among the ethnic Nepalese in Bhutan. The Royal Government's initiative on the front of *Driglam Namzha* falls under the same framework of streamlining the system and the administration. Some say—perhaps rightly—that a country of the size and population of Bhutan cannot afford the same kind of diversity and pluralism as in India or other big countries of the world. Bhutan has got to face the problem of national identity with all seriousness. In fact, it becomes all the more essential because of its landlocked character and physical similarities of its people with the people of Nepal and China (Autonomous Region of Tibet in this case).

The critics of this system and practice allege that it is an attempt at Bhutanization and was introduced in 1989 by King Jigme Singye Wangchuck with a view to reviving Bhutanese culture and tradition. But the Secretary of the Special Commission for Cultural Affairs, who mainly oversees this programme's implementation, stated that there is nothing new in *Driglam Namzha.* He stated that this was nothing but national etiquette and centuries' old. When I asked as to why did it become pronounced in 1989, the Secretary replied that it had been neglected during the past 25 years of socio-economic developments and it was now decided to execute it vigorously. He stressed that the programme was related to Bhutan's national identity.[39]

It is also alleged that the programme was launched with a view to imposing the Drukpa culture on the ethnic Nepalese in Bhutan. However, its protagonists emphasize that the word "Drukpa" stands for the Bhutanese of all hues, colours and creeds. Mentionably, the programme was not sought to be executed all of a sudden. It was only after the forceful advocacy of this programme during the 68th session of the *Tshogdu* by the representatives of Gaylegphug, Sarbhang and Kalikhola (all in southern Bhutan), recommendations of the District Development Committees and various requests by the people of southern Bhutan made to the King that this programme came to be implemented.[40] On the other hand, there had been earnest and consistent demand for this during the various tours of the King of southern Bhutan.[41]

True, the *Driglam Namzha* programme earned some notoriety because of the overenthusiasm shown by the Bhutanese police. I found most of the Bhutanese officials and ministers accepting this charge to some extent. The overenthusiasm shown by the Bhutanese police is not difficult to explain. In actuality, a man not wearing *Gho* and a woman not wearing *Kira* were to be fined Nu. 100 each and 50 per cent of this amount was to go to the police as incentive. The result was that for some time the Bhutanese police used to catch hold of any man or woman at a time when he or she was not supposed to wear that to impose the fine. This made the measure unpopular, especially in Southern Bhutan, to a very great extent. However, it need to be mentioned that the Royal Government of Bhutan had to spend a large amount in providing *Gho* an *Kira* to the people at subsidised rates.

Not that the government is very adamant on the execution of this programme. There seems to be sufficient relaxation on this front. Of course, the dress norms are supposed to be adhered to strictly in various government offices in Bhutan. Palpably, while the government sought to use this programme with a view to achieving greater national integration, the ethnic Nepalese found in it a godsend opportunity to create problems of nation-building and state-building. Alienation of the ethnic Nepalese, if anything, increased further.

No Objection Certificate (NOC)

Like the census exercise and the practice of *Driglam Namzha,* the Royal Bhutan Government's introduction of the No Objection Certificate—introduced after the increase of terrorism in Bhutan—also became a subject of serious controversy. It pertained to clearance for transfer of students and various operations of Bhutanese farmers. While the ethnic Nepalese claim that this system was introduced with a view to creating various obstacles for the Nepalese, the government claims that it had become quite essential after the terrorists raised their ugly heads.

The government claims that despite the limitation of seats, students from schools in southern Bhutan were transferred to schools in other parts of the country. To ensure that all bona fide Bhutanese children received the first preference for admission in the schools, a No Objection Certificate was made essential for the transfer of students. According to the government, NOCs would not be issued to those students who have been actively involved in anti-national activities and to children of illegal immigrants.

One further requirement for the NOC was for the release of cheques to farmers for the sale of their cash crops. NOCs would not be issued to people whose immediate family members are actively involved in terrorist activities. This was a necessary precaution to ensure that the terrorists did not receive the money to purchase arms and explosives. "It must be made clear that the money due to the owners of these cash crops is merely frozen and not confiscated". The government also asserts that the "amounts due to them will be released once the current disturbed situation is resolved".[42]

Not that the government is unaware of the problems of the formalities of obtaining an NOC. It knows that some incovenience is natural. However, it asserts that many children from southern Bhutan have been accommodated in schools all over the country despite the limited number of seats in these establishments. The Royal Government also asserts that "several crores of Rupees have been released to southern Bhutanese farmers who have sold their cash crop through the STCB".[43]

All this goes to show that the Royal Government of Bhutan took some measure to streamline the administrative machinery and dilute, if not completely preclude, the advantages to non-nationals or anti-nationals (called *ngolops)*. No government in the position of the Bhutanese government can afford to sit idle in the developing situation. Perhaps, any group of anti-national people would have grabbed such a situation to use for propaganda purposes. That is what the *ngolop* Nepalese in Bhutan are doing today. Obviously, this does not augur well for national unity and integrity. Therein lies the crux of the problem. The Royal Government has doubtless to make efforts to grapple with the situation.

The ethnic Nepalese got an opportunity to articulate and aggregate their interests and show to the world that they were being harassed and victimized in Bhutan. A number of political parties and other organizations have come into existence either in India or in Nepal, where very many of the ethnic Nepalese of Bhutan have been taking refuge. While the number of refugees are sought to be exaggerated in every possible way by the ethnic Nepalese in Bhutan, the Royal Government does not accept that all the Nepali-speaking refugees are necessarily from Bhutan or they are Bhutanese nationals.

New organizations formed by the ethnic Nepalese of Bhutan

Let us now take up for discussion the various organizations that have been formed by the ethnic Nepalese living in exile in India and Nepal. Let us first take up the political parties. A political party is an organized group, made up of members who subscribe to some common set of values or policies, which has as its fundamental aim the attainment of political power and public office, generally by constitutional means, in order to implement these policies. It differs from lobbies, pressure groups and interest groups, since these are concerned with influencing government decisions or legislative proposals in some specific cases, or over a limited range or cases, whereas a party seeks to implement its policies over the whole spectrum of public affairs. A party differs from a movement by virtue of its more formal organizational structure, the more specific nature of its aims, and its broad acceptance of the methods of obtaining political power that currently prevail in the system.

The exercise of governmental power is not the only function which a political party performs and fulfils. It is an agency for political recruitment, an instrument of political socialization, a channel for political communication étc. In terms of the political system, it has "gatekeeping" and interest-aggregative roles, among others.

A party system is the complex interrelationship between political parties, the political community, the political public and the functions which parties perform. The party systems vary according to major dimensions of these components.[44]

It is difficult to say how many of these features and functions apply to the political parties of the Bhutanese Nepalese. What is, however, certain is that the political parties have been marked by ethnic specificity. Let us now take up in turn various political parties that have been formed by the ethnic Nepalese.

The Bhutan People's Party (BPP): The Bhutan People's Party (BPP) was formed on 2 June 1990. According to its President R.K. Budathoki, it was formed because a politcal platform was needed "to intensify our pro-democracy agitation". According to him, on 19 September 1990, the government killed 327 people at a rally organized by pro-democracy activists. Many were injured in the police firing. He asserted that the BPP "became the target of the Government's attacks".[45] According to him, the party's supporters are being hounded out. There are over 2,500 political prisoners in Bhutan. "We received report that the bodies of those killed by torture are being disposed of in the Sunkosi river", said Budathoki.

The government has been denying these allegations. It is quite difficult to believe that the killing of 327 people would have been such a normal matter and the international community, including India and Bhutan's other neighbours, would not have come to know about it. Moreover, it is difficult to believe the number of political prisoners, as stated by Budathoki. According to a government statement only 42 people were arrested in Bhutan between October and December 1989 for being involved in anti-national activities.[46]

Be that as it may, the BPP president says, his party is determined to continue the struggle to establish a "secular parliamentary democracy in Bhutan and ensure that human rights are protected". Adult franchise, fundamental rights of the citizens and an independent judiciary and an election commission are among its other aims. But the King will have his constitutional role.[47]

Budathoki asserted in an interview that if the government persists in its reign of terror, discrimination against ethnic Bhutanese who lived with other communities in harmony for centuries, a civil war may break out. He however asserted that the "BPP is committed to a non-violent struggle. We will pursue our democratic agitation against the Government".[48] While asserting that there are no splinter groups in the BPP, Budathoki averred:

> We are ready for a negotiated settlement, but have received no invitation from the Government. We have accepted the Government's code of national dress, but it should not be made compulsory. We are not against the King. We want him to be the pivot for national integrity and unity. But we are opposed to discriminations against southern Bhutanese.[49]

Overall, the BPP seems to be interested in dialogue with the authorities in Thimphu and it has also shown its predilection for tripartite talks, making India a party to such talks. India, however, has not shown any such willingness. From time to time various government functionaries in India have been asserting that India's relations with Bhutan cannot be allowed to be strained by the activities of the BPP from Indian territory.

According to the version of the Royal Government of Bhutan, R.K. Budathoki was an Assistant Director in the Department of Customs who had been terminated from service for corruption.[50] Commenting on various demands of the BPP the Ministry of Home Affairs of the Royal Government of Bhutan stated:

> The true aim and objective of the terrorist movement in southern Bhutan has been revealed in demand Nos. 2 and 4 of the 13-point demands of the so-called BPP. Demand No. 2 calls for the establishment of constitutional monarchy with the election of a prime minister and proportional ethnic representation in the National Assembly and the cabinet based on population. Demand No. 4 calls for the amendment of the 1985 Citizenship Act. While these two demands are of direct importance towards the fulfilment of the true objectives of the terrorist movement, all other demands are merely cosmetic and meant for propaganda as they centre around the popular catch phrases of democracy and human rights. While most of the issues and grievances enumerated in the 13-point demands are non-existent, some other issues such as democratic rights are in actual fact enjoyed by all sections of the Bhutanese people both in practice and spirit, although they may not be institutionalized in form.[51]

Bhutan Congress : According to news reports in a section of the Indian press, Bhutan's "outlawed premier political party, Bhutan Congress, has resurfaced after staying underground in India for decades".[52] We have, already seen that the party that had come into existence in 1952—the first to do so—was called the Bhutan State Congress. Either there is some confusion about the nomenclature or some misinformation. According to the reports, the "leadership mantle has now fallen on the 66-year-old self-styled Father of Bhutani Democracy, Devi Bhakta Lamitare, who has his headquarters at Hardwar, Uttar Pradesh and 11 members in the party's executive committee mostly based in the Doors region of North Bengal bordering Bhutan."[53]

Obviously, the emergence of a new party or the reemergence of an old party was indicative of a rift among the ethnic Nepali agitators. Lamitare termed the BPP and the People's Forum for Human Rights (PFHR) as "Communist stooges dancing the tune of Indian and Nepali Marxists." It was a wrong step, he opined, to have obtained political asylum in Nepal, even though the self-exiled BPP and PFHR leaders have successfully campaigned among both the ruling Nepali Congress and the Opposition CPN (UML) and a combined Bhutan support group is in the offing.[54]

Lamitare, who was reportedly associated with the Nepali Congress for 22 years, condemned the BPP and PFHR leaders for launching a violent movement in Bhutan and then taking shelter in Nepal. He felt that these leaders should have based themselves in India. "We don't want to obtain any material help from the Indian government, but we have every right to take any help from the Indian people. It is the Indian tax payer's money that goes to maintain Bhutan", Lamitare said in a recent interview.[55]

Curiously, he had sent telegrams to the prime ministers of India and Nepal seeking their intervention "to stop suppression of democratic movement in Bhutan". Averse to being called a Nepali, he insists that he is a "Bhutani Gorkha and his entire thrust behind the finest political rhetoric is to save the Hindu Gorkhas from the stranglehold of the ruling Drukpa Buddhists and capture political power in the kingdom".[56]

Though nothing has come to light about the political and economic programmes of the party thus far, what is palpable after the emergence of this organization is the fact that not all ethnic Nepalese in Bhutan or even their so-called leaders think even wellnigh alike.

The [Bhutan] National Democratic Party (BNDP)

In a series of formation of political parties by the ethnic Nepalese of Bhutan, an organization called the "Bhutan National Democratic Party" came into existence in February 1992. One wonders why the word "Bhutan" has been inserted in brackets by the party founders. A document entitled "[Bhutan] National Democratic Party Ideology, Manifesto and Organization Structure" with its headquarters at Thimphu was issued on 5 February 1992.

At a press conference held in New Delhi on 7 February 1992, D.N.S. Dhakal, general secretary of the party said that the new party would work for instituting a secular constitution and restoring human rights in all parts of Bhutan as per the 1948 UN Declaration of Human Rights.[57] Speaking further, Dhakal said that the King of Bhutan had since long unleashed a "reign of terror" on the Nepalese Bhutanese who constitute 53 per cent of the total population in the country. He alleged that the King had declared them as migrants in their own country. He averred that the feudal institution in power was incapable of adapting to the changing aspiration and it must be replaced by a system of government that takes into account the will and desire of Bhutanese people. Dhakal also said: "We are not against the King but the system."[58] According to Dhakal, the BNDP would fight for the establishment of "constitutional monarchy in Bhutan with a multi-party democratic set-up".[59]

The document of the party, which we have already referred to, is an elaborate and detailed information about its ideology, programme and organizational structure. The addresses of its president, R.B. Basnet, and general secretary, D.N.S. Dhakal, were also mentioned. A list of 29 people was mentioned as the founding members of the party. Of them there are 14 such officials who left the country in the aftermath of the agitation. Very many of such officials are facing corruption charges. Significantly, very many of them are related to one another. Among such officials Bhim Subha, R.B. Basnet, B.L. Sharma, Mandoj Tamang, P.S. Gurung, D.P. Basnet, Usha Tamang and others had notoriously figured in the news after they had left the country in the aftermath of the beginning of the audit process. Very many of them were held guilty of corruption and embezzlement charges by the government in Thimphu.[60] Among the founder members there were 8 former National Assembly Members, 3 former businessmen and 2 ex-college students.[61]

Without doubt, the manifesto of the party has been couched in catchy words and written in chaste English. Comprising 25 pages in all, it deals with the organizational structure, the background information giving reasons for democratic reforms. It talks of the feudal institution and economic interest of the members of the royal family. It also laments the fact that the southern Bhutanese have been made "scapegoats to the problem".[62] Besides, it stresses political reforms as the need of changing time. It is on this score that it talks about multi-party democracy as an alternative to monarchy.[63] On the economic front, the manifesto talks about "Mutually Beneficial Capitalism" (MBC), human capital formation, economic development for a natural resource and generating adequate income. It also talks about making Bhutan "an active participant within and outside the economies of the Indian sub-continent".[64]

On the front of foreign policy, the manifesto talks of the maintenance of "warm and friendly diplomatic relationship" with India. It promises to honour the 1949 Treaty, while trying to strengthen and establish diplomatic relationships outside the SAARC region "keeping in view Bhutan's long-term interest in business and economic cooperation".[65]

On the front of employment, the manifesto talks of employment to non-Bhutanese and job-reservation scheme and better paying jobs.[66] The manifesto also talks of right to education and mix of public and private schools, high teaching standards, Education Insurance Scheme, Common Board of Examinations, result-oriented training, higher education fee etc.[67]

Besides, the manifesto talks in detail of Health Care Policy and

Tourism Policy promising reforms on both these fronts. While talking of population policy, it talks about population planning and control and family planning education in the country. It also throws light on its environment policy, immigration and census policy, language policy, cultural integration and national identity policy, culture and tradition policy, monastic institution policy, ethnic minority policy and women development policy.[68]

Thus the newest party of the ethnic Nepalese of Bhutan is different from others—which we alluded to earlier—in several ways. Most of its founder members are well-educated, having been sent abroad on the grants and scholarships of the Royal Government of Bhutan. Very many of them have had the experience of administration. It was rather startling that the leader of a party, very many of whose leaders are facing corruption charges, dared to organize a press conference in India's capital, a country whose government or even the Opposition is not supposed to be sympathetic to their cause. This has, in fact, left many observers and analysts baffled.

The ethnic Nepalese of Bhutan have also formed several other human rights organizations in India and Nepal to focus on the treatment meted out to the group in Bhutan. Such organizations include :

The People's Forum for Human Rights (PFHR);
The United Liberation People's Front (ULPF); and
The Students' Union of Bhutan (SUB).

According to the information given by the Royal Bhutanese Government, the PFHR was led by Gopal Sharma, and based in Garganda (India). According to this source, Gopal Sharma, who used to work as an extension worker in the Agriculture Department, is not even a bona fide Bhutanese national but an immigrant who was illegally registered in the past records of Samchi district with the connivance of some of the villagers and the block mondal.[69] On the other hand, S.N.M. Abdi wrote in *The Illustrated Weekly of India*, that at first the PFHR was floated, incredibly enough by a British couple! Malcolm and Marjorie Jack taught at the National Institute of Education in Samchi under the Voluntary Service Overseas (VSO) scheme. They were assisted by an Indian teacher, Augustine Issac, whose role in the writing of anti-national literature has now been established by the Home Ministry. The British couple handed over the leadership of the PFHR to Gopal Sharma.[70]

Soon enough, other organizations like ULPF and the SUB also came into existence to oppose various measures adopted by the government in Thimphu in recent times. According to the information given by the government, the ULPF is lead by Balram Poudyal based in Siliguri. According to this information Poudyal "is an ordinary criminal who embezzled Nu. 97,865 from public funds and private individuals while he was mandal of Bara block in Samchi".[71]

Thus more and more organizations for the purpose of interest articulation and interest aggregation of the Bhutanese of Nepali extraction are surfacing and indulging in propaganda against the government in Thimphu. Some view the surfacing of various organizations as a split in the ranks of the agitating Nepalese. Some view it as a sign of growing frustration among the Nepalese operating in exile in India and Nepal. Some view it as a sign of growth of more pressure on the Royal Government of Bhutan. It will be time before one could say things conclusively or even tangibly on this front. Writing in *The New York Times International* Barbara Crossette rightly observed:

> The small Buddhist kingdom of Bhutan has become the target of a well-organized campaign, based in India, to stir up violent opposition to the country's moves to protect itself and its culture from illegal immigration.[72]

Modus operandi of ethnic Nepalese in exile

The modus operandi of the Nepalese of Bhutan in exile in India and Nepal could be said to be mainly consisting of propaganda campaign against the Royal Government, extortions from and robbing and maiming of the Nepalese in Bhutan who do not see eye to eye with them and destroying of census records.

On the front of propaganda, various Bhutanese groups in India and Nepal have been holding rallies and demonstrations at various places, including New Delhi and Kathmandu, with a view to attracting the attention of the leaders and people of these countries to the plight of and discrimination against the Nepalese in Bhutan. These groups have also been holding press conferences at various places in India and Nepal where they have thrown light on the harassment of ethnic Nepalese in Bhutan. They seem to have impressed some sections of the Indian press, where news about the alleged harassment and torture of the ethnic Nepalese in Bhutan figure again and again. They also appear to have succeeded in convincing some human rights organizations in India about the plight of Nepalese in Bhutan. However, by and large people in India feel chary about the political activities of the Bhutanese Nepalese in India. Some even feel that all this has in itself the design of Pan-

Nepalism on the part of the Nepali Bhutanese. It, of course, remains to be seen how things shape eventually on this front.

The Bhutanese of Nepali extraction in India and Nepal are, according to various information given by the Royal Government of Bhutan from time to time, indulging in extortions from and kidnapping of those Nepalese who do not see eye to eye with them and who want to live in their own country with peace. Thanks to the *modus operandi* of the Bhutanese in exile in India and Nepal, the process of census initiated in 1988 has been badly affected. They are now indulging in the destruction of whatever records are traceable with relevant officials and people in southern Bhutan. This makes their objective and intention quite palpable. There is little doubt that the administration in Bhutan, especially in the southern part, has been badly affected and very many innocent people have either lost their lives or been maimed. The leaders of various organizations in exile, however, blame the police and the army of Bhutan for all these acts. There seems to be few takers for such charges.

Exodus of refugees in India and Nepal

As things developed in Bhutan during 1988 and 1989, it was expected that some Nepalese would leave their country either in sympathy with the leaders of various organizations or out of fear and threat given to them by various leaders and operators in exile. However, the number of ethnic Nepalese from Bhutan living as refugees in India and Nepal has often remained a matter of controversy. At a Press conference in New Delhi, the general secretary of the newly-formed BNDP, D.N.S. Dhakal, asserted that since 1990 "nearly 40,000 people had fled the country and sought refuge in Nepal and India". At the same time, he asserted that India has not allowed refugee camps to be set up here.[73]

Significantly, India has never given any figure of Nepali refugees from Bhutan living in exile in this country. Nepal, however, keeps on giving the number of refugees from Bhutan from time to time. According to the figure mentioned in the government-controlled *Gorkhapatra* of 1 February 1992, the "number of Bhutanese refugees in Kankai and Timai camps in Jhapa was said to have reached 14,567 and about 150 more were said to be arriving everyday". This figure, according to sources from Kathmandu, increased subsequently. According to an official of the Home Ministry in Kathmandu, there were now about 25,000 Bhutanese refugees in Nepal and as many as 30,000, if refugees living outside camps were also counted. He further added that about 200 to 500 more refugees were coming in everyday.[74]

As for the Royal Government of Bhutan, it has not given any figure of Bhutanese who have left the country. However, it does not accept that several thousands of Nepali-speaking Bhutanese have left the country in the aftermath of terrorist activities. There were reports that very many of them had, at one point of time or another, returned to Bhutan. Overall, despite the claims of various political organizations headed by Nepalese from Bhutan, the figure of Bhutanese refugees living in India and Nepal has remained a matter of controversy and not many believe in the figures given by leaders of various political organizations. On the other hand, many tend to believe that many refugees in Nepal have gone there from various parts of north-eastern Indian states, rather than from Bhutan. So mobile have been the people of Nepali origin that the number of genuine Bhutanese refugees in Nepal and India is bound to remain controversial.

Officials' desertions

As terrorist and political activities by the ethnic Nepalese increased the instances of several highly-placed Nepali officials quitting the country—especially for Nepal—came to light. According to the government, several of them were facing corruption and embezzlement charges. Very many of them had received their education and training abroad at the expense of the Royal Government of Bhutan. Very many of them subsequently became founder members of the BNDP, a political party that came into existence in February 1992, which we have already referred to.

According to the Secretary of the Royal Civil Service Commission, Dasho Khandu Wangchuk, a total of 354 civil servants, 26 forest guards and 99 personnel from the services have absconded from the country so far. Dasho Khandu Wangchuk pointed out that out of 12,023 civil servants, 5,383—or 39.23 per cent—are from southern Bhutan. The Secretary said: "We are concerned about more southern Bhutanese civil servants leaving the country at a time when we need every Bhutanese because we are short of trained and skilled manpower".[75]

Bhutanese government's response

The response of Royal Government of Bhutan has been quite balanced amidst all these provocations. It has so far adopted a low profile. For instance, the King has been counselling the army and the police personnel not to open fire on the *ngolops* and terrorists until and unless such an eventuality becomes completely unavoidable. This attitude of His Majesty King Jigme Singye Wangchuck has produced serious criticism—albeit *sotto voce*—even by the system supporters. But the government has maintained a remarkable balance in giving safety and security to the citizens and dealing with ngolops and terrorists.

On the other hand, the Royal Government has shown no allergy to the concept of human rights. In an exclusive personal interview to me at his Tashichho Dzong office at Thimphu on 21 October 1991, King Jigme Singye Wangchuck said: "As a Buddhist, and also as a member of the United Nations, I fully support the Universal Declaration of Human Rights and I respect all genuine human rights organizations". But at the same time the King showed his reservations to the PFHR by stating: "However, so-called human rights organizations such as the People's Forum for Human Rights (PFHR), which are merely a front for terrorist outfits, must be recognized for what they are". Commenting on the activities and reputation of this body, the King said: "Perhaps it was in recognition of the bad reputation earned by the PFHR due to its dubious activities that its members have recently decided to make a cosmetic change and rename it the Human Rights Organization of Bhutan".

Unlike several other political systems, the Royal Government of Bhutan also does not appear to be allergic to political parties. The names of various political parties have not non—pulsed the government. About political parties, and human rights, groups chances of functioning in Bhutan, King Jigme Singye Wangchuck told me in an exclusive interview at Thimphu on 21 October 1991:

> I have always said that the future of Bhutan lies in the hands of the Bhutanese people. If the people feel there is a need for human rights groups and political parties or constitutional monarchy, it is for them to decide. As the King, my main concern and cherished wish is to ensure that the security and well-being of Bhutan will always be safeguarded. For me the interest of the nation always comes first.

In a daring act, the Royal Government of Bhutan invited the Amnesty International's team to visit Bhutan and see for itself the state of human rights in the kingdom. On 10 January 1992, King Jigme Singye Wangchuck granted an audience to a delegation from Amnesty International, the eminent human rights organization, which came on a 6-day visit. Led by the secretary general of the Amnesty International, Ian Martin, the 3-member delegation included Derek G. Evans, head of the Asia and Pacific Research Department and Elizabeth Roswell, also of the same department. Ian Martin said in a press interview that the delegation had come to Bhutan to meet government officials to express Amnesty's concern about 6 persons who had been detained in connection with the disturbances in southern Bhutan. These included the three detainees who were pardoned by the King on 17 December 1991. Martin further stated that the Amnesty delegation would also like to assess the human rights situation in Bhutan and, in this regard, ascertain what measures were being taken by the Bhutanese government to prevent excesses by the security forces. Martin also stated that the Amnesty was also "concerned about the killings and torture by people who are fighting the government".[76]

The 3-member delegation of the Amnesty left Bhutan with a much better understanding of the whole context of human rights problems in the kingdom. It was the view expressed by the secretary general, Ian Martin, in Thimphu before the team's departure. Martin said in an interview: "This visit has certainly enabled us to understand the perspectives of various people at different levels of Bhutan on that matter." He further stated: "It is not for us to make judgement—we are outsiders and our only specialization is in the protection of human rights—but of course it is important for us understand the context in which human rights is under pressure".[77]

Martin described his visit to Bhutan as a significant and important first visit and expressed his hope that it would be a part of an increasing discussion about human rights issues and how human rights can be best protected in the country. "What is important is that this continuing dialogue goes on between our organization, the government, and also the people", he stated. He further stated: "We have found in the course of this visit both that some of the allegations about human rights violations made outside Bhutan are untrue and some that have been made to us have been substantiated".[78]

In addition, the Bhutanese government has shown its magnanimity by releasing more and more political prisoners and giving them amnesty. So far the King has granted royal pardon to a total of 1,348 people who had been detained for their involvement in anti-national activities.[79] In an exclusive interview to me on 21 October 1991 at Thimphu, King Jigme Singye Wangchuck said that he did not want to send prisoners on trial quickly so that the High Court pronounces harsh judgment, which law requires, and then he has to intervene. He stated that by intervening after court's verdicts, he did not want to belittle that body. This obviously reflected his desire to be as lenient as possible.

Moreover, the Royal Government has shown its willingness and readiness to intervene whenever there has been any complaint about harassment to the ethnic Nepalese by the members of the Bhutanese administration. A high-level investigation team was sent by King Jigme Singye Wangchuck to Chirang and Dagana to investigate some excesses committed by the civil servants against the natives, who were all Nepalese. The investigation team which left Thimphu on 13 January 1991 comprised Home Minister Lyonpo Dago Tshering, Chief Justice Dasho Sonam Tobgye, Royal Advisory Council Chairman Dasho Kunzang Tangbi, High Court Judges Dasho Phub Dorji and Dasho D.N. Katwal, Police Chief Colonel Tandin Dorji and Tashi Gyelsthen of Immigration and Census.[80]

The investigation team received allegations of forced eviction by the civil administration. Investigating all allegations of eviction, the team discovered that two families had already left under such intimidation and that in the case of one, Bachala Maya Acharya of Lamidara, representatives of the thrimkhang and dzongkhag administration had visited her houses to list all her property even before she had applied to leave the country.[81]

Lyonpo Dago Tshering said in an interview that the team had found the activities of the members of the civil administration in Chirang, led by the senior thrimkhang officials, extremely questionable. The officials, he said had lost all direction and were involved in grabbing land and buying buildings from the emigrants who were leaving the country. Some of the officers of the Royal Bhutan Police and the security forces were also involved in purchasing land and houses.

Obviously, these steps of the Royal Bhutan Government, show that it wants to preserve national unity and integrity, while maintaining the honour of all law-abiding Bhutanese, regardless of their ethnicity.

External dimensions to the ethnic Nepalese problems: Support and sympathy in India and Nepal

The geography of southern Bhutan and the kingom's open borders with India and Nepal could have easily added regional, if not also international, dimensions to the problems articulated by the ethnic Nepalese and their exodus in large numbers to India and Nepal. That is what subsequently happened when more and more Nepalese Bhutanese (especially the vocal ones) arrived in India and Nepal. True, they received some sympathizers both in India and Nepal—more in the latter.

In India, the initial sympathies came more from the parties other than the ruling one at the centre. However, the sympathies lessened subsequently even on those fronts as more and more real information became available. Perhaps, the Indian political parties could see the designs of the ethnic

Nepalese sooner than later and they could realize that by using catchy phrases of multiparty democracy, constitutional monarchy and human rights, they were trying to institutionalize the ethnic invasion in Bhutan. Though various political parties' leaders might have met the leaders and workers of various political groups of Bhutan operating in India and the Indian soil might have been used by these groups for indulging in various methods of attention-attraction, it is obvious that so far the various segments of Indian political life have given a mature response to the whole problem.

The various important political and administrative functionaries whom I met in Thimphu during my visits of October 1990 and October 1991, including King Jigme Singye Wangchuck, gave the impression that they were satisfied with the Indian leaders perceptions of the current situation in Bhutan. The Bhutan government has been apprising the governments of West Bengal, Assam and India of the day-to-day developments and no communication gap had ever occurred.[82] West Bengal Chief Minister Jyoti Basu paid a 4-day visit to Bhutan in response to an invitation from the King in June 1990. On his return from the mountain kingdom, Basu described his trip as "friendly and cordial".[83]

The then Minister of State for Foreign Affairs, Hari Kishore Singh, said on 19 October 1990 that the government would not allow the Nepalese in India to carry out an agitation against Bhutan. He made it clear that the Nepali-speaking people were free to live and work in India but "they have no political right to agitate against a friendly neighbour".[84] More importantly, replying to a question, Singh said that the Bhutan government was competent enough to tackle the situation arising from the agitation launched by a section of the Nepali-speaking people living in that country. He emphasized that "those who are not citizens of Bhutan have no right to agitate against that country".[85] Relevantly, the Minister denied that asylum had been given to agitators said to be operating from the border areas of North Bengal districts. Several thousand Nepalese were working in India, particularly in West Bengal, as they were free to come under the Indo-Nepal Treaty, but it would be embarrassing to the government if they were found involved in agitations against the Bhutan government, with which India had excellent ties, the State Minister stressed.[86]

The then Indian Foreign Secretary, Muchkund Dubey, appeared more forceful. He conveyed to the Bhutanese King the Government of India's decision to provide all possible assistance, including communication and logistics, to bolster his kingdom's law and order machinery and also counter the acts of violence which shook it recently. Also conveyed to the Bhutanese monarch was the message that India was considering the possibility of opening armed outposts along the Bhutanese border to stop illegal entry of foreigners into the kingdom. India, the then Foreign Secretary said in Calcutta on 21 October 1990, was considering the proposal since it did not want the recurrence of foreigners illegally crossing over to Bhutanese territory and engaging in acts of violence.[87]

Dubey further asserted that he had assured the King that India would never allow its territory to be used against Bhutan. The Indian government had already initiated action against those who were engaged in such activities, besides sending back 6,000 Bhutanese of Nepalese origin, who had come across to North Bengal at the height of political turmoil. He averred that he had told the King that India would not "tolerate any threat being posed to Bhutan's stability and it would take prompt and effective action, if Bhutan could point out that Indian territory was being used against the country's interest". More importantly, Dubey added that he had told the King that "we have conveyed to the Nepalese settlers in India that we will not tolerate their joining any anti-Bhutan activity". He asserted that the King "was convinced of our best intentions and appreciative of our stand".[88]

However, the case in Nepal appears quite different. The two main political parties—the ruling Nepali Congress and the main Opposition United Marxist Leninist—have tried to vie with each other in sympathizing with and giving moral support to the Bhutanese refugees of Nepali extraction. It is widely believed in Bhutan that the Nepali government is supporting the dissidents from the south. Prime Minister G.P. Koirala, who prides himself on being associated with the formation of the first political party in Bhutan in the early 50s, i.e. the Bhutan State Congress, has no confusion or hesitation in giving political asylum to a number of Nepali Bhutanese who have defected to Nepal and are indulging in political activities in that country. Thus, many vocal ethnic Nepalese have found a safe haven in Nepal. G.P. Koirala has stressed time and again that his government was committed to human rights and since Bhutanese people, according to him, were fighting for democracy and human rights, "our moral support is with the people of Bhutan". Though Koirala reiterates that Nepal will not interfere in the internal affairs of Bhutan, it does not dilute, much less solve, the problem. Instead, the ethnic Nepalese have been emboldened because of Koirala's attitude and statements. Koirala has also been making statements about his sentimental and emotional attachment with the "Bhutanese people" ever since the formation of the Bhutan State Congress in the early 1950s. Significantly, he does not take the corruption charges made against several Nepali civil servants who defected to Bhutan seriously and insists that a dictatorial regime often indulges in such things. Being hopeful of liberalization in Bhutan, Koirala also emphasizes that relations between Nepal and Bhutan are not bad.[89]

It was widely believed first during Koirala's state visit to India in December 1991 and secondly, during the SAARC Summit in Colombo in the same month that his talks with the Indian Prime Minister and subsequently the Bhutanese King would improve this situation. But the ethnic Nepalese from Bhutan are feeling more and more encouraged in Nepal and their political activities have increased.

However, it cannot be said that the views or enthusiasm of Koirala are supported by all Nepalese. People from southern Nepal, i.e. the Terai, and leaders and workers of the Nepal Sadbhavana Party feel that instead of taking up the cause of the people of another country, the Nepali government should improve the human rights records of its own in southern Nepal and bring to an end severe discrimination meted out to the *Madheshis*, who preponderate in southern Nepal. It is discernible even to a casual observer that the *Madheshis* enjoy much less privileges (even though they are the genuine citizens of Nepal) in comparison to the ethnic Nepalese in Bhutan in every sphere of life. Many in the Terai also feel apprehensive of the camping of the Nepali refugees in their region.[90]

Summing-up

In sum, Bhutan's problems of national and territorial integration and law and order have assumed deep and serious proportions during the past couple of years. The problems, which emanated from the government's desire to streamline the country's administration and have a proper counts of its citizens have not looked back thereafter. Instead, they have been accentuated and aggravated. With the formation of more and more political organizations, including parties, and more and more *Tshogdu* members and absconding civil servants joining political activities outside the kingdom with a view to establishing constitutional monarchy and multiparty system in the kingdom, the movement no longer seems to be led by the non-nationals or economic refugees.

The north-south divide, has of course, made Bhutan newsworthy. But a small country like Bhutan should have the right and opportunity to maintain its cultural indentity. Not that the Royal Government of Bhutan has not tried devolution of politico-economic powers and liberalization on the whole. As we saw, it has also been making essential and and serious efforts to incorporate the ethnic Nepalese in the administrative and political mainstream from the earliest possible time. But the over-ambitiousness and over-politicization of the ethnic Nepalese in every possible way and the overjealous steps of some segments of the Bhutanese administration have brought Bhutan to the crossroads. Continuous illegal immigration has only accentuated the problem.

One hopes that the politics of agitation and terrorism is replaced by the politics of dialogue and discussion sooner than later. One wishes that Bhutan continues to move on the path of progress and prosperity retaining its national unity and integrity and its cultural specificity. But democracy and human rights have to be the concern of the entire Bhutanese people. Various happenings in the recent past have shown that no system can suppress the will of the people for long. But who constitute the "people" always remains a relevant question. That remains an important and relevant question in Bhutan. It is this state of things that gives rise to doubts about the genuine desire of the slogan-mongers of democracy and human rights.

Notes and References

1. See Gabriel A. Almond and G. Bingham Powell, Jr., *Comparative Politics: A Developmental Approach*, Amerind Publishing Co. Pvt. Ltd., New Delhi, 1975, 16-41.
2. Manash Ghosh, "Bhutan's survival at stake", *The Sunday Statesman*, Delhi, 26 January 1992, 10.
3. *The Concise Oxford Dictionary of Current English*, Oxford University Press, Delhi, 1990, 401.
4. *The New Lexicon Webster's Dictionary of the English Language: Deluxe Encyclopedic Edition*, Lexicon Publications Inc., New York, 1987, 324.
5. Department of Information, *Anti-National Activities in Southern Bhutan: A Terrorist Movement*, n.p., 1991, 1.
6. See B.S. Das, "Economic Development and Social Change in Bhutan", in Urmila Phadnis, S.D. Muni and Kalim Bahadur, eds., *Domestic Conflicts in South Asia: vol. 2: Economic and Ethnic Dimensions*, South Asian Publishers, New Delhi, 1986, 84.
7. See Kapileshwar Labh, "King and Country-I: Why Bhutan Needs Peace", *The Statesman*, Delhi, 4 January 1991, 6. Also see Manash Ghosh, n. 2.
8. Nari Rustomji, *Bhutan : The Dragon Kingdom in Crisis*, Oxford University Press, New Delhi, 1978, 7.
9. Ibid., 7-8.
10. Cited in Sunanda K. Datta-Ray, "Druk Past & Present-II : Strategies for Survival", *The Statesman*, 11 July, 1983, 6.
11. Manash Ghosh, n. 2.
12. Kapileshwar Labh, n. 7.
13. See Manash Ghosh, n. 2.
14. *The Gurkha People of Southern Bhutan Must Unite and Fight For Our Rights*, Place and date not mentioned, 6.

15. Kedar Nath Pandey, "Bhutan Today: anguished voices of a double tragedy", *Alive,* New Delhi, June (Second) 1991, 20.
16. Approximation based on calculation of 1981 ethnicwise population figures cited in B.S. Das, n. 6, 86.
17. Manash Ghosh, n. 2.
18. See Parmanand, "India-Bhutan Friendship and Bhutan's Problem of National Integration", *Strategic Analysis,* New Delhi, vol. 13, n.12, March 1991, 1414.
19. Das, n. 6, 86.
20. *Kuensel,* Thimphu, vol. 9, nos. 1-2, 6 January 1974, 2. Also see Kapileshwar Labh, "Monarchical System of Bhutan: Challenges of Modernization", in Urmila Phadnis, S.D. Muni and Kalim Bahadur, eds., n. 6, 191.
21. Department of Information, Ministry of Development, Royal Government of Bhutan, *Our Beloved King,* Thimphu, 1979, 25.
22. Ibid., 25-26.
23. B.S. Das, n. 6, 97.
24. Sunanda K. Datta-Ray, n. 10.
25. Ibid
26. Narendra Kumar, "Uneasy Lies The Head. . .", *The Sunday Statesman Miscellany,* Delhi, 14 July 1991, 5.

26a. Ibid.

27. Department of Information, n. 5, 2.
28. *Facts on The Situation in Bhutan* (Circulated by the Royal Government of Bhutan), n.p., n.d., 6.
29. Ibid. Also see Sonam T. Rabgye, "Current Developments on Bhutan and its implications", *Unity International,* New Delhi, vol. 15, no. 4, April 1991, 7-8.
30. The Secretary of the Royal Civil Service Commission, Dasho Khandu Wangchuk, told me in an exclusive personal interview in his office at Thimphu on 22 October 1991. Also see Parmanand, "Bhutan: Phoney Crisis of Integration", *The Times of India,* New Delhi, 20 November 1991, 6.
31. *Kuensel,* vol. 6, no. 41, 19 October 1991, 12.
32. King Jigme Singye Wangchuck told me in an exclusive interview in his Tashichho Dzong office in Thimphu on 21 October 1991.
33. Kapileshwar Labh, n. 7.
34. Leo E. Rose, *The Politics of Bhutan,* Cornell University Press, Ithaca, 1977, 111.
35. Sunanda K. Datta-Ray, n. 10.
36. *Facts on the situation in Bhutan,* n. 28, 2.
37. The Home Minister, Lyonpo Dago Tshering, told me in an exclusive interview on 21 October 1991 in his Tashichho Dzong office at Thimphu. Also see Ram Bahadur Rai, "Dakshin Bhutan Ki Sthiti: Rajshahi Ke Khilap Bagawat Ki Awaj" (The Situation in Southern Bhutan : Voice of Rebellion Against the Monarchy), *Navbharat Times,* New Delhi, 17 September 1990, 1-8.
38. Narendra Kumar, n.26,4.
39. Dasho Rigzin Dorji, Secretary, Special Commission of Cultural Affairs, Royal Government of Bhutan, told me in an exclusive interview at Thimphu on 14 October 1990.
40. *Facts on the situation on Bhutan,* n. 28, 9.
41. Lyonpo Om Pradhan, Minister for Trade and Industry, who himself is a Nepali Bhutanese and who toured Southern Bhutan along with the King several times, told me in an exclusive interview on 12 October 1990 at Thimphu.
42. Royal Bhutanese Embassy, *Press Release,* New Delhi, 7 June 1991, 5.

43. Ibid., 6. King Jigme Singye Wangchuck told me in an exclusive interview at Thimphu on 21 October 1991 that:
The No-objection Certificate was introduced in connection with transfer of students to other schools and appointments to new jobs. It applies to all Bhutanese equally. It was felt necessary in the wake of the large-scale violence and terrorism unleashed last year to ensure that persons having direct connections with known anti-nationals and terrorists are not given employment in sensitive posts or the opportunity to subvert fellow students in educational institutions.
44. Geoffrey K. Roberts, *A dictionary of political analysis,* Longman, London, 1971 145-6.
45. M. Vinayak, "Unrest in Bhutan: The voice of a people uprooted", *Frontline,* Madras, 27 April 1991, 110.
46. *Facts on the Situation in Bhutan,* n. 28, 1.
47. M. Vinayak, n. 45, 111.
48. Ibid.
49. Ibid.
50. Department of Information, n. 5, 5.
51. Ibid., 7.
52. See *Sunday Mail,* New Delhi, 6 October 1991, 2.
53. Ibid.
54. Ibid.
55. Ibid.
56. Ibid.
57. See *The Hindu,* New Delhi, 8 February 1992, 3.
58. Ibid.
59. Ibid. Also see *Indian Express,* New Delhi, 8 February 1992, 14.
60. See "When crooks become patriots", *The Statesman,* 6 September 1991, 5: "Bhutan officials' extradition sought", *The Times of India,* 11 September 1991, 9; and the Royal Bhutanes Embassy, New Delhi, n. 42.
61. *[Bhutan] National Democratic Party Ideology, Manifest, and Organization Structure,* place not mentioned, 1992, 23-25.
62. Ibid., 7.
63. Ibid., 9.
64. Ibid., 10-11.
65. Ibid., 12.
66. Ibid., 15.
67. Ibid., 15-16.
68. Ibid., 16-21. Also see Savitri Choudhury, "Democracy for dragon kingdom", *The Sunday Times of India,* New Delhi, 16 February 1992, 14.
69. *Facts on the Situation in Bhutan,* n. 28, 2.
70. S.N.M. Abdi, "Rumblings of Discontent", *The Illustrated Weekly of India,* Bombay, 4-10 November 1990.
71. *Facts on the Situation in Bhutan,* n. 28, 2.
72. Barbara Crossette, "India Based Groups Seek to Disrupt Bhutan", *The New York Times International,* 7 October 1990, 22.
73. *Indian Express,* 8 February 1992, 14.
74. Rising Nepal, Kathmandu, 31 March 1992, 1.
75. *Kuensel,* vol. 6, n. 44, 9 November 1991, 1.
76. Ibid., vol. 7, no. 2, 11 January 1992, 1.
77. Ibid, vol. 7, no. 3, 18 January 1992, 1.
78. Ibid.
79. Ibid., vol. 7, no. 5, 1 February 1992, 1.
80. Ibid., vol. 7, no. 4, 25 January 1992, 1.
81. Ibid.

78. Ibid.
79. Ibid., vol. 7, no. 5, 1 February 1992, 1.
80. Ibid., vol. 7, no. 4, 25 January 1992, 1.
81. Ibid.
82. King Jigme Singye Wangchuck and Home Minister Lyonpo Dago Tshering told me in exclusive separate interviews at Thimphu on 21 October 1991.
83. *The Hindu,* 10 June 1990, 1.
84. *The Hindustan Times,* New Delhi, 20 October 1990, 6.
85. Ibid.
86. *The Hindu,* 20 October 1990, 3.
87. *The Statesman,* 24 October 1990, 5. Also see *Kuensel,* vol.5, no. 43, 27 October 1990, 1.
88. Ibid.
89. See Parmanand, "Friendly Neighbours: India and Nepal Come Closer", *The Statesman,* 17 December 1991, 6; *Kuensel,* vol. 6, no. 43, 2 November 1991, 1, and BBC interview of G.P. Koirala of 25 October 1991.
90. I have gathered this impression on the basis of my talks with various people from Nepal's Terai.

6

Bhutan In Global Politics

Without doubt, a country of the nature, size and population of Bhutan cannot be expected to play any serious role in global politics. Small Bhutan is a landlocked country as also sandwiched between two Asian giants India and China and this reality hampers an international role for it in a variety of ways. On the other hand, the land of the Thunder Dragon does not possess a very strong position in terms of the most of elements of power, which, according to a great analyst of international politics, Hans J. Morgenthau, include: Geography, Natural Resources (including food, raw materials and industrial capacity), Military Preparedness (including technology, leadership, quantity and quality of armed forces), Population (including distribution and trends), National Character, National Morale (including its instability, the quality of society and government), the Quality of Diplomacy, the Quality of Government (including the problem of balance between resources and policy, the problem of balance among resources and the problem of popular support and the domestic government and foreign policy).[1] Bhutan is weak on some of these planes, even if its is doing quite well on some of them.

Perhaps, Bhutan's long-maintained seclusion was also guided by this reality. This, however, does not mean that Bhutan has no meaningful role to play in international or regional politics. It has made its voice heard effectively from time to time and there is no reason why it should not continue to do so in future. Once Bhutan decided to give up its policy of isolationism in the early 1960s, it as never looked back.

Bhutan's role in global politics can be seen and assessed in terms of its membership of various regional international organizations and establishment of diplomatic relations with various states of the world. It can also be seen in adoption of various independent stands on several issues of importance.

Membership of various world bodies

Bhutan has by now joined a large number of international organizations. It joined the Colombo Plan in 1962. It became a member of the Universal Postal Union in 1969. Most significantly, in 1971, Bhutan became a member of the United Nations by unanimous decision of the General Assembly, and opened the Permanent Mission of the Kingdom of Bhutan to the United Nations in New York. The same year Bhutan also joined the Group of 77 and, in December, became the second of the world's governments to recognize the newly independent state of Bangladesh.

Bhutan joined the ECAFE (now called ESCAP) in 1972. It became a member of the Non-Aligned Movement (NAM) in 1973. Bhutan has been a member of the South Asian Association for Regional Cooperation (SAARC) since its inception in 1985. Earlier Bhutan had been associated with the process of regional cooperation under the auspices of the South Asian Regional Cooperation (SARC) since its inception in 1983.

On the other hand, Bhutan is also a member of the World Bank and the Asian Development Bank and this position enables it to supplement financial and technical assistance received from the United Nations system and friendly countries. By 1989, Bhutan was a member of nearly all organizations affiliated with the UN.[2]

Bhutan fully subscribes to the purposes and principles of the United Nations and the NAM, and has, accordingly, continued to play an active and committed role in both these international organizations. The foreign policy of Bhutan is based on the principles of peace, friendship and non-alignment. A significant event in the evolution of Bhutan's foreign policy was the attendance of His Majesty King Jigme Singye Wangchuck at the 5th summit conference of the NAM at Colombo in 1976.[3]

Mentionably, King Jigme Singye Wangchuck is the only head of state or government who has thus far attended all the six summits of the SAARC heads of state or government since its inception in 1985. Significantly, the 6th SAARC summit in Colombo had to be postponed because of his inability to attend the summit slated for November 1991. Subsequently, the summit was held in December 1991.

The process of involvement of Bhutan in international affairs can be gauged from the fact that Bhutan attended no fewer than 67 international conferences, seminars and workshops during 1982-83.[4]

In carrying out far-reaching programmes for the social and economic development of the kingdom in the last two decades, Bhutan has received the generous assistance of its neighbour, India, with whom it enjoys close and friendly relations, and from various bodies of the United Nations such as the UNDP, the UNICEF, the WEP, the CDF and the UNFPA. In view of the enlarged participation of the UNDP in the developmental activities of the kingdom, an office of the UNDP Resident Representative was established in Thimphu in 1979. Bhutan also receives some development assistance from friendly countries such as Australia, Switzerland, Japan, United Kingdom, Singapore, New Zealand and Austria.[5]

Bhutan's diplomatic relations

Bhutan formed a Department of Foreign Affairs in 1970 and it was accorded ministerial status in 1972. Thereafter started the process of establishing diplomatic relations with a number of countries. 1971 saw the establishment of the Royal Bhutan Mission in New Delhi. It was redesignated as the Royal Bhutanese Embassy on 8 August 1978. Today Bhutan has its embassies in India, Bangladesh and the UNO. Besides, it has a Consulate General in Kuwait. It has its honorary consuls in Hongkong and Singapore. All in all, Bhutan has diplomatic relations with 21 countries, including India, Bangladesh, Nepal, Sri Lanka, the Netherlands, South Korea, Japan, Switzerland and the countries of the European Community.

More and more countries are showing their desire and willingness to establish diplomatic relations with Bhutan. This, if anything, shows its credibility and acceptability in the international community. On his part, the King has emphasized the concepts of sovereignty and self-reliance of Bhutan. In an address to the people, King Jigme Singye Wangchuck once said:

> Sovereignty and self-reliance are two important goals. Whatever we do in the government, it is aimed towards the strengthening and the attainment of these two objectives. But government alone cannot make the country self-reliant. The people have an important role to play. It is important that whatever we do ensures that we retain our sovereignty and helps us become self-reliant.[6]

Bhutan's role in regional and international affairs

Ever since the beginning of the process of Bhutan's internationalization, the country has been playing its role quite meaningfully at various fora.

For instance, speaking at the first meeting of Foreign Ministers of the South Asian countries in New Delhi on 1-2 August 1983, Bhutan's Foreign Minister, Lyonpo Dawa Tsering, said:

> The fact that seven Foreign Ministers of South Asia are meeting for the first time in a purely regional context, presents both opportunities and challenges. The opportunities are evident. The implementation of the Integrated Programme of Action in nine areas to begin with should be the prelude to greater and more varied cooperation in the years to come. Regional cooperation can make a countribution to improving the quality of life of our peoples through social, economic and cultural development of the region. It should help to strengthen collective self-reliance among our countries. Also, to the extent we can harmonize our positions on various issues as a group, it would enable us to have a greater say in the councils of the world.[7]

Lyonpo Dawa Tsering has the distinction of being his country's Foreign Minister for a much longer duration in comparison to any of his South Asian counterparts. In fact, his tenure must be longer than most of the foreign ministers in the present-day world. He has a unique capacity of maintaining a low profile based on profundity. This has augured well for Bhutan in ways more than one.

How Bhutan's young and energetic monarch, His Majesty King Jigme Singye Wangchuck, has understood the political reality of the region and the globe is obvious from his various statements at various fora. The King (then only 30), while speaking at the inagural meeting of South Asia's foreign ministers on 13-14 May 1985 at Thimphu, *inter alia,* said:

> No other region in the world needs harmonious and cooperative relations among its states more than South Asia. Despite the historical and cultural bonds which have existed between our countries through the ages, several forces have emerged since the end of the colonial era to sow seeds of dissension, suspicion and hostility in our ranks. Nationalism for instance, which has given each of us such a strong sense of nationhood, of freedom and pride and self-respect, has often stood in the way of regional cooperation. The deep-seated desire to safeguard the right to an independent foreign policy, which is in the ultimate analysis the test of a country's independence, has sometimes created obstacles in the development of mutual cooperation between our countries. . . In my view we have already implicitly come to accept the fact that political heterogeneity and independent national

foreign policies are compatible with close regional cooperation. Our collective efforts over the past four years bear eloquent testimony to this new attitude and approach.[8]

While most of the heads of state or government talked of high ideals during the first SAARC summit at Dhaka on 7-8 December 1985, His Majesty King Jigme Singye Wangchuck's address was refreshing inasmuch as he chose to call a spade. The King *inter alia* said:

> . . . Mr Chairman, it may neither be possible nor desirable to limit discussions in our meetings to issues of non-political nature, for the political climate of our region will undoubtedly cast a long shadow over our deliberations. In the geopolitical realities of our region, it would be unrealistic to ignore the primacy of the political factor, as, in the final analysis, it will be the political environment of the region, which will determine the shape and scope of regional cooperation in South Asia.[9]

Showing his predilection for concrete achievements in place of formal deliberations, King Jigme Singye Wangchuck said during the second SAARC summit at Banglore on 16-17 November 1986:

> . . . We should devote less time to workshops and seminars and concentrate more on concrete regional projects. The selection of such projects must be carried out carefully in order to ensure that benefits will accrue to all member states. The goals we set for ourselves must be realistic and time-bound. This will impart strength and vigour to our activities and make SAARC a result-oriented body.[10]

Striking a note of realism, King Jigme Singye Wangchuck, *inter alia*, said at the 5th SAARC summit at Male on 21 November 1990:

> During the Islamabad Summit, we directed the Secretary General to submit recommendations to the Standing Committee on how to streamline SAARC activities and make them more effective. I would like to emphasize once again that it is not the number of acitivities but their successful implementation that is important for the credibility of SAARC. Some of us still face serious difficulties in meeting the financial and manpower resources to participate in all the ongoing activities. I therefore believe that a further streamlining and even more careful selection of activities would prove to be more beneficial in the long run. We must remember that the peoples of South Asia

> will expect tangible and concrete benefits from regional cooperation. We should also take note of the fact that although seven years have passed since the Integrated Programme of Action was launched in 1983, we have yet to move to the core economic areas of trade, industry, energy, money and finance.[11]

Attending the one-day 6th SAARC summit at Colombo on 21 December 1991, King Jigme Singye Wangchuck emphasized the need for concerted action against the growing menace of terrorism in South Asia. He said that the countries of the region had already launched crusade against that evil. He stressed: "We must now work together to eradicate this menace before it engulfs our societies and tears our nations apart."[12] His Majesty pointed out that to eradicate the scourage of terrorism, it was vital that no member state extended any form of support to terrorist organizations and that the principle of non-interference in the internal affairs of member-countries, as enshrined in the SAARC charter be fully respected.[13]

Mentionably, the summit of Colombo endorsed His Majesty the King's proposal to set up a South Asian Development Fund. The proposal envisages mobilization of external resosources to finance national efforts at industrialization, poverty alleviation, environmental protection, and balance of payment support. The Secretary General of SAARC was directed by the summit to form an Experts Group to examine the matter in all its aspects and to submit their recommendations to the 7th summit.[14]

Apart from playing a meaningful role in the regional and international affairs, Bhutan has also established a place for itself by signing the Nuclear Non-Proliferation Treaty. This step fits into the country's professed belief in the teachings of Lord Buddha.

Overall, the small country, despite being circumscribed by a variety of factors, has given a good account of itself in the regional and global politics. One striking feature in Bhutan's foreign policy has been continuity in action as also in the functionaries of foreign policy making and execution. While King Jigme Singye Wangchuk has been taking keen interest in his country's foreign policy-making and its execution, his low-profile but immensely articulate foreign minister, Lyonpo Dawa Tsering, has always given a good account of himself. The wavelength between the two, if anything, is ideal. One could expect Bhutan to continue to play a meaningful role in the regional and global affairs.

Notes and References

1. See Hans J. Morgethau, *Politics Among Nations: The Struggle for Power and Peace*, Fifth Edition (Indian reprint), Scientific Book Agency, Calcutta, 1976, 112-49.
2. Francoise Pommaret, *An Illustrated Guide To Bhutan: Buddhist Fort of the Himalayas*, The Guidebook Company, Hongkong, 1990, 66.
3. See The Royal Government of the Kingdom of Bhutan, *Bhutan Himalayan Kingdom*, Thimphu, 1979, 30 and Dasho Rigzin Dorji, *A Brief Religious, Cultural and Secular History of Bhutan*, The Asiatic Society Galleries, New York, 1989, 15.
4. Sunanda K. Datta-Ray, "Druk Past & Present-I: Catching Up With The 20th Century", *The Sunday Statesman*, Delhi, 10 July 1983, 6.
5. Francoise Pommaret, n. 2.
6. The Royal Government of Bhutan, n.3.
7. Royal Government of Bhutan, Ministry of Foreign Affairs, SAARC Division, *Major Statements Made By Bhutanese Delegations On SAARC 1981-1991*, Thimphu 1991, 12.
8. Ibid., 41.
9. Ibid., 60.
10. Ibid., 91
11. Ibid., additional 4-5.
12. *Kuensel* (Bhutan's National Newspaper), Thimphu, vol. 6, no. 51, 28 December 1992, 1.
13. Ibid.
14. Ibid.

7

Bhutan-China Relations: An Exercise in Tightrope Walking

The People's Republic Of China (PRC)—having the largest population, the second largest area of land (after the break-up of the USSR) and common borders with the largest number of states of the world—is Bhutan's northern giant neighbour. This geostrategic and geopolitical reality cannot but be a constant variable in the determination of Bhutan's foreign policy and to some extent that of the PRC because of its being an Asian giant with no stated or even hinted desire to desist from the politics of the South Asian region. If this nitty-gritty creates for Bhutan a situation of a tightrope walk, it presents China with a situation meriting moves with care and caution. However, it is to be noted here that China and Bhutan are important for each other primarily because of the annexation of Tibet by China. It is the Autonomous Region of Tibet which is located in the north of Bhutan and its Chumbi valley is only 6 miles away from Bhutan. Besides, there is a great deal of cultural and religious similarity between the people of Bhutan and Tibet. Consequently, there have been natural interactions between the people of Tibet and Bhutan since time immemorial.

In order to appraise the present-day, and attempt a prediction of the future, relations between Bhutan and China, it would be in order to have a background of Bhutan's relations with Tibet, on the one hand, and China, on the other. Not unnaturally, at several points such an analysis will find both Tibet and China converging.

Bhutan-Tibet Relations:A historical perspective

At the beginning of the 8th century, when Tibet was at the zenith of its military might, Tibetan armies invaded Bhutan. There was little resistance. Some of the inhabitants fled to the plains of Assam. The rest submitted to the Tibetan rule. The Tibetan Lamas and hoi polloi followed their army. They settled down in Bhutan and intermarried with the local people. The western region of Bhutan, thus, came to be inhabited predominantly by people to Tibetan and mixed Tibetan-Bhutanese extraction.

However, the military might of Tibet declined in the 9th century, and consequently, it withdrew from Bhutan. Unfortunately, the central authority, which was sought to be established there by the Bhutanese themselves, also lost its hold over the state. In fact, Bhutan relapsed into a state of fragmented sub-regions with no control of any central agency. Predictably, topographical oddities led to the growth of numerous cultural and linguistic sub-regions in Bhutan. Some Lamas came intermittently from Tibet during this period and exercised some temporal authority over the western part of the country, though only briefly. Nevertheless, these visits kept up the flow of cultural, especially Lamaistic, ideas.[1]

As a matter of fact, ever since the 13th century, the Tibetan Lamas migrating into *Druk-yul* were instrumental in the large-scale conversion of the local people to Buddhism. Perhaps, it is because of this that many in Bhutan accept Tibet as their spiritual guide at a point of time in history. Till the very recent past, Bhutan continued to maintain its tributary relationship with Tibet. "Lhasa was the sacred land for the Bhutanese and a visit to Lhasa was the cherished desire of practically every Bhutanese".[2]

However, the event of the greatest importance and consequence on the plane of interaction between Tibet and Bhutan was the arrival of the prince-abbot Shabdung Ngawang Namgyal (1594-?1651)[3], destined to be individually most instrumental in unifying the kingdom and giving it its present shape. He arrived there as a refugee from Tibet in 1616. He discovered a land, whose multiple barriers had already been partly eroded by a uniform set of religious institutions implanted from Tibet, by a common agricultural livelihood prone to yield profits and by a framework of cultural and trade contacts, which had begun to link the main valleys. These contacts had been effected by the construction of iron chain suspension bridges by the famous saint Thangtong Gyalpo (1385-1464).

The Shabdung, as he is popularly known, was able to use the monasteries of his own school already founded in the area as a power base from which he extended his control over all the western valleys. He successfully contended not only with rival lamas in the region but also with several Tibetan invasions, especially those of 1639 and 1647, mounted against him by the Tangspa and Gelukpa rulers of Tibet.[4] Most visibly, his achievement remains the construction of a series of fortified monasteries located in each valley. Those located in central and eastern Bhutan were built in the 1650s shortly after his death. These imposing edifices serve even today both as state monasteries as also centres of local government and administration.[5] Palpably, this was the most important and lasting interaction between the people of Tibet and Bhutan and the Shabdung is still remembered in Bhutan with great respect and feeling.

In 1731, the Tibetan ruler, Polhane, succeeded in imposing suzerainty on Bhutan, and this relationship was in turn formally passed on to Tibet's own overlord, the Ching dynasty of China. Although there is no evidence of either Tibet or China ever having implemented their rule in Bhutan, both occasionally claimed a legitimate right to interfere in local politics. However, their attempts were rarely successful.[6] Nevertheless, it is significant to mention that as a part of their tributary relationship to Tibet, a Bhutanese representative was posted in Lhasa up to 1959. From 1950 to 1959, the Bhutanese were in regular contact with the Chinese authorities in Tibet.[7]

A letter by the then King of Bhutan to the Viceroy and Governor General of India on 17 May 1946 stated that Bhutan was very close to Tibet and China and that Bhutan had "acknowledged Tibetan sovereignty" up to 1860. He also added that an annual payment was still being paid to Tibet in recognition of its suzerainty.[8]

There is, thus, no denying the fact that Bhutan had close relations with Tibet on various planes, not excluding political, and in a variety of ways. These relations had, not unexpectedly, their ups and downs. But various available facts bear out that relations between Bhutan and Tibet were more of cultural and religious nature and less of political character. For political relations were skin deep or formal.

Bhutan-China relations:A look into history

It will be difficult to say that Bhutan's relations with China had been of the same nature and level as those with Tibet. However, even if one were not to accept the closeness of Bhutan with China, as mentioned in the then Bhutanese King's letter of 17 May 1946 to the Viceroy and Governor General of India, there can be no doubt about the various interactions between the two.

In 1736, the Chinese Emperor invested the ruler of Bhutan with a seal and patent of office and according to Chinese sources, from the early 18th century onwards Bhutan was a vassal of China.[9] Sunanda K. Datta-Ray, on the other hand, refers to the "seal and hat with false coral button" gratuitously bestowed by the Amban in 1891 on the Deb Raja.[10] But Leo E. Rose, Kapileshwar Labh and Ram Rahul all find little significance in Bhutan's repeated acceptance of Chinese seals and patents of office.[11] Agreeing with these authors, Sunanda K. Datta-Ray observes:

> The historical connexion was not particularly close or harmonious. Bhutan had no direct relations with China until the 18th Century, when Ambans (Residents) were appointed in Lhasa: contact was purely ceremonial even then, and, unlike the Nepalese, the Bhutanese never sent mission that the Chinese might have described as tributary. Neither did the Deb Raja ever use the "seal and hat with false coral button" gratuitously bestowed by the Amban in 1891. When the latter sent Ma Chifu with a premptory letter nine years later, the envoy was allowed only a few miles into the kingdom and King Ugyen Wangchuck, the first hereditary Druk Gyalpo and His Majesty's great-grandfather, refused to receive him.[12]

There seems some palpable discrepancy in Sunanda K. Datta-Ray's account, for in 1900 (the year that he alludes to) Ugyen Wangchuck had not become the first hereditary Druk Gyalpo. It was only in the year 1907 that he assumed the throne. Ugyen Wangchuck might, therefore, have acted in his capacity as the Penlop of Tongsa at that time. However, what is of importance is that Bhutan did not attach the same significance to China as the latter may have thought of and demanded.

But, nevertheless, it would not be proper to conclude that China kept quiet *vis-a-vis* Bhutan over the years. The former intervened in Bhutan in 1830, 1876, 1885, 1889 and 1905.[13] In fact, in February 1910, the Manchu Government of China laid claim to Bhutan along with Nepal and Sikkim.[14] As a matter of fact, Bhutan entered upon a new phase of its history at the turn of the 20th century. Its relations with the neighbouring countries hastened its modernization. The post-1904 developments in Tibet were rather ominous for Bhutan. For no sooner had the troops of Zhao Erh-feng, Warden of the Szechwan marches of China, occupied Lhasa on 12 February 1910 and compelled the 13th Dalai Lama to seek refuge in India than the Manchu Government laid claim to Bhutan along with others.[15]

There were, on the other hand, direct contacts between Bhutan and China in 1940, 1943, 1947, 1951 and 1953. More importantly, a Bhutanese representative was permanently posted in Lhasa, where he regularly met Tibetan and on occasions Chinese officials.[16]

There are some scholars who tend to believe that China imposed its suzerainty on Tibet in the late 18th century, and this in turn, was extended to Bhutan from 1793, when Bhutan become a vassal of both Tibet and China.[17] This relationship, of course, never meant that Bhutan was a sovereign part of China, but simply that it was like Tibet, suzerain to China. It is equally important to note that from 1875 onwards, China's agent in Lhasa had been voicing the sentiment that Nepal, Bhutan, Tibet and Sikkim all formed parts of the Chinese empire. Consequently, the relations between Bhutan and the British Government were governed by several serious considerations and they reduced their action in Bhutan to the barest minimum.[18]

How China had viewed Bhutan as early as 1907 is clear from the statement of the Chinese Amban in this context. He said :

> China, Nepal, Tibet, Bhutan and Sikkim might be compared to the five principal colours, viz., yellow, red, blue, black and green. A skilful painter may so arrange the colours as to produce a number of beautiful designs or effects. In the same way if we would cooperate with one another, we may presumably promote the interests of all.[19]

On the other hand, though the Bhutanese authorities had rebuffed Ma Chifu in 1900, as we saw earlier, rebuffs did not prevent the Wai-wu-pu (Board of Foreign Affairs) and Prince Ch'ing from claiming suzerainty during 1910-12. Commenting on this episode Sunanda K. Datta-Ray writes:

> They argued that Ambans had always employed the mainfesto style in addressing Bhutan, replies allegedly being couched as petitions to the Celestial Throne. The assertion outraged the Viceroy, Lord Hardinge, Sir Edward Grey in London, Sir Charles Bell, the Political Officer in Gangtok, and King Jigme Singye's maternal grandfather, the far-sighted Raja Ugyen Dorji, then Bhutan's Agent in Kalimpong. They rightly pointed out that the question of suzerainty could not possibly arise since Bhutan had never paid tribute to China or Tibet, and the courtesy gifts to the Dalai Lama (or even the Amban) had no political significance.[20]

However, that was not the end of the matter. No less a person then Mao Zedong, who was the undisputed leader of the Chinese Communist

Party till his death in 1976 and who had the privilege of becoming the first President of the People's Republic of China, once wrote that the Western imperialists detached Vietnam, Burma, Korea, Nepal and Bhutan from the Chinese empire, which, he said were states tributary to China and that this was the first dismemberment of the Chinese empire.[21] In 1930, Mao openly declared that the correct boundaries of China would include Burma, Bhutan, Nepal, Taiwan, Korea and Ryykyu islands.[22] The original remarks of Mao were contained in the original version of the *Chinese Revolution and the Communist Party,* but were deleted from later versions of the book with a view to avoiding suspicions in the minds of the leaders of these countries. What lesson, however, this drives home is that only a man deeply immersed in the Chinese tradition could have made such a statement. Nor was the so-called Chinese empire ever a geographical reality. It was at best a cultural expression. Nor were these areas the dependencies of China in the sense that the word in normally use in modern parlance. They only paid occasional tribute to the superior culture of China. However, the very assertion of no less a person than Mao in this regard makes one view it seriously.

Besides, there was time when fears were being created with some reports that China was contemplating to form "a Himalyan Federation" under its leadership. Manorama Kohli has commented on this problem in the following words:

> Such statements and reports did undoubtedly threaten both Nepal and Bhutan who felt the need to protect their independent existence. The possibilities of subversive Communist activities in the valleys of Bhutan loomed so large on the horizon that the economic hardships which followed from the closure of trade links with Tibet got ignored and the Dragon Kingdom closed its doors to Tibet.[23]

This aside, there were other complexities that China was creating in its relationships with Bhutan, at times even to the chagrin of India. Intriguingly, these things were being done during the "Hindi-Chini Bhai-Bhai" phase. After consolidating its own position, China endeavoured hard to treat Bhutan as an independent identity beyond the framework of the Treaty between India and Bhutan in 1949. In 1953, the Chinese attempted to send gifts to the Druk Gyalpo. Chinese officials in Lhasa started issuing visas directly to the Bhutanese citizens in 1955. In 1959, the PRC forcibly occupied Bhutanese enclaves in Tibet. Bhutan withdrew its representative in Lhasa and its officer in Western Tibet, and sealed its frontier with Tibet. In 1960, China refused to discuss with the officials of the Government of India in Rangoon any question relating to Bhutan's boundary with Tibet.[24]

Though the misgivings about Bhutan being a part of what Mao had described as "lost territories" were removed subsequently, Premier Zhou Enlai in one of his communications with Nehru on the question of boundary dispute expressed China's desire to "live together in friendship with Sikkim and Bhutan, without committing aggression against each other." In 1961, China made offer of assistance to Bhutan but was spurned by the Druk Gyalpo.[25]

All this clearly shows that China has been very keen to have close relations with Bhutan regardless of the status of Tibet in its own framework. China, as we have seen thus far, tried to avail itself of every opportunity to get closer to Bhutan. However, it seems instructive that while trying to befriend Bhutan or getting close to it, China did not try to use force. Instead it chose the method of diplomacy for establishing friendship with Bhutan. This was probably a part of the strategy to show to the states of the region as also the international community that China was not a hegemonic power and that it was more desirous of accommodating small neighbours in its dealing with them.

An important question arises at this point: was China trying to befriend or getting closer to Bhutan unilaterally and that Bhutan never took any initiative? This question cannot be replied to in the positive, for there are instances showing that from time to time Bhutan, too, took initiatives to have good relations with China. Srikant Dutt states that a Bhutanese lama was present in Tibet in an informal capacity all through the 1960s. Tashi Dorji, while in exile in Hong Kong, according to press reports, met Chinese representatives from both Taiwan and China, as did her brother Lhendup in Kathmandu.[26] However, it is obvious that Bhutan's attempts were of only casual nature.

But there is the other side of the coin as well. The British Government in India had been very careful and cautious in maintaining friendship with Bhutan. And, while doing so, it had always taken the China factor into account. This is, in fact, borne out by the treaties of 1865 and 1910, which the British government entered with Bhutan. The British strategy in this regard was continued by the independent India, when it signed another Treaty with Bhutan in 1949. It was not for nothing that Nehru said in Bhutan in 1958—which was his first visit to Bhutan as also the first visit of any foreign leader to that country—that:

> . . .We are members of the same Himalyan family and should live as friendly neighbours, helping each other. The freedom of both Bhutan

> and India should be safeguarded, so that no one from outside can do any harm to them.[27]

Without doubt, Nehru's visit's timing and words were aimed at driving the lesson home that India considered Bhutan to be an object of protection from any onsalught. His visit and speech also coincided with the growing anxiety in India about Chinese designs of expansion expressed more definitely on the Sino-Indian boundary dispute. However, the fact that a map published in July 1958 in the*China Pictorial* magazine denoting large tracts of not only Indian but also Bhutanese territory as belonging to China, involved the territorial integrity of Bhutan as well. As if the events in Tibet in 1959 were not enough, reports of Chinese troops' movement on the border caused serious concern. It was incumbent upon India to take action, not only in its own security interests but also for Bhutan as per the 1949 Treaty obligations, whereby it was responsible for Bhutan's foreign affairs.[28] It was in this context that Nehru said in the Lok Sabha (India's Parliament's lower and popular house) on 28 August 1959 that:

> The Government of India is responsible for the protection of the borders of Sikkim and Bhutan and of the territorial integrity of these two states and any aggression against Bhutan and Sikkim will be considered as aggression against India.

He added:

> We shall abide by the assurances we have given to them. How we shall abide by them and in what manner if circumstances arise is a matter of careful consideration. It is not a matter of direct statement in this House or elsewhere, but of action, if necessity arises . . . very difficult aciton.[29]

On the other hand, in his letter of 26 September 1959 to Chinese Premier Zhou Enlai—which was a response to the latter's letter of 7 September 1959—Nehru objected to China's map showing several parts of Bhutan as those of Tibet as also to China's viewpoint that the boundaries of Sikkim and Bhutan did not fall within the scope of the boundary discussion.[30]

Not unexpectedly, then, Bhutan-China relations—or whatever was visible and perceptible of them—took a new turn with the increasing tension in the relations between the two Asian giants because of the border dispute. Bhutan's concern and worries increased. Bhutan had to take a stand. It was apparent from the outset that Bhutan considered the security calculus of India more to its liking, even though it was quite conscious of the fact that the crisis situation was also an opportunity to reiterate its sovereign position.

In a statement on 28 August 1959, Bhutanese Prime Minister Jigmie Dorji welcomed Nehru's assurances, as he said, "the Government of Bhutan situated as it is, does not possess the means to repel any large-scale attack on its territories". He, however, made it clear that "Bhutan is not an Indian protectorate, nor is there any clause in the Treaty between India and Bhutan relating to defence".[31] Bhutan's stress on its sovereignty was obviously aimed at proving that it was sensitive to be totally dependent on India. The Indian government had to take this aspect of relations carefully into its strategic calculus. A. Appadorai and M.S. Rajan are of the opinion that this "insistent clarification however may have also arisen from a genuine fear of China and an eagerness demonstrate obliquely its objectivity in Sino-Indian affairs".[32]

Bhutan's cautious approach was, in fact, more visible in a statement of King Jigme Dorji Wangchuck in 1961 during his visit to India. The King said: "We do not want to be either friends or enemies of China".[33] On its part, China, too, was willing to take Bhutan to its side, if possible. During the 1962 Sino-Indian war, it was willing to accord Bhutan, which it had formally claimed and coveted, a sovereign status when the Indian government had in a note to the Chinese government lodged a protest on behalf of the Bhutan government against "repeated violations of the air space of Bhutan by Chinese aircraft". In a reply note China vehemently denied the charge and blamed India for sowing "discord in the friendly relations between China and Bhutan".[34] Clearly, this statement of China was aimed more at creating a confusion in India than showing any genuine warmth or respect for Bhutan.

Be that as it may, Bhutan had to move differently under altogether altered circumstances. In 1960, trade between Bhutan and Tibet was stopped by Bhutanese Prime Minister Jigmie Dorji. It meant closing the traditional outlet for the kingdom's surplus rice and depriving weavers around Bumthang with wool until Australia stepped in with supplies. He also placed the Bhutanese army at India's disposal in 1962.[35] However, Bhutan seemed to have decided to adopt a low profile in a dispute between the two Asian giants. Perhaps, it was strategically correct. King Jigme Dorji Wangchuck in remarks made in March 1960 said that Bhutan's relations with China were "friendly and peaceful" and that Bhutan had no defence agreement with India. On its part, China did not lag behind. At his press conference in New Delhi in April 1960, Zhou

Enlai said that there was no dispute between Bhutan and China.[36] He announced in New Delhi: "We have no claim with regard to Bhutan, nor do we have any dispute with it" adding that there were no boundary disputes between China and Sikkim or Bhutan.[37]

However, Sunanda K. Datta-Ray has rightly commented on the Chinese *modus operandi* in the following terms:

> But such affirmations are open to more than one interpretation since the Chinese will admit no dispute over what they insist, however wrongly, is theirs. Nor is the assurance easily reconciled with theories of the five affiliated races, blending of five colours (Wu Ts'ai), or of the five fingers of China's Tebetan palm. Some Bhutanese may remember too that one of the Shabdung's Thu (mind) incarnations is a Chinese protege.[38]

Towards opening relations

But closure of trade with Tibet could not have been the last word on Bhutan-China relations. It is true that like another Himalyan kingdom of South Asia, Nepal, Bhutan did not play the China card in its relations with India, but it would not have been possible for Bhutan to indefinitely ignore interactions with China. Then, there were pressing reasons for Bhutan, too, to change the status quo.

It was incumbent upon Bhutan to do something about the loss of 8 Druk enclaves during 1959. These enclaves in Western Tibet were given by a 17th century Ladakhi ruler, Sengye Namgyal, to a Bhutanese lama, whose prayers are said to have resulted in the birth of a royal heir. But the Royal government could justifiably refuse to transfer *de jure* sovereignty, which was confirmed by the 5th and 13th Dalai Lamas, until China evacuated occupied territory and recognized the traditional border.

There were other serious problems, too. There were reports of China building roads and setting up military installations in the extensive areas. Traditional grazing, along the Chumbi valley, formerly a Sikkimese possession, where yak and cattle follow the pasture, creates friction between the two. Even in the East, a prominent Bhutanese nobleman was not long ago asked to pay tax for grazing in an area now claimed by China. Besides, Issue No. 95 of the *China Pictorial*, published in 1958, shows the entire Tashigang region in the east and a substantial slice of territory in the north-east as Chinese. According to European sources, Beijing claimed about 300 square miles in the north-eastern Bhutan and a considerable tract north of the old capital of Punakha.[39]

There were other reasons, too, that would have made the Bhutanese authorities rather careful in dealing with China. There were rumours of the involvement of some pro-Chinese elements in the assassination of Prime Minister Jigmie Dorji, though there has been no substantial proof to that effect. For instance, Nari Rustomji, writes:

> . . .The Chinese had thrown out feelers to Bhutan more than once in their endeavours to bring Bhutan within the orbit of their influence. The Bhutanese owe it to Jigmie that he did not succumb to their enticements, but was firm in maintaining an independent stand for his country.[40]

A scholar tends to believe that there was some attitudinal change among the Bhutanese elite *vis-a-vis* China particularly after 1964. According to him: "Some success in diluting the influence of India was achieved particularly between 1964-72 when the Bhutanese elite softened their attitude towards China.[41] Morever, during 1966, there were some incidents on the border owing to the Cultural Revolution in China and the resulting turmoil in Tibet. China, however, declared that any dispute between itself and Bhutan was a purely bilateral matter.[42] However, China's emphasis on bilateralism seemed instructive inasmuch as it seemed determined to talk to Bhutan without any *locus standi* for India. In 1970, there were more incidents. Though the border remained calm and the incidents did not escalate, it was apparent that China was determined to get to Bhutan without India's support in any possible manner and by means, fair or foul.

We have already seen how China had been consistently insistent on not recognizing any role for India in having any negotiations with Bhutan. To that extent, China has been quite oblivious of the implications of the 1949 Treaty. We have already seen how 8 enclaves in Western Tibet given to the then Bhutanese ruler more than 300 years ago were taken over by China. Reportedly, at the third Druk Gyalpo's request two Indian notes in August 1959 "represented to the Chinese Government to restore the rightful authority of the Bhutanese Government over their enclaves."[43] Apparently, China did not respond to this request. Perhaps, it made Bhutan concerned about having some kind of working relationship with the PRC.

It was against this background that Bhutan got an opportunity to have an interaction with China. The opportunity came when China, along with various other states, was invited to the coronation of King Jigme Singye Wangchuck in 1974. Indeed, it was a godsend opportunity for

China. It showed some desire on the part of the Bhutanese elite to make attempts to normalize relations with their giant northern neighbour, albiet without establishing diplomatic relations. It was also a proper opportunity for Bhutan to internationalize its personality. In the event, an official Chinese delegation led by Ma Mo Ming visited Bhutan after a lapse of about 65 years. The *New China News Agency* described the visit as a "new page in the friendly contacts of the two countries". It was a chance for China to revive broken bridges of communication with Bhutan. The Chinese congratulatory message took special notice of the "desires of the Bhutanese government in developing its economy and safeguarding its national independance".[44]

Significantly, Chinese Premier Zhou Enlai sent his congratulations on this occasion. In his message, he emphasized Bhutan's moves to safeguard its "national independence". The occasion witnessed the first public reception of a Chinese official since 1908. At the coronation ceremony itself, only the representatives of Bangladesh, China, India, Sikkim, the Soviet Union, and the United States were allowed as witnesses.[45] Apparently, it was aimed at giving the PRC its due place among the states Bhutan had interactions with.

Obviously, it was a new phase in Bhutan-China relations. It could have been utilized as an opportunity by both these states. Had Bhutan learnt some lessons from the Sikkim episode? The questions seems to be relevant. But still Bhutan did show its adroitness by not going out of the way to follow China or by trying to play the China card *vis-a-vis* India. Therein lies the crux.

Apart from the visit of the Chinese delegation at the coronation of King Jigme Singye Wangchuck, Bhutanese ping pong teams went to China in 1977 and 1979 and that also provided the two countries opportunities to interact with each other.[46]

Several things followed the presence of the Chinese delegation at the coronation ceremony of King Jigme Singye Wangchuck—and they made Bhutan move further in the direction of normalization of relations with China. China was creating every kind of subtle pressure on Bhutan so that the latter felt the necessity of talking to it. Chinese intrusion into the Bhutanese territory was increasing. It used to be in the form of graziers coming to the Bhutanese territory.

In 1974, Bhutan's Survey Department—then only 2-year old—examined claims and historical records. Negotiations were even then seen as a practical necessity.[47] The Bhutanese *Tshogdu* began discussing the problem and prospects of negotiations in 1976. The initiative had not been taken earlier because data had not been collected. Also, King Jigme Singye Wangchuck would not begin discussions until New Delhi's relations with Beijing improved.[48] In any case, Bhutan, as a small country could not have afforded an undemarcated border. That is what Druk Gyalpo Jigme Singye Wangchuck told an Indian political analyst in 1981.[49]

What happened in 1979 perhaps advanced the talks between the two countries. During the rainy season that year some Tibetan graziers had entered into the Bhutanese territory. Though it was, more or less, construed to be an annual feature, the 1979 intrusions were found to be on a larger scale than in the former years.[50] However, according to another account, the 1979 alarum was not caused by Chinese soldiers disguised as graziers, as Indian reports suggested at that time, but by the Chinese surveyors, some of whom might have carried small arms for protection in wild uninhabited terrain.[51] Be that as it may, the incident was seen as the increasing desire of China to enter into negotiations with Bhutan on the demarcation of border.

The important question now was: who should talk on behalf of Bhutan? Many might have thought that India would talk directly to China on behalf of Bhutan or would do so along with the Himalayan kingdom because of the special relations existing between the two on the plane of foreign policy. Of course, nowhere does the 1949 Treaty say, that India would act on behalf of Bhutan in such matters. True, the "tactfully acquiescent" King Jigme Dorji Wangchuck, was "probably perfectly willing to be represented by India".[52] However, the Chinese adamantly maintained that Bhutan-Tibet border did "not fall within the scope of the Sino-Indian boundary question" and was therefore "irrelevant to the task of the officials of the two countries".[53]

It was against this background that when in 1979 both India and China protested to Bhutan against the intrusion by graziers in that year, Beijing responded to the note sent by Thimphu but no reply was sent to New Delhi. Obviously, China construed the matter as falling within Bhutan's exclusive jurisdiction.[54]

Preparations and talks

Quite predictably, now Bhutan started preparing itself for negotiations with China. In any case, it would have been undesirable to leave its borders with its giant northern neighbours undemarcated indefinitely, especially so when both China's willingness to talk and its pressure on Bhutan to do so were quite evident. Now that it was clear that India would not be allowed to play any direct role in these negotiations, it was perhaps incumbent upon Bhutan to make its stand clear. In the event, Bhutan chose to take India into confidence over the talks on the Bhutan-China borders. In an interview to an Indian political analyst, King Jigme Singye Wangchuck said in 1981 that talks would be held with India's full trust and confidence.[55]

It was not for nothing that the announcement of talks with China was made just after the then Indian Minister for External Affairs, P.V. Narasimha Rao, visited the Himalayan capital and before Huang Hua was to arrive in New Delhi. In fact, so close was and still is the bond that His Majesty King Jigme Singye Wangchuck had no problems to discuss with the visiting Indian External Affairs Minister.[56]

Lyonpo Dawa Tsering, Foreign Minister of Bhutan, informed the *Tshogdu* at the end of June 1981 that:

> Bhutan would like to start direct and bilateral negotiations with China to delineate and demarcate the Bhutan-China boundary, and that the status quo on the present traditional border should be maintained until such time as the border negotiations have been concluded.[57]

In fact, there were talks about getting to China in Bhutan even during the Janata regime. In 1979, as the Janata government in India, in pursuit of its policy of "beneficial bilateralism," took some forward steps towards normalization of relations with the PRC, some concerns were expressed in the Bhutanese *Tshogdu*. A few members expressed their desire for establishing direct communication with China. Commenting on this Foreign Minister Lyonpo Dawa Tsering stated:

> Some National Assembly members felt that if China and India became friends Bhutan would lose all importance for Peking and New Delhi. They thought that we should make our own efforts to develop ties with China or be left out in the cold.[58]

Having prepared itself for several years, Bhutan eventually started talking to its northern giant neighbour. So far 7 rounds of talks have been held between Bhutan and China. The first round of talks were held in Beijing in April 1984. The second round of talks took place in Thimphu in April 1985. The third round of talks were held in Beijing in June 1986. The fourth round of talks were arranged in Thimphu in June 1987. The two sides met for the fifth round of talks in Beijing in May 1988. The sixth round of talks were held again in Beijing in November 1989. The seventh (and the last so far in the series) round of talks took place in Thimphu in August 1990.

From the first to the fifth round of talks, the Bhutanese side was led by the Bhutanese Ambassador in New Delhi. On the other hand, the Chinese side was led by a Vice Foreign Minister. Subsequently the level of the talks was upgraded. During the sixth and seventh rounds of talks, the Bhutanese side was led by the country's Foreign Minister, Lyonpo Dawa Tsering, and the Chinese side was led by a Senior Vice Foreign Minister.[59]

Several rounds of talks between Bhutan and China have proved beyond doubt that the two are capable of dealing with each other without any outside interference or any third party arbitration. It is, indeed, remarkable that no controversy in any round of talks has come to the notice of the press or the public. The various rounds of talks between Thimphu and Beijing and Bhutan's continuing and growing friendship with India also show that over the years Indo-Bhutan relations have become sufficiently, if not also completely, mature to preempt any kind of confusion. In fact, some analysts tend to feel that the Sino-Bhutan talks have not so far succeeded finally in clinching the border problem because China tends to suspect that Bhutan passes to India the details about these talks.

While the talks between the South Asian Himalayan state and the Asian giant go on, many tend to ask whether this would result in establishing diplomatic relations between the two. In fact, many tend to believe that China is pressurizing Bhutan to establish diplomatic relations sooner rather than later. Politics is the art of the possible and one cannot rule out any development therein. But Bhutan certainly does not seem to be keen on or even willing to establish diplomatic relations with the PRC. Various statements by Bhutanese leaders bear this out.

In a statement in September 1979, Druk Gyalpo Jigme Singye Wangchuck denied having any intention of establishing diplomatic contacts with China since he called it "utter nonsense".[60] During his state visit to India in February 1980, King Jigme Singye Wangchuck was asked by S. Venkat Narayan, *India Today's* Excutive Editor, about his country's relations with China. The Druk Gyalpo asserted: "Our National Assembly had decided not to have any diplomatic relations with China".[61]

During two exclusive interviews to me in October 1990 and October 1991, Druk Gyalpo Jigme Singye Wangchuck seemed to be more cautious on this issue. In any case, Bhutan is doing a tight-rope walking as far as its talks with China are concerned. It calls for political and diplomatic maturity and the Druk Gyalpo has shown that he is not wanting in it. Without doubt, the question of the establishment of diplomatic relations with China would remain a vital issue not only for the Chinese but also for the political analysts and observers outside.

Speaking to presspersons on 16 May 1985 in Thimphu, who had assembled for the SARC meeting's coverage, Bhutanese Foreign Minister Lyonpo Dawa Tsering said that Bhutan had no plans to establish diplomatic relations with China. He added that due to resource constraints Bhutan did not visualize setting up new missions "for years to come". He further added that Bhutan was short of financial resources as well as qualified manpower and expansion of diplomatic ties was not in the list of its priorities.[62]

In the light of all kind of talks and negotiations between Bhutan and China during the regime of Druk Gyalpo Jigme Singye Wangchuck, it seems quite unlikely that Bhutan would explore the possibility of using China to balance relations with India, as scholars like Ram Rahul and Manorama Kohli would like one to believe.[63]

An overview

In fine, then, the relations between Bhutan and China have been from the outset those of care and caution and not without any interaction. And care and caution still remain the watchwords of these relations. Bhutan could have tried to remain oblivious of the existence of the PRC for all practical purposes, had Tibet not been annexed by China. But the changed political-geographical reality had to have its impact on *Druk-yul* or *Shangri-La*, as it is called.

Bhutan could not have been expected to reconcile to the loss of its enclaves. Nor could have it left the border with the PRC (particularly the part of the Autonomous Region of Tibet) undemarcated *ad infinitum*. Besides, talks with China add a new and positive dimension to Bhutan's international personality, and, mentionably, that status has not been achieved by any questionable means. A very significant aspect of this development is the fact that India does not feel to have been marginalized or sidelined, although it has no *locus standi* in this matter in China's eyes.

Several questions arise in this context. Why have these talks lingered so long without achieving anything tangible? Would, Bhutan establish diplomatic ties with China eventually? Would in that event, Bhutan play the China card to balance or influence India? These are some of such questions.

Talks on border and other disputes between any two neighbours, who are closely linked geographically, usually span over years. What is happening at the talks between India and the PRC or for that matter between India and Pakistan or even India and Bangladesh? There is generally no quick-fix solutions to the wheels-within-wheels problems between any two neighbours. Bhutan and China are no exception.

As for the establishment of diplomatic ties between the two, the possibility cannot be ruled out for all time to come. Politics is the art of the possible: it applies to Bhutan-China relations and emerging dimensions thereto. If India and Israel can establish diplomatic ties, why can Bhutan and China not do so? However, it is not to suggest that there are any chances of that happening in the near future. No straws in the wind indicate that currently.

Regarding the use of the China card by Bhutan, there seems little possibility of that in the foreseeable future. Bhutan must not be oblivious of the role played by China in Nepal's politics and the consequence thereof. In fact, the governing elite of Bhutan appears enlightened enough to know the nitty-gritty of this complexity. More closeness with China would create more problems for Bhutan's internal politics and that cannot be imagined to be to Bhutan's advantage. On this front, Bhutan cannot also be careless about the possibility of the Tibetans or Chinese moving to Bhutan as the Land of the Thunder Dragon is faced with the problem of the paucity of manpower.

In one word, Bhutan has to continue its interactions with China with immense care and caution. It is precisely doing that.

Notes and References

1. R.C. Misra, "Bhutan-China Relations", *China Report*, Delhi, vol. 17, no. 2, March-April 1981, 45.
2. Manorama Kohli, "Bhutan's Strategic Enviroment : Changing Perceptions", *India Quarterly*, New Delhi, vol. 42, no. 2, April-June 1986, 143.
3. Even his date of birth remains disputed and some consider it to be 1534. See Manorama Kohli, *India And Bhutan : A Study In Interrelations 1772-1910*, Munshiram Manoharlal Publishers Private Limited, New Delhi, 1982, 6-7.
4. R.C. Misra, n. 1.
5. Michael Aris, "Bhutan : internal development and relations with outside power to 1952", in Francis Robinson, ed., *The Cambridge Encyclopaedia of India, Pakistan, Bangladesh, Sri Lanka, Nepal, Bhutan and Maldives*, Cambridge University Press, Cambridge, 1989, 161-62.
6. Ibid., 162-63.
7. Srikant Dutt, "Scholarship on Bhutan", *China Report*, vol. 17, no. 5, September-October 1981, 61.
8. Srikant Dutt, "Bhutan's International Position", *International Studies*, New Delhi, vol.

20, nos. 3-4, July-December 1981, 604.
9. Ibid., 605.
10. Sunanda K. Datta-Ray, "Return Of The Dragon-I : Bhutan Prepares To Talk To China", *The Statesman*, Delhi, 17 July 1981, 6.
11. See Leo E. Rose, *The Politics of Bhutan,* Cornell University Press, Ithaca, 1977; Kapilesnwar Labh, "Bhutan's International Position Prior to 1947", *International Studies,* New Delhi, vol. 13, no. 1, January-March, 1974 and Nirmala Das, *Dragon Country*, New Delhi, 1973.
12. Sunanda, K. Datta-Ray, n. 10.
13. Srikant Dutt, n. 7, 60.
14. Ram Rahul, "Making of Modern Bhutan", *International Studies*, vol. 19, no. 3, July-September 1980, 225-26.
15. Ibid.
16. Srikant Dutt, n. 7, 58.
17. Josef Kolmas, *Tibet and Imperial China : A Survey of Sino-Tibetan Relations up to the end of the Manchu Dynasty in 1912,* ANU, Canberra, 1967 ; L. Petch, *China and Tibet in the Early 18th Century,* Leiden, 1972. Cited in Ibid.
18. R.C. Misra, n. 1, 48.
19. Cited in Manorama Kohli, n. 2, 144.
20. Sunanda K. Datta-Ray, n. 10.
21. V.P. Dutt, *China's Foreign Policy : 1958-62,* Asia Publishing House, Bombay, 1964, 19-20.
22. K.P.S. Menon, *China : Past And Present,* Asia Publishing House, Bombay, 1968, 21.
23. Manorama Kohli, n. 2, 144.
24. Ram Rahul, *The Himalaya as a Frontier,* Vikas Publishing House Pvt. Ltd., New Delhi, 1978, 93.
25. Manorama Kohli, n. 2, 145.
26. Srikant Dutt, n. 7, 61.
27. Cited in A. Appadorai and M.S. Rajan, *India's Foreign Policy and Relations,* South Asian Publishers Private Ltd., New Delhi, 1985, 173.
28. Ibid.
29. Ibid., 173-74.
30. Ibid., 174.
31. Ibid.
32. Ibid.
33. Cited in Manorama Kohli, n. 2, 145.
34. Cited in A. Appadorai and M.S. Rajan, n. 27, 175.
35. Sunanda K. Datta-Ray, n. 10.
36. Srikant Dutt, n. 8, 611.
37. Sunanda K. Datta-Ray, n. 10.
38. Ibid.
39. Ibid.
40. Nari Rustomji, *Bhutan : The Dragon Kingdom in Crisis,* Oxford University Press, Delhi, 1978, 14-15.
41. R.C. Misra, n. 1, 50.
42. Srikant Dutt, n. 8, 617.
43. Sunanda K. Datta-Ray, "Flight of The Dragon-II : Challenge of Settlement With China", *The Statesman,* 28 April 1984, 6.
44. Cited in Manorama Kohli, n. 2, 147.
45. Srikant Dutt, n. 8, 618.
46. Srikant Dutt, n. 7, 62.

47. Sunanda K. Datta-Ray, n. 10.
48. Ibid.
49. Ibid.
50. Manorama Kohli, n. 2, 148.
51. Sunanda K. Datta-Ray, n. 10.
52. Sunanda K. Datta-Ray, "Flight Of The Dragon-I : Bhutan's Three-Pronged Strategy", *The Statesman*, 27 April 1984, 6.
53. Ibid.
54. Manorama Kohli, n. 2, 148.
55. Sunanda K. Datta-Ray, n. 10.
56. Druk Gyalpo Jigme Singye Wangchuck told me in an exclusive interview at his Tashichho Dzong Secretariat in Thimphu on 13 October 1990.
57. Cited in Sunanda K. Datta-Ray, n. 10.
58. *The Tribune*, Chandigarh, 5 November 1979, cited in Manorama Kohli, n. 2, 150, and Manorama Kohli, "Dragon Kingdom's Urge For International Role", *India Quarterly*, New Delhi, vol. 37, no. 2, April-June 1981, 237.
59. This information is based on the data supplied by the Foreign Secretary of Bhutan, Dasho T. J. Rixin, on 11 March 1992.
60. See *Indian Express*, New Delhi, 11 September 1979.
61. "Interview of The Fortnight : Jigme Singye Wangchuck : A Neighbour Without Problems", *India Today*, New Delhi, 1-15 March 1980, 90.
62. L.K. Sharma, "No diplomatic ties with China : Bhutan", *The Times of India*, New Delhi, 16 May 1985, 16.
63. See Ram Rahul, *Royal Bhutan*, Motilal Banarsidass, Delhi, 1983, 68 and Manorama Kohli, n. 2, 150.

8

Bhutan-India Relations: The Importance of Being Matured

Relations between the tiny Himalayan state of Bhutan and the large-sized South Asian core state of India are bound to be one of the most important issues—perhaps the most important issue-in the calculations of the foreign policy-makers of *Tashichho* Dzong (the headquarters of the Royal Government of Bhutan. On the other hand, the foreign policy-makers of India's South Block (the headquarters of the Ministry of External Affairs) seem to be more careful and cautious to see that nothing is done—even unwittingly—to hurt the ruling elite or even hoi polloi of Druk-yul in any thinkable manner on any front.

It is, therefore, rightly felt that regardless of the wording of the India-Bhutan Treaty of Friendship, 1949—which forms the basis of the formal and institutionalized relations between the two South Asian states—relations between them have over the years grown from maturity to maturity. It is not for nothing, then, that the Bhutanese leaders often stress that this pattern of relationship is worth emulating by other South Asian states *vis-a-vis* India. It is not without reason that His Majesty Druk Gyalpo Jigme Singye Wangchuck takes keen and personal interest in shaping his country's relations with India and perhaps leaves nothing to chance.

Only recently, Bhutanese Foreign Minister Lyonpo Dawa Tsering said in an interview: "Unlike other SAARC (the seven-nation South Asian Association for Regional Cooperation) countries, we have always followed a positive approach towards India and cashed on it".[1]

It is widely and rightly believed that a country's foreign policy changes less often than its domestic policies. Based as a country's foreign policy, *inter alia,* is on its regional and international settings, its national interest and its day-to-day requirements, there is a palpable continuity on this front. Bhutan has shown this continuity also in the form of retaining a foreign minister ever since the Ministry of Foreign Affairs was established in that country. The wavelength between the Druk Gyalpo and his Lyonpo dealing with foreign affairs, if anything, is complete and perfect. This augurs exceedingly well for the conduct of Bhutan's foreign policy, in general, and the shaping of Bhutan-India relations, in particular.

The ties between Bhutan and India could be said to have been best portrayed in a story that is traced back to the 8th century, when Guru Padmasambhava, an Indian saint, was preaching Buddhism in *Druk-yul*. A scholar on Bhutanese affairs writes:

> The legend of Sindhu Raja of Bumthang and his battles with Na'u-che (big Nose), a neighbouring Indian ruler warns "that if Mon (Bhutan) succeeds, all of the India will be conquered, if India succeeds all of Mon will be conquered". The warning was really an exhortion to peace; it persuaded the two princes to meet under Guru Padmasambhava's benign aegis and swear everlasting amity at the oathstone pillar which was thereafter known as Powerless since the kings relinquished their own power for the sake of eternal friendship between the two countries.[2]

British involvement with the Himalayan kingdom of Bhutan began in the 1770s and 1780s with a number of missions sent by Warren Hastings after a conflict between Bhutan and Cooch Behar. The sympathetic accounts left by these missions show that they were motivated as much by a desire to extend the frontier of knowledge as to open trade route to Central Asia. By contrast, the British mission of the nineteenth century were aimed at containing the predatory activities of the border Bhutanese in the frontier regions of Assam and Bengal. While the kingdom of Bhutan had won for itself various traditional rights over these areas (called Duars), apparently the centre had little control over their exploitation by local officials and raiding parties. That does not, however, mean that the state remained without any benefit. The income derived from these areas helped it to maintain the state monks in the capital and provincial dzongs. On the other hand, Indian slaves captured in the plains, or descended therefrom, were employed both by the state and its taxpayers.[3]

However, the interactions between them in the 1770s and 1780s could only be called an involvement. The direct contact was yet to be established. Indeed, it came to be established in 1826, after the British annexation of Assam. The British grip over Cooch Behar in 1773-74 and the British victory over Nepal in 1815-16 had strengthened Bhutan's suspicions of British objectives. Eventually, the Bhutanese and the British confronted each other on the question of the Assam Duars, which had normally been under the control of the erstwhile Ahom rulers of Assam and which had been occupied by the Bhutanese in the first half of the 18th century. Several events on the frontier of Assam with Bhutan in the 1830s made it necessary for the British to throw out the Bhutanese and to extend their own powers as far as the Duars. The British tried to settle the dispute respecting the Assam Duars and to make Bhutan the medium of renewing commercial relations with Tibet and West China. However, the Bhutanese refused to play such a role.[4]

The British-Bhutan relationship, as it developed during the last quarter of the 18th and through the 19th century, was not an isolated affair. The eyes of the British government in India were fixed not only on the mountainous region, comprising Bhutan, Sikkim, Nepal and Tibet, but on the entire subcontinent of India. Its policy of conciliation, at times, and of aggressiveness, at others, was shaped by considerations which had little to do with Bhutan *per se*. In fact, the British were busy in other parts of India and waging wars with Mysore and then with Maharashtra and other powers and ultimately with the Sikhs. As such, it considered it expedient to maintain peace in the northern mountainous region.[5]

After the annexation of Assam, however, the situation changed substantially. Now Bhutan was the next-door neighbour of the British government in India. Complaints about depredations by the Bhutanese nationals in British Assam poured it. Consequently, the attitude of the British towards Assam stiffened. However, the British maintained the policy of peaceful coexistence, not because they were very fond of Bhutan, but because they were preoccupied with various other problems in other parts of the country. Nevertheless, the Assam Duars were annexed by the British in 1841 and a sum of Rs. 10,000 was sanctioned to be paid to the Bhutanese government as compensation for the loss incurred by it on that count.[6]

During the period that followed this event there were minor confrontations between the two. However, what was of consequence from the point of view of Bhutan's political history was that the kingdom was moving towards a state of political anarchy owing to the lessening hold of the Dharma Raja and the Dev Raja on the powerful penlops and dzongpens. Bhutan was encouraged to encroach on Assam and Cooch Behar after the 1857 revolt in India. After the British government in India quelled the rebellion of 1857, it decided to annex the Bhutanese territory of Ambari Falakak. The decision was reportedly taken in 1857 but was kept in abeyance owing to the problems in India. The territory of Ambari Falakak was annexed in 1859. Quite expectedly, relations between the Bhutanese and the British government in India became strained.

However, after 1857, the attitude of the British government in India underwent a marked change. It indulged in annexation even on the slightest pretext earlier: now annexation became an avoidable proposition. In fact, even the Duars were not really annexed. They were only taken for administrative efficiency to arrest incrusions by the Bhutanese. On the other hand, as we saw, compensation was paid for the loss of the territory. Indeed, it was the policy of no annexation and no territorial expansion, emphasized in the Queen's Proclamation of 1858, that came to the rescue of Bhutan in maintaining and retaining its independent and distinct political entity.[7]

Things changed thereafter in such a manner that relations between Bhutan and India came to be institutionalized further and farther. This trend could be seen emerging on several fronts. One could see three clear methods in the direction of institutionalizing and strengthening these relations: 1. Treaties, 2. Visits, and 3. Aids. We can take up each of them in turn.

Treaties

Towards the 1865 Treaty: In 1845, the Bhutanese authorities demanded an increase in the amount of the annual payment of Rs. 10,000. The British rejected the demand. Consequently, the Bhutanese commenced hostile activities in the Assam and Bengal Duars. With a view to settling the differences, the Government of India sent Ashley Eden, Secretary to the government of Bengal, to Bhutan in the winter of 1863. Eden failed to persuade the Bhutanese to accept the British stand in the matter. Instead, he provided them with an opportunity to extract from him an agreement which postulated surrender of all the Assam and Bengal Duars as well as the political offenders and runway slaves to Bhutan.

The Indian governmment repudiated the agreement and declared war on Bhutan on 22 November 1864. Initially the British suffered a set-back particularly at Dewangiri, which then formed the southern tip of Bhutan. They beat a retreat from there in haste under the cover of night. They had not yet perfected their military system to defend the uncertain and difficult northeast frontier. However, the Bhutanese were eventually defeated.

The two parties concluded at Sinchula in Bhutan on 11 November

1865 a treaty of peace. It was, indeed, very hard for the Bhutanese. The British retained possession of the entire strip of the Assam and Bengal Duars from the Dhansiri river in the east to the Tista river in the west, the low-country lying along the foothills, together with the Daling hills tract, contiguous with the Bengal Duars. The British also retained Dewangiri and the area around it.

On the other hand, the British agreed to pay Bhutan a subsidy of Rs.25,000 in the first year, Rs.35,000 in the second, Rs. 45,000 in the third and Rs. 50,000 every year thereafter. The harshness of the British was clearly due to a desire to punish the Bhutanese for their sympathetic attitude towards the Indian rebels in 1857.

The Treaty of 1865 made the British the sole arbiter of Bhutan's relations with Cooch Behar and Sikkim. It also stipulated free trade between Bhutan and free India. However, it left Bhutan's relations with Tibet undefined. This had serious political implications and these came into sharp focus during the civil war of 1884-86 in Bhutan. The Manchu China showed little concern for the happenings between Bhutan and the British as in 1774, even though the Manchu Amban in Lhasa had been charged in 1793 with exclusive responsibility for the conduct of Tibet's relations with Bhutan, as with Sikkim and Nepal.[8]

Article 1 of the 1865 Treaty talked about "perpetual peace and friendship between the British Government and the Government of Bhootan". Various Articles of the 10-Article Treaty were rather humiliating for the Bhutanese authorities. For instance, Article 2 stated:

> Whereas in consequence of repeated aggression of the Bhootan Government and of the refusal of the Government to afford satisfaction for those aggressions, and of their insulting treatment of the officers sent by His Excellency the Governor-General-in-Council for the purpose of procuring an amicable adjustment of differences existing between the two States, the British Government has been compelled to seize by an armed force the whole of the Doars and certain Hill Posts protecting the passes into Bhootan and whereas the Bhootan Government has now expressed its regret for past misconduct and a desire for the establishment of friendly relations with the British Government, it is hereby agreed that the whole of the tract known as the Eighteen Doars, bordering on the Districts of Rungpoor, Cooch Behar and Assam, together with the Talook of Ambaree Fallacotah and the hill territory on the left bank of the Teesta up to such points as may be laid down by the British Commissioner appointed for the

> purpose is ceded by the Bhootan Government to the British Government for ever.[9]

The Bhutan Government (Article 3) also agreed to surrender all British subjects as well as subjects of the Chiefs of Sikkim and Cooch Behar who were detained in Bhutan against their will, and to place no impediment in the way of the return of all or any of such persons into British territory. Article 4 talked about the payment of subsidy to the Bhutanese authorities in various instalments, which we have already referred to. But Article 5 was again an attempt to belittle Bhutan. It stated:

> The British Government will hold itself at liberty at any time to suspend the payment of this compensation money, either in whole or in part, in the event of misconduct on the part of the Bhootan Government or its failure to check the aggression of its subjects or comply with the provisions of this Treaty.[10]

The 1865 Treaty also enhanced the power of arbitration of the British government *vis-a-vis* disputes between Bhutan and other states. Article 8 stated, thus:

> The Bhootan Government hereby agree to refer to the arbitration of the British Government all disputes with, or causes of complaint against, the Rajahs of Sikkim and Cooch Behar, and to abide by the decision of the British Government; and the British Government hereby engage to enquire into and settle all such disputes and complaints in such manner as justice may require, and to insist on the observance of the decision by the Rajahs of Sikkim and Cooch Behar.[11]

The Sinchula Treaty of 1865 also provided for free trade and commerce (Article 9) between the two governments. No duties were to be levied on Bhutanese goods imported into British territories, nor was the Bhutanese government to levy any duties on British goods imported into, or transported through, the Bhutanese territories. More importantly, the Bhutanese subjects residing in British territories were to have equal justice with British subjects, and British subjects residing in Bhutan were to have equal justice with the subjects of the Bhutanese government.[12]

Needless to state, the 1865 Treaty was in every sense of the term an imposed treaty on Bhutan—an imposed peace on the mountain kingdom. But, perhaps, there was little that the small kingdom could have done.

Besides, the timing of the Treaty was also significant inasmuch as it was signed at a time when Bhutan was moving towards more internal clashes among the power-holders and power-wielders. The importance of the Treaty lies in the fact that it institutionalized relations between the two states for the first time and it led to the continuation of that process in future as well.

The 1910 Treaty: Bhutan entered a new phase of its history with the turn of the 20th century. It felt impelled and compelled to take to modernization, albeit in limited doses, because of its problems and relations with its neighbouring countries. What happened in Tibet after 1904 was rather ominous for Druk-yul. Hardly had the troops of Chao Erh-feng occupied Lhasa on 12 February 1910 and compelled the 13th Dalai Lama to seek refuge in India when the Manchu government made its claim over Bhutan along with Nepal and Sikkim. With a view to preempting Bhutan's movement into China's sphere, the British Government in India revised the 1865 Treaty on 8 January 1910. The Treaty was signed at Punakha in Bhutan.

The most important aspect of the Treaty of Punakha was the revision of Article 8 of the 1865 Treaty. By revising this Article, the British Government in India enhanced its power from an arbitrator to an adviser. Article 8 of the Sinchula Treaty was revised and the revised Article ran as follows:

> The British Government undertakes to exercise no interference in the internal administration of Bhutan. On its part, the Bhutanese Government agrees to be guided by the advice of the British Government in regard to its external relations. In the event of disputes with or causes of complaint against the Maharajas of Sikkim and Cooch Behar, such matters will be referred for arbitration to the British Government which will settle them in such manner as justice may require, and insist upon the observance of its decisions by the Maharajas named.[13]

Through this Treaty the Government of India also increased the annual subsidy to Bhutan from Rs. 50,000 to Rs. 1,00,000. This was the result of an addition made to Article 4 of the Sinchula Treaty.

"This treaty was a turning-point in the history of modern Bhutan. It placed Bhutan as far as the management and conduct of its foreign relations were concerned, on the same footing as Sikkim."[14]

Before the Treaty was signed, Druk Gyalpo Ugyen Wangchuck had emerged as a strong personality on the political scene of Bhutan as a result of his election as the Druk Gyalpo of the kingdom in 1907. A question arises at this point: why did Ugyen Wangchuck throw in his lot with the British in India? The reasons are not far to seek. First, the British success against the Tibetans in the very heart of Tibet in the summer of 1904 had left a strong imprint on his mind. Secondly, Ugyen Wangchuck wanted protection against Manchu expansionism in Druk-yul. Thirdly, under the then prevalent circumstances, he realized the difficulty or impossibility of Bhutan's existence as a separate political entity without the British pleasure.[15] In any case, Ugyen Wangchuck showed his capacity of rising to the occasion by signing this Treaty.

Needless to say, the 1910 Treaty brought Druk-yul further under the influence of the British authorities in India. However, the situational difference was of importance. Whereas the 1865 Treaty was an imposed one and was, to a very great extent, the outcome of Bhutan's diplomatic *fau pax*, the Treaty of 1910 seemed more of a balanced *quid pro quo*. Apparently, Bhutan needed the support of the British authorities. By the time of the signing of the Treaty of 1910, sufficient rapport and confidence had developed between the British authorities in India and Druk Gyalpo Ugyen Wangchuck. The British had, in fact, conferred the title of the Knight Commander of the Indian Empire (KCIE) on Ugyen Wangchuck before he was elected *Druk Gyalpo*. Indeed, the British were supposed to be instrumental in getting Ugyen Wangchuck elected as the Druk Gyalpo of Druk-yul to a very great extent, for they were tired of dealing with various centres of power in the kingdom. This, of course, is not to suggest that his political clout and military might inside the kingdom were inferior to any other personality.

India-Bhutan Treaty of Friendship, 1949: Circumstances, quite expectedly, changed in the region after the signing of the 1910 Treaty. Bhutan could not have remained oblivious of these changes. The circumstantial changes eventually led to the signing of the India-Bhutan Treaty of Friendship of 1949, which, to this date formalizes and institutionalizes the relationship between the big (India) and the small (Bhutan). Let us first have a look into the circumstances that resulted in the signing of the Treaty of 1949.

In 1946, on the occasion of the British Cabinet Mission's visit to India, the Government of Bhutan presented a memorandum. It affirmed its separate identity from the other princely states in India, but confirmed its special ties with India. The Cabinet Mission made no commitment beyond reaffirming Bhutan's political status in line with the minute of the Secretary of State for India in 1924. After the British withdrew from India on 15 August 1947, the status of Bhutan was undecided and, therefore, a matter of conjecture. Druk-yul was not a part of India: it was autonomous. Its position was between Nepal and Sikkim. It was less independent than Nepal but more free than Sikkim. In the event, Bhutan's relations with independent India began in a climate of suspicion and misunderstanding.[16]

It was in this context that Ram Rahul wrote:

> Owing to certain extraneous reasons, the Bhutanese authorities felt that new India would be imperialistic towards their country. They, therefore, thought of forging a federation of Sikkim and Bhutan in association with Tibet as a counter-weight to India. Towards the end of 1948, a Bhutanese delegation visited India to discuss Bhutanese relations. The Government of India assured Bhutan that it would respect Bhutan's autonomy if it maintained the same relationship with independent India as with British India.[17]

It was under these circumstances that Druk Gyalpo Jigme Wangchuck, the second Wangchuck King of Bhutan, decided to renew Bhutan's connection with the new and independent India and signed the Treaty of 1949 on 8 August of that year in Darjeeling.

In a way, the new 10-Article Treaty was the continuation of the 1910 and 1865 Treaties as far as the foreign affairs of Bhutan were concerned. Article 2 of the 1949 Treaty states:

> The Government of India undertakes to exercise no interference in the internal administration of Bhutan. On its part the Government of Bhutan agrees to be guided by the advice of the Government of India in regard to its external relations.

Article 1 states: "There shall be perpetual peace and friendship between the Government of India and the Government of Bhutan".

The annual subsidy was further enhanced to Rs. 5 lakhs from Rs. 1 lakh (as mentioned in the 1910 Treaty). It was agreed that the annual payment shall be made on the tenth day of January every year, the first payment being made on the tenth day of January 1950. This payment is to continue so long as this "Treaty remains in force and its terms are duly observed". (Article 3).

Article 4 talks about the return of 32-square miles of territory to Bhutan within one year of the signature of the Treaty. It was to "mark the friendship existing and continuing between the said Governments". The said territory was in the area known as Dewangiri. The Government of India, in this connection, undertook to appoint a competent officer or officers to mark out the area so returned to the Government of Bhutan.

Article 5 talks about free trade and commerce between the territories of the two governments in the following words:

> There shall, as heretofore, be free trade and commerce between the territories of the Government of India and the Government of Bhutan; and the Government of India agrees to grant the Government of Bhutan every facility for the carriage, by land and water, of its produce throughout the territory of the Government of India, including the right to use such forest roads as may be specified by mutual agreement from time to time.

Article 6 talks about the transportation of arms and ammunition through the Indian territory in the following words:

> The Government of India agrees that the Government of Bhutan shall be free to import with the assistance and approval of the Government of India, from or through India into Bhutan, whatever arms, ammunition, machinery, warlike material of stores may be required or desired for the strength and welfare of Bhutan, and that this arrangement shall hold good for all time as long as the Government of India is satisfied that the intentions of the Government of Bhutan are friendly and that there is no danger to India from such importations. The Government of Bhutan, on the other hand, agrees that there shall be no export of such arms, ammunition, etc., across the frontier of Bhutan either by the Government of Bhutan or by private individuals.

Article 7 talks about equal justice to the people of each other's country in the following terms:

> The Government of India and the Government of Bhutan agree that Bhutanese subjects residing in Indian territories shall have equal justice with Indian subjects and that Indian subjects residing in Bhutan shall have equal justice with the subjects of the Government of Bhutan.

Article 8 talks about the extradition of people involved in criminal activities in either of the two countries. Article 9 is more important from the view of ironing out of differences, if any, regarding the application or interpretation of the Treaty. It says:

> Any differences and disputes arising in the application or interpretation of this Treaty shall in the first instance be settled by negotiation. If within three months of the start of negotiations no settlement is arrived at, then the matter shall be referred to the Arbitration of three

arbitrators, who shall be nationals of either India or Bhutan, chosen in the following manner:

> (1) One person nominated by the Government of India; (2) One person nominated by the Government of Bhutan; (3) A Judge of the Federal Court, or of a High Court in India, to be chosen by the Government of Bhutan, who shall be the Chairman.
>
> The judgement of this tribunal shall be final and executed without delay by either Party.

This Treaty is to "continue in force in perpetuity unless terminated or modified by mutual consent". (Article 10).[18]

The 1949 Treaty—especially its Article 2— is viewed by many as a device that impedes the political sovereignty of the Himalayan kingdom. Many feel that even Article 9—which deals with the method to iron out differences between the two countries *vis-a-vis* the Treaty—favours India in comparison to Bhutan. It is because of this that many treat it as an unequal Treaty. As late as 1960, Druk Gyalpo Jigme Dorji Wangchuck had asserted: "We are not hundred per cent independent because of the 1949 Treaty".[19]

However, Nagendra Singh, who had the privilege of serving as the Constitutional Adviser to the Royal Government of Bhutan, is of the opinion that the Indo-Bhutan Treaty of 1949 was the result of negotiations in which the mountain kingdom found that it was to her advantage to get aid of free India "in guiding her external relations" once it was clearly established that Bhutan was no part of India. It was in contravention of how the British had treated the kingdom. Singh also stresses that as the Bhutanese delegation had pointed out that they did not like the use of the title "Maharaja"—which was uniformly borne by the rulers of Indian states—the 1949 Treaty takes "good care to recognise the title of Druk Gyalpo". He further emphasizes that whereas the "instruments of accession and merger agreements signed by the Government of India with the Indian rulers were all solemnised by the signature of the Ruler himself and not by his representative, the treaty of 1949 between India and Bhutan does not bear the signature of the Druk Gyalpo himself". In fact, it bears the signature of his representatives who had full powers to sign on behalf of the Druk Gyalpo's government.[20]

Be that as it may, Articles 2 and 9 are construed by many— especially Bhutanese with nationalistic fervour and scholars with objective attitude, even if *sotto voce*—as a device to dilute Bhutan's sovereignty. It is difficult to believe now that Bhutan cannot take care of its foreign policy independently of the aid and advice of India. Thanks to the continuity in the Foreign Ministry of Bhutan, the Foreign Minister of the kingdom, Lyonpo Dawa Tsering, is quite adept in the nitty-gritty of regional and international politics. His knowledge of international affairs, if anything, is commendable. The young and energetic Druk Gyalpo, under whose enlightened supervision every lyonpo works, is a mine of knowledge and information. This, without doubt, augurs well for the conduct of the foreign policy of Druk-yul.

It is only because of the liberal attitude and interpretation adopted by the Government of India *vis-a-vis* the Treaty that relations between the two have remained ideal: they have, in fact, moved from maturity to maturity. Whenever there has been any wavering on this front, protest and displeasure have also become visible. When a case of ham-handed diplomatic dealing with Bhutan came to light during the regime of Janata Party(S) government led by Charan Singh, Bhutan did not leave its attitude unknown. When Foreign Secretary Jagat Mehta visited Bhutan in 1978, he was in for a bit of surprise. Not only did Bhutan take a strong line on the Treaty of 1949 and the need to revise it; there were indications that fresh demands were taking shape, which would include the right of independent access to and from Bhutan to third countries and perhaps even a new trade and transit treaty.[21] In September 1979, King Jigme Singye Wangchuck had said that he wished the Indo-Bhutanese Treaty of 1949 to be updated. His speech at the Havana summit of the Non-Aligned Movement, on the other hand, had caused some discussion.[22]

Mercifully, Bhutan-India relations did not deteriorate further, thanks to the growing understanding between the two governments that followed after Indira Gandhi returned to power in New Delhi. Druk Gyalpo Jigme Singye Wangchuck paid a 4-day offical visit to New Delhi in February 1980, and had frank discussions on the entire gamut of Bhutan-India relations with various leaders, including Prime Minister Indira Gandhi. On 25 Ferbruary 1980, the Government of India welcomed the statement of the Bhutanese King that there was no need to discuss the provisions of the Indo-Bhutanese Treaty of 1949. The two sides agreed that the treaty, as it stands, serves the mutual interests of Bhutan and India and, as such, there was no question whatsover to go into it again.

A spokesman of the External Affairs Ministry, who conveyed the government's reaction to the King's statement to a group of newsmen on 24 February 1980, said: "As far as Indo-Bhutanese relations are carried on within the traditional framework in a spirit of friendship, trust and cooperation, they are bound to expand and grow as was evidenced in the recent round of talks the King had with the Prime Minister, Mrs Indira Gandhi, and other leaders". The spokesman said the Government of India agreed with the King that there were no issues which could not be discussed between the two countries if the need arose. Prime Minister Indira Gandhi, who went along with President N. Sanjiva Reddy to see off the royal visitor, told newspersons at Delhi Airport that the King's visit was a "normal one". She added: "It is important that we keep meeting frequently to exchange views on bilateral and other matters".[23]

Visits

Apart from the Treaty provisions, the two countries have strengthened their relations through the visits of dignitaries of one country to the other. Such visits have been quite frequent and both official and non-official. They have been occasions of reaffirming of friendship between the two as also of assurances of various kinds, even outside the Treaty provisions and requirements.

In 1911, Druk Gyalpo Ugyen Wangchuck visited Delhi for the Durbar of King George V, formerly His Royal Highness the Prince of Wales, whom the former had first met in Calcutta in 1906, when he was yet to ascend the Bhutanese throne. In 1924, the Secretary of State for India defined the political status of Bhutan as an autonomous state under British suzerainty but not as an Indian princely state, though its transition to that stauts could have been easily affected then with the concurrence of both the parties.[24]

After the death of Druk Gyalpo Ugyen Wangchuck on 21 August 1926, his eldest son, Jigme Wangchuck, ascended the throne of Bhutan on 14 March 1927. In his reply to the speech of Colonel F.M. Bailey, Political Officer in Sikkim, and leader of the British party, the young Druk Gyalpo expressed his determination to follow in the footsteps of his father in his loyalty to the British connection. He chose to speak in Hindi—a pretty compliment to India in the existing climate—on that occasion. Druk Gyalpo Jigme Wangchuck, accompanied by the Queen, paid his first visit to India in December 1934, which went a long way in strengthening the ties between the then Indian and Bhutanese governments.[25]

Druk Gyalpo Jigme Dorji Wangchuck, who took over the throne, after the death of his father, Jigme Wangchuck, in 1952, visited India in the summer of 1954.[26] In June 1955, India's Foreign Secretary, R.K. Nehru, travelled to Bhutan. Up to that time, India's contacts with Bhutan had been exclusively through its Agent posted in Sikkim. In 1956, India renewed its offer of aid, and the King toured India.[27]

Indian Prime Minister Jawaharlal Nehru visited Bhutan via the Chumbi valley of Tibet. In a public address in Paro on 23 September 1958, he ruled out any pressure on Bhutan which might impair its independent status. On 28 August 1959, he stated in the Lok Sabha (lower house of Indian Parliament) that the protection of the territorial integrity and frontiers of Bhutan was the responsibility of the Government of India. Thus, India committed itself to maintain the integrity of the Himalayan kingdom, even though the 1949 treaty had no clause relating to Bhutan's defence and security.[28]

On 18 September 1959, a Bhutanese delegation headed by Prime Minister Jigmie Palden Dorji visited New Delhi for discussing with the Government of India the development needs of Bhutan. Accordingly, India gave a sum of Rs. 150 million as aid to the Himalayan kingdom for taking up road projects in the country. Since 1949, India had been paying to Bhutan ad hoc grants for various developmental purposes.

Druk Gyalpo Jigme Dorji again visited New Delhi in February 1960, specially for discussing Bhutan's defence and economic development. He was a popular figure: he was warmly welcomed wherever he went in India.[29]

Druk Gyalpo Jigme Dorji Wangchuck paid a state visit to New Delhi on the eve of Bhutan's admission to the United Nations from 6 to 12 April 1971. The visit was quite significant. Indeed, it marked a milestone in the relations between the two South Asian states. Speculation was gaining ground that the 1949 Treaty between Bhutan and India would need to be revised after Bhutan had joined the United Nations. The Druk Gyalpo set such speculation to rest by expressing satisfaction with the 1949 Treaty and firmly ruled out any revision to it. King Jigme Dorji, in fact, affirmed that Bhutan's advent in international affairs would be gradual, and as a friend and partner of India.[30] In any case, ironing out of differences, if any, was badly needed at that juncture and the visit of King Jigme Dorji achieved that objective.

In an interview to an Indian journalist, King Jigme Singye Wangchuck talked about the relations between Bhutan and India after India's independence and opined that Jawaharlal Nehru and Jigme Dorji Wangchuck were the architects of this relationship. He said:

> . . . My father had a warm and very firendly relationship with Pandit Jawaharlal Nehru. It was they who built up strong foundations on which Indo-Bhutan firendship has grown and flourished over the

years. . . . India has always been Bhutan's closest friend and neighbour. The architects of India-Bhutan friendship were Pandit Nehru and my father.[31]

Indeed, on 6 April 1971, a few months before Bhutan became a member of the United Nations, King Jigme Dorji Wangchuck said in course of a speech in New Delhi at the banquet given in his honour by President V.V. Giri: "The destiny of Bhutan is intimately bound with that of India and it is our mutual interest to still further strengthen the existing bonds of friendship and understanding between our two countries".[32]

Indeed, King Jigme Dorji Wangchuck collaborated with Indian leaders, like Jawaharlal Nehru, Indira Gandhi and others, in building a strong foundation for strong links between India and Bhutan. Just as he was the author of Bhutan's modernization on the domestic plane, he was also the author of making Bhutan an international personality, while strengthening bilateral relations with India.

Druk Gyalpo Jigme Singye Wangchuck ascended the throne consequent upon the death of Druk Gyalpo Jigme Dorji Wangchuck in Kenya on 21 July 1972. The young and energetic Druk Gyalpo has been able to pay more frequent visits to India than his predecessors for a variety of reasons. The process of internationalization of the small kingdom has continued unabated during his regime: India's role has been of great significance in this process. This has obviously brought him to India more frequently. On the other hand, there has been a remarkable change for the better in the transport system and biweekly flights of Druk Air to New Delhi has facilitated his frequent visits to this country. Also, ever since his accession to the throne, politics in Delhi *per se* has become more dynamic and Bhutan has to take it into account. Of course, it augurs well for Indo-Bhutan relations that change in Delhi does not effect them. What happened during the foreign ministership of S.N. Mishra was, of course, an exception.[33]

The developments in Sikkim, in Bhutan's close neighbourhood, also increased the frequency of His Majesty King Jigme Singye Wangchuck's visits to India during those days. Doubts persisted in Bhutan about its close southern neighbour, i.e. India. Bhutan had to be reassured by India on this count. In the event, King Jigme Singye Wangchuck came to New Delhi on an informal visit in September 1975. This was followed by two formal visits—one in August 1976 and another in April 1977.[34]

In a way, there is little difference between the King's official and private visits. For in both cases he has been having through and deep interactions—based on warmth—with people from various walks of life, including politics, civil service, the press and the academic world. The King gives the impression of eagerness to know more and more about various aspects of Indian life. I got this impression during my previleged audience with King Jigme Singye Wangchuck at the Rashtrapati Bhavan in New Delhi during his visit to the country in September 1991. In an exclusive interview with me, Bhutanese Foreign Minister Lyonpo Dawa Tsering said that his official visits are not different from his private visits, for during both kinds of visits he avails himself of meeting as many people from India as possible. This, if anything, shows the intimacy between the governments and the people of the two countries.

It is not for nothing that King Jigme Singye Wangchuck said in an interview on the status of Indo-Bhutan relations that:

> . . .The Indian leadership, not only Presidents and Prime Ministers but also ministers and senior bureaucrats, have always shown firendship and goodwill towards Bhutan and have contributed to the growth of Indo-Bhutan friendship and understanding. Indo-Bhutan relations, based on mutuality of interests, have developed to such an extent that they are no longer dependent on individuals in the leadership of both the countries.[35]

In yet another interview to a noted Indian political analyst, the King said: " The stronger we are the more happy India should be. We will give unstinted support in times of crisis". "Bhutan's aspirations can be best fulfilled through maintaining the closest of relations with India", said Lyonpo Dawa Tsering.[36]

Needless to emphasize, King Jigme Singye Wangchuck's frequent visits to India—both official and private—have continued contributing to the Indo-Bhutan firendship and removal of misunderstandings. King Jigme Singye Wangchuck had not a moment's hesitation about accepting, when he was invited at short notice, King Hussein of Jordan having dropped out, to be the chief guest at the 1984 Republic Day celebrations. It meant advancing an already planned state visit by a few days. The King stressed that friends do not stand on ceremony.[37]

On their part, the Indian leaders have also not lagged behind in visiting Bhutan. They have shown a special affection towards Bhutan. The hospitality that the Indian leaders receive in the mountain kingdom are bound to move them. They are really moved.

We have already seen how much warmth had the first Indian Prime Minister, Jawaharlal Nehru, shown towards Bhutan and its people during his visit in 1958. On that occasion he was accompanied by Indira Gandhi, who subsequently became the Prime Minister of India. In fact, Nehru was very eager to make another visit to Bhutan, but he could not do so because of his failing health and the poor transport system that existed at that time. Indira Gandhi was also very friendly to Bhutan and cherished visting that country.

Indian Prisident V.V. Giri went to Bhutan to attend the coronation ceremony of King Jigme Singye Wangchuck in June 1974. He received a grand ovation on that occasion. Giri had firendly talks with the new King on 4 June 1974 in Thimphu. He invited the young king to visit India. The Indian President also announced that India had agreed to help in the construction of hydro-electric project and a cement factory in Bhutan.[38]

Prime Minister Rajiv Gandhi had a deep and personal friendship with King Jigme Singye Wangchuck—and during his prime ministership Indo-Bhutan cooperation flourished. He visited Bhutan in 1985, and 1988.[39] During Prime Minister Rajiv Gandhi's visit of 1985, the Indian Prime Minister and the Bhutanese King together resolved to further consolidate the close and warm friendship that existed between India and Bhutan. Expressing their desire to build further "on the excellent foundations that have been laid", the two leaders in their respective banquet speeches noted with satisfaction that it was possible for a large country like India and a small neighbour like Bhutan to "coexist in perfect harmony, trust and cooperation". They also gave a call for peace in the world and stability in "our region" for genuine progress of the South Asian countries. King Jigme Singye Wangchuck said he was happy to note that "at this point of time Indo-Bhutan relations enjoy a level of complete trust and friendship." There was "close understanding on all issues of mutual concern and interest", he added. In his speech, Rajiv Gandhi reaffirmed India's commitment to Bhutan's development and said: "We do not regard our involvement in Bhutan's development programmes as extending assitance or aid". He said the help extended to Bhutan by India "is considered by us as sharing of resouces for common benefit". He stated that Indo-Bhutanese relationship also showed that when there was true respect and understanding, differences of size did not come in the way of equality.[40] This was a remarkable statement indeed—a remarkable gesture, without doubt.

During his visit to the mountain kingdom in 1985, Rajiv Gandhi on 29 September received the kingdom's highest "Druk Wangysl' award given posthumously to his mother, Indira Gandhi, at a function in the ornated throne room of the sprawling Tashichho Dzong at Thimphu. The prestigious award of a gold medal and citation was presented to Rajiv

Gandhi by King Jigme Singye Wangchuck. Speaking on the occasion, the King said his country was honouring a "true and dear friend" of Bhutan. He said Mrs Gandhi was a great leader.[41]

President R. Venkataraman visited Bhutan in 1988 to inaugurate the Chukha Hydel Project. It is considered a great testimony to Indo-Bhutan friendship and cooperation. Among other things, the King and the President discussed continuing Indo-Bhutanese cooperation, especially in econommic development, education and health. On this occasion, stressing the age-old harmonious relations between the two countries, the King said, it "demonstrates the wisdom of farsighted leadership and enlightened perception in inter-state relations."

The Druk Gyalpo asserted: "We in Bhutan draw much satisfaction from India's achievements both at home and abroad under a succession of dynamic and dedicated leaders". He further said that the Indian President's visit following so shortly after the Prime Minister, Rajiv Gandhi's visit was a testimony to the "very close friendship between India and Bhutan".[42]

Apart from the visits of Indian Presidents and Prime Ministers and Bhutan's Kings, other Ministers and Chief Ministers of India and various Lyonpos (Ministers) and Deputy Ministers of Bhutan keep on visiting each other's country for various official and private purposes. Such visits lead to strengthening of friendship, on the one hand, and ironing out of misunderstandings, if and when they crop up, on the other. Officials of these two countries are in constant touch with one another's counterparts. This obviously augurs well for the establishment of better mutual understanding.

It is significant and relevant to mention here that the process of Bhutan's internationalization began with the visit to that country by the first Indian Prime Minister, Jawaharlal Nehru. Without doubt, Bhutan has not looked back thereafter on this front.

Economic aids and assistance

India has been the largest aid-giver to Bhutan ever since the mountain kingdom started moving on the path of modernization and internationalization. This should not be seen as a gesture of kindness or mercy to Bhutan. In fact, India could be said to be doing so in its own interest. We have already seen how Zhou Enlai had made an offer of economic assistance to Bhutan in 1961. India's security and strategic perceptions rather impel it to help Bhutan to the maximum possible extent. India has so far given over $ 300 million to Bhutan and has almost completely executed its first 3 5-year plans. For the 7th Plan, beginning this year (1992), India has pledged a grant of over $ 250 million, besides loans for various projects, including cement and hydro-electric plants.[43]

It was in this context that Bhutanese Foreign Minister Lyonpo Dawa Tsering told me in an exclusive interview in New Delhi on 10 Feburary 1992 that Bhutan had "integrated" its economy almost completely with India to "our great benefit". In fact, the Foreign Minister believes that if other countries of this region adopt the model of Bhutan-India economic cooperation, it would lead to a new era of economic prosperity in this part of the globe. His assessment does not seem to be erroneous. Maybe economic nitty-gritty one day forces the countries of South Asia to follow the model of Bhutan-India economic relations.

It would be in order here to mention Prime Minister Rajiv Gandhi's assurance to the Bhutanese *Tshogdu* during his visit to that country in 1985. Addressing a special session of the *Tshogdu* on 30 September 1985, Rajiv Gandhi assured that India would be associated with the kingdom's planning process and finance a portion of the 6th Plan beginning in 1987. He stated that India would finance the improvement of the electricity distribution system in the capital and the country's air link gateway town Paro, the construction of mini-hydro electric projects at Gyesta and Khaling in eastern Bhutan. India, he said, would also assist the construction of a broadcasting station and river training works in the southern Bhutan.

In a reference to the negotiations underway about the collaboration for setting up another cement plant at Dungsum, he indicated that support would be forthcoming for this and other new areas during Bhutan's Sixth Plan.[44]

Significantly, the visit of an Indian Planning Commission team to Paro in 1961 initiated the process of India's deep involvement in Bhutan's development. 6 5-year Plans and a countrywide infrastructure of roads, schools, hospitals, farms, industries and power projects testify to India's generous commitment to Bhutan's advancement.

Bhutan-India Relations in Trade and Commerce

The economic interactions between Bhutan and India are also reflected in the relationships in the spheres of trade and commerce between the two countries. Significantly, before 1978, Bhutan's trade contracts were exclusively with India, except those under the aegis of the Colombo Plan, which permitted only limited contacts with countries like Australia, New Zealand, Japan etc. On the basis of an agreement signed between Bhutan and India in 1978, the former was permitted to sell its exportable surpluses to third countries, if and when India was not in a position to buy them.[45]

It is mentionable here that India's active endorsement of Bhutan's diversification of trade and commerce is more directly evident in a series of interlocked arrangements that will permit the landlocked kingdom to expand and diversify exports and imports, if only it can think of the right kinds of merchandise in sufficient quantities. In 1980, trade agreement with Bangladesh—the first of its kind—was elaborated in a protocol signed in February when King Jigme Singye Wangchuck paid a state visit to the nascent state. Besides listing commodities, it mentions routes. It would not have been possible, if India had not guaranteed transit rights and customs facilities in a memorandum of understanding signed with Bangladesh at the end of January 1980. This, in turn, flowed from the new Indo-Bhutan Trade and Commerce Agreement of 27 December 1983, explicitly recognizing the kingdom's right to trade with third countries through Indian territory, and not only granting road, rail and river routes to Bangladesh but also transit via Panitanki to Nepal as well as the use of ports and air terminals.[46]

Obviously, New Delhi recognized the aspirations of Druk-yul in the spheres of trade and commerce and by so doing showed its full trust in the mountain kingdom.

The latest Agreement on the front of trade and commerce between the Government of the Kingdom of Bhutan and the Government of the Republic of India was signed at Thimphu on 2 March 1990. Lyonpo Om Pradhan, Minister for Trade and Industry, Government of the Kingdom of Bhutan, signed the agreement on behalf of his country. Arun Kumar Nehru, Minister for Commerce and Tourism, signed on behalf of the Government of India. The 12-Article Agreement, comprising the protocol and import procedure is to remain in existence for a period of 5 years from the date of signature. The agreement "may be renewed by mutual consent subject to such changes and modifications as may be agreed upon between the two countries".

Article 1 of this Agreement states that there shall, "as heretofore, be free trade and commerce between the territories of the Government of the Kingdom of Bhutan and the Government of the Republic of India". Article 2 is more realistic inasmuch as it says:

> Notwithstanding Article 1, the Government of the Kingdom of Bhutan may, henceforth, impose such non-tariff restrictions on the

entry into Bhutan of certain goods of Indian origin as may be necessary for the protection of industries in Bhutan. Such restrictions, however, will not be stricter than those applied to goods of third countries.

Article 4 talks of "annual consultations" in view of "free movement of goods following between the two countries and the possibility of the flow from one to the other of goods of third country origin".

Article 6 talks of such measures of restrictions as are necessary for the purposes of protecting public morals, protecting human, animal and plant life, safeguarding implementation of laws relating to import and export of gold and silver bullion and safeguarding such other interests as may be mutually agreed upon. It says, notwithstanding the foregoing provisions, either contracting party may maintain or introduce such measures or restrictions. Significantly, Article 7 states that the trade "between Bhutan and India will continue to be transacted in Bhutanese Ngultrums or Indian Rupees".[47]

Palpably, the Agreement on Trade and Commerce between India and Bhutan augurs well for institutionalized, and yet, unhindered economic interaction between them. In fact, the two countries have shown how balanced and purposeful economic and political relationships could be maintained between two countries having different political, social and cultural systems, if there is perfect trust between the two. This phenomenon, if anything, has been mutually beneficial to both these countries. And there is no reason why it should not remain so in future.

The current problems of ethnic divide and terrorism and India's role therein

What has been happening in Bhutan currently on the planes of ethnic divide and national disintegration in the names of human rights, constitutional monarchy and political pluralism has again brought India's role therein into sharp focus. Clearly, India cannot remain unaffected in or oblivious of such a situation because of its open border with Bhutan as also because of its open democratic political system—based on competitive political pluralism and the freedom of the press. But India has been rather quick and prudent to grasp this reality. The comments of its political leaders and officials have shown that they know the reality full well.

In fact, the various important political and administrative functionaries whom I met in Thimphu during October 1990 and October 1991 gave the impression that they were satisfied with the Indian leaders, perceptions of the current situation in Bhutan. Such Bhutanese leaders included:

King Jigme Singye Wangchuck, Lyonpo Dawa Tsering, dyonpo Dago Tshering, Lyonpo C. Dorji, Lyonpo Om Pradhan and Dasho Rigzin Dorji. The Royal Bhutanese Government has been apprising the Governments of West Bengal, Assam and India of the day-to-day developments and no communication gap has ever occurred.[48]

West Bengal Chief Minister Jyoti Basu paid a 4-day visit to Bhutan in response to an invitation from the King in June 1990. On his return from the mountain kingdom, Basu described his trip as "friendly and cordial".[49] During my sojourn in Thimphu in October 1991, I found Nirmal Bose, a former West Bengal Minister, visiting Bhutan and he too seemed to be veering round the view that the crisis was artificial sought to be utilized by anti-nationals and non-nationals.

The Indian Minister of State for External Affairs, Hari Kishore Singh, said on 19 October 1990 that the government would not allow the Nepalese in India to carry out an agitation against Bhutan. He made it clear that the Nepali-speaking people were free to live and work in India but "they have no political right to agitate against a friendly neighbour". More significantly, replying to a question, Singh said that the Bhutan Government was competent enough to tackle the situation arising from the agitation, launched by a section of the Nepali-speaking people living in that country. He emphasized that "those who are not citizens of Bhutan have no right to agitate against that country".[50] Relevantly, Singh denied that asylum had been granted to the agitators said to be operating from the border areas of North Bengal districts. Several thousand Nepalese were working in India, particularly in West Bengal, and they were free to do so under the Indo-Nepal Agreement, but it would be embarrassing to the Government, if they were found involved in agitations against the Bhutanese government, with which India had excellent ties, the Minister stressed.[51]

Indian Foreign Secretary Muchkund Dubey appeared more forceful. He conveyed to the Bhutanese Druk Gyalpo the Government of India's decision to provide all possible assistance, including communication and logistics, to bolster the kingdom's law and order machinery and also counter the acts of violence which shook it recently. Also conveyed to the Bhutanese monarch was the message that India was considering the possibility of opening armed outposts along the Bhutanese border to stop illegal entry of foreigners into the Kingdom. India, the Foreign Secretary said in Calcutta, was considering the proposal since it did not want the recurrence of foreigners, illegally crossing over to Bhutanese territory and engaging in acts of violence as happened recently.[52]

In an interview in Calcutta on 21 October 1990, on his way back to Delhi from Thimphu, Dubey said that he had assured the King that India would never allow its territory to be used against Bhutan. The Indian government had already initiated action against those who have engaged in such activities, besides sending back 6,000 Bhutanese of Nepalese origin, who had come across to North Bengal at the height of political turmoil.[53] Dubey further stated: "I told the King that India would not tolerate any threat being posed to Bhutan's stability and it would take prompt and effective action if Bhutan could point out that Indian territory was being used against the country's interest." Clearly, such an assertive assurance was called for and it was reassuring when it came from the Foreign Secretary of India. Dubey added: "I told the King that we had conveyed to the Nepalese settlers in India that we will not tolerate their joining any anti-Bhutan activity. The King was convinced of our best intentions and appreciative of our stand."[54]

Obviously, India does not have any doubt about its role in the matter at any level. It augurs well for the relationship between the two countries. If India has come to the rescue of states like Maldives, Sri Lanka and Nepal at one time or another, there is no reason why should it not help maintain Bhutan's integrity.[55]

Differences between Bhutan and India

By now, we have seen how Bhutan and India have shaped and developed their relations based on mutuality and maturity. We have also seen how devices like treaties, visits, economic cooperation and trade and commerce have institutionalized the relationship between the two and how they have been brought closer and closer to each other. It would be rather preposterous to expect Bhutan to agree to India's perceptions on each and every issue in regional and global politics. Not even all the states (provinces) in India—even if the governments at the centre and the states belong to the same political party—think alike on each and every issue of the national politics. Obviously, various factors are in conflict with each other between the local and the national interests. We have already seen, how Bhutan thought afresh of the 1949 Treaty at a particular point of time and how it soon realized that it was not needed. However, it would be in order to make an assessment of various problems where the two intimately friendly states differed from each other and to what effect.

It is worth mentioning that during the tenure of Shyam Nandan Mishra as the Minister for External Affairs, the relationship between the two soured, thanks to his ham-handed approach *vis-a-vis* Bhutan. For all practical purposes, Article 2 of the 1949 Treaty is now "obsolescent except for the purpose of regular consultations in which the King declares himself as an enthusiastic believer".[56] When during the differences with the Indian Foreign Minister India seemed to be insistent on the application of Article 2, Bhutan had started thinking of Article 9 of the Treaty which provides for negotiations followed by arbitration in case of difference and disputes over interpretation.

Mercifully, this prospect does not seem likely to become pronounced in the near future, for more and durable understanding has developed after the beginning of the misudnerstanding and communication gap.

Bhutan signed the Nuclear Non-Proliferation Treaty (NPT) in 1985, contrary to India's position over the issue. Many considered it as Bhutan's step to adopt an independent stand. India does not seem to have made it a prestige point: in fact, there appears to be some understanding between the two over the issue. Bhutan does not have any stake in this issue. In a personal and exclusive interviews Bhutanese Foreign Minister Dawa Tsering told me that as a Buddhist state Bhutan naturally does not believe in nuclear proliferation: hence this step.

Bhutan's support to the ousted Pol Pot regime of Kampuchea during the Havana summit of NAM in 1979 is seen as another point of difference between the two countries. Of course, that difference became quite pronounced at that time. But what should not be forgotten is the communication gap and bitterness created by the then Indian External Affairs Minister.[57]

Then, there were reports of Bangladesh's advice to Bhutan to seek a revision of the 1949 Treaty with a view to excluding its security from the purview of India. Diplomatic sources reported in Calcutta that Humayun Rashid Chowdhary, adviser to President Ershad on Foreign Affairs, and Farrukh Ahmad Chaudhury, Foreign Secretary of Bangladesh, during their stay in Thimphu in 1985, stressed the necessity for Bhutan to seek a revision of the treaty in order to take security out of its purview. In this connection, much significance was attached to the airdashing of Indian Foreign Secretary Romesh Bhandari to Thimphu and the anouncement of Indian Prime Minister Rajiv Gandhi's visit to the Hinalayan kingdom. Besides, the circles also noted the obvious extra care New Delhi took during King Jigme Singye Wangchuck's routine visit earlier in July 1985. The sources pointed out that Bangladesh had been apparently zealous in following its policy of uniting the smaller South Asian states into a composite group in order to raise their bargaining strength *vis-a-vis* India.[58]

No matter whatever the basis of this story, subsequent events have shown that no such thing has happened in Indo-Bhutan relations and their friendship has withstood such manipulations, no matter who engineered them.

On the other hand, several steps taken by Bhutan, including the rechristening of Bhutan's embassy in New Delhi as the Royal Bhutanese Embassy (1978), opening of diplomatic relations with Bangladesh (1979), a major breakthrough in the expansion of Bhutan's external contacts with the inauguration of Druk Air Service (1983), were seen by many analysts and observers as a sign of Bhutan's assertiveness *vis-a-vis* India. When in 1978, presumably at the request of the Government of Bhutan, the Bhutan Mission in New Delhi, as it was known till then, was renamed as the Royal Bhutanese Embassy. Commenting on the change in the nomenclature of the Bhutan Mission, a leading Indian daily wrote: "The revised nomenclature is not without significance, especially since it should logically lead to a qualitative change in the Indo-Bhutanese connection".[59]

It is difficult to say what qualitative change has come in the Indo-Bhutan relations. What, however, is obvious is that Bhutan has not done anything to damage India's interest in any sense of the term. In fact, whenever Bhutan and India have differed that difference has been characterized by maturity. Also, that difference has not hindered India's interest in any sense of the term. Equally importantly, it has helped Bhutan acquire an international personality of its own. Nevertheless, it has also prempted criticism that Bhutan is India's satellite.

An analyst has also seen some significance on the front of relations between Bhutan and Bangladesh and India's attitude thereto. Commenting on the presentation of credentials by Bangladesh's Ambassador to Bhutan, Sunanda K. Datta-Ray wrote in July 1981:

> It was not wholly agreeable to India which might explain why Bangladesh ambassador presented his credentials just six days before Mrs. Gandhi was sworn in last year. The Bhutanese insist that the timing was only a coincidence, and that New Delhi's response is now even more friendly and cooperative than before; but the Bhutan Bangladesh trade agreement, signed last September, had to be twice deferred because of Indian reservations.[60]

An overview

The relations between India and Bhutan have, thus, grown from maturity to maturity. The relations had their past: at times demoralization and bitterness of one party were too obvious to be brushed aside. But with the passage of time and with a variety of developments taking place in international politics, these countries have come closer to each other. The relations are, if anything, intimate, cordial and deep, not only at the government level but also at the people-to-people level. This is so mainly because a large number of Bhutanese come for school and higher-level education in India. Thanks to the paucity of manpower in *Druk-yul*, a large number of Indians—both skilled and unskilled—go to the mountain kingdom for employment.

All these have contributed to—and probably would continue to contribute to—the strengthening of relations between the big (India) and the small (Bhutan). It is also worth mentioning that it is the only state in the region without a substantial "Indian" component in its population, which is inhabited almost entirely by Tibeto-Burman speaking groups and some late 19th and early 20th centuries' immigrants from Nepal. Of course, the latter component also has in its fold immigrants from hilly India, like Darjeeling and Sikkim. Writing in 1984, I.J. Bahadur Singh, who had at one point of time in his distinguished and varied career the privilege of serving as Political Officer in Bhutan, stated that Bhutan "has about 45,000 Indian nationals of *Nepalese origin* (emphasis mine) settled contiguous to the Indian borders".[61] Singh further wrote that some of the Indians with their families "have gone to Bhutan for short-term assignments", "for a period between 2 and 3 years to serve under the Royal Government of Bhutan and other India-based organizations." "About 100 Indians including their family members mostly belonging to neighbouring State of Sikkim have taken Bhutanese citizenship".[62] Fortunately, because of Bhutan's nearness to India, no cultural aberration has confronted the Indian community in Bhutan, as has been the case with the people of Indian extraction in the countries of the Caribbean. It is believed that "if they in turn try to understand Bhutan and its people they would find them to be even more generous sometimes than their own people".[63]

This aspect of the population migration also augurs well for Bhutan-India relations. One could see for oneself at various places in Bhutan that the Indian community and the Bhutanese complement and supplement one another.

It is worthwhile to mention that even in 1926, when relations between the British Government in India and its counterpart in Bhutan were not so good, the former rose to the occasion in helping the latter. When Sir Ugyen Wangchuck, the first Druk Gyalpo of Bhutan died, in 1926, the

British government at once recognized his 21-year-old son, Jigme Wangchuck as the Druk Gyalpo. Thus the problem of succession was solved peacefully. Dorji Rapden's dream to succeed as the ruler of Bhutan remained unfulfilled. Dorji Rapden even went to Tibet to seek help, but on the advice of the Government of India Tibet refused to interfere. Had the British Government in India avoided a timely action, there was every chance of a civil war over the issue of succession.[64]

It would be unreasonable or even unthinkable to avoid a mention of Article 2 of the 1949 Treaty, while taking into account the relations between the two countries. In fact, the content of this Article had also formed part of the Treaties of 1910 and 1865 in one form or another. This provision is often cited—not illogically—as an example of India's stronger and Bhutan's weaker positions. However, even a scholar like Michael Aris feels that "the relevant clause now seems to be regarded by both parties as a colonial fragment that is best forgotten".[65] Leo E. Rose, on the other hand, opines that India has "demonstrated a greater liberality, or perhaps a greater sense of confidence, in its dealings with Bhutan, over the years agreeing to virtually every concession that a cautious and sensible Thimphu government has sought."[66] The manner in which the Western scholars like Rose and Aris have construed the provisions of Article 2 of the 1949 Treaty apparently dilutes the scope of much controversy over the issue. What has now become important is not the letters of the Treaty but the growing spirit of friendship and cooperation between India and Bhutan.

We have seen how Bhutan and India have adopted different lines on issues like the NPT and Kampuchea etc. These differences have probably been magnified by some scholars and analysts. On one of these issues, India could claim to have faced an embarrassing situation because of Bhutan's role therein. But what is forgotten in the process of laying stress on such differences is Bhutan's role in supporting India on various crucial issues. Three examples appear to be of great significance and consequence.

First, Bhutan played a commendable role in recognizing Bangladesh soon after the recognition accorded to that country by India. India's position in that matter seemed unreasonable or even untenable to many of its critics. A friendly Bhutan proved beyond doubt that it was a friend in need and deed.

Secondly, when India's position was becoming increasingly embarrassing at various regional and international fora because of its non-recognition to Nepal's proposal of the kingdom being declared and recognized a Zone of Peace, Bhutan was one of the few countries not to fall in line with others. Not less than 115 states had recognized that proposal by 1990. Much significance should be attached to Bhutan's role on this front, for the provisions of the proposal were seen as a device to, *inter alia,* strengthen the monarchy of Nepal. That a monarchical Bhutan adopted the Indian line to the chagrin of monarchical Nepal was indeed remarkable. It showed Bhutan's closeness with India.

Thirdly, by offering its land and other facilities for talks between the various militant Tamil groups, including the LTTE, of Sri Lanka and the island's government under the good offices of India in 1985, Bhutan proved beyond doubt that it can rise to the occasion, whenever India needed its help and support. Needless to state, India's position had become quite unenviable over the issue.

It is thus obvious that Bhutan-India friendship has over the years grown and matured. No segment of Bhutanese or Indian society seems to have been offended by this growth. Therein lies the test. Differences between them, if any, have always been eclipsed by the thorough understanding.

Notes and References

1. Tarun Basu, "Trouble in a Himalayan kingdom", *India Abroad,* New York, vol.22, no. 23, 6 March 1992, 25.
2. Sunanda K. Datta-Ray, "India's Closest Friend:Ancient Oath On Ties with Bhutan", *The Stateman,* Delhi, 20 July 1983, 6.
3. Michael Aris, "Bhutan: internal development and relations with outside powers to 1952", in Francis Robinson, ed., *The Cambridge Encyclopaedia of India, Pakistan, Bangladesh, Sri Lanka, Nepal, Bhutan and The Maldives,* Cambridge University Press, Cambridge, 1989, 163-64.
4. Ram Rahul, "Making Of Modern Bhutan", *International Studies,* New Delhi, vol.19, no.3, July-September 1980, 522.
5. R.C. Misra, "Bhutan-China Relations", *China Report,* Delhi, vol.17, no.2, March-April 1981, 46.
6. Ibid
7. Ibid.
8. Ram Rahul, *The Himalaya as a Frontier,* Vikas Publishing House Pvt. Ltd., New Delhi,1978, 86-87.
9. Cited in Manorama Kohli, *India And Bhutan: A Study in Interrelations 1772-1910,* Munshiram Manoharlal Publishers Pvt. Ltd., New Delhi, 1982, 209.
10 Ibid., 210.
11. Ibid., 211.
12. Ibid.
13. Cited in Ibid., 214.
14. Ram Rahul, n.8, 89.
15. See Ibid., 90.
16. Ibid., 91.

17. Ibid.
18. For the text of the 1949 Treaty see Ram Rahul, n.8, Manorama Kohli. n.9 and Nagendra Singh, *Bhutan: A Kingdom in the Himalayas,* Thomson Press India Limited, New Delhi, 1978.
19. *The Hindu*, Madras, 3 June 1960.
20. Nagendra Singh, n.18,103-107.
21. "Bhutan: Quiet Assertion", *Economic And Political Weekly,* Bombay, vol.13, no. 37,16 September 1978, 1571.
22. Interview of the Fortnight: "Jigme Singye Wangchuck: A Neighbour without problems", *India Today,* New Delhi, 1-15 March 1980,90. Also see Sunanda K. Datta-Ray, "Flight of the Dragon-I: Bhutan's Three-Pronged Strategy", *The Statesman,* 27 April 1984, 6.
23. *Indian Express,* New Delhi, 26 February 1980, 7.
24. Ram Rahul, n.8, 90.
25. Ibid.
26. Ibid., 92.
27. Srikant Dutt, "Bhutan's International Position", *International Studies,* vol.20, nos. 3-4, July-December 1981, 609.
28. Ram Rahul, n.8, 92.
29. Ibid.
30. Ibid., 93-94.
31. See Narendra Kumar, "Uneasy Lies The Head ...", *The Sunday Statesman, Miscellany.* Delhi,14 July 1991, 4.
32. Ram Rahul, n.4, 528.
33. See Sunanda K. Datta-Ray, n.21.
34. Manorama Kohli, "Bhutan's Strategic Environment: Changing Perceptions", *India Quarterly,* New Delhi, vol.42, no.2, April-June 1986,147.
35. Narendra Kumar, n.31.
36. Sunanda K. Datta-Ray, n.2.
37. Sunanda K. Datta-Ray, n.22.
38. See Nagendra Singh, n.18,153.
39. Samir Pal, "A significant upswing", *The Hindustan Times,* New Delhi, 17 December 1991,18.
40. K. Sriram, "India, Bhutan for world peace", *Indian Express,* 30 September 1985,1.
41. Ibid.
42. *The Times of India,* New Delhi, 19 October 1988,1.
43. For figures see Tarun Basu, n.1.
44. See Samir Pal, "PM: India will finance part of Bhutan Plan", *The Hindustan Times,* 1 October 1985,1.
45. Manorama Kohli, "Dragon Kingdom's Urge For An International Role", *India Quarterly,* vol.37, no.2, April-June 1981, 231.
46. Sunanda K. Datta-Ray, n.22.
47. For details see *Agreement On Trade And Commerce Between The Government Of The Kingdom Of Bhutan And The Government Of The Republic Of India.*
48. His Majesty King Jigme Singye Wangchuck and Home Minister Lyonpo Dago Tshering told me in separate interviews in October 1991 at Thimphu.
49. *The Hindu,* New Delhi, 10 June 1990, 1.
50. *The Hindustan Times,* 20 October 1990, 6.
51. *The Hindu,* 20 October 1990, 3.
52. *The Statesman,* 24 October 1990, 5. Also see *Kuensel,* Thimphu, vol. 5, no. 43, 27 October 1990, 1.

53. Ibid.
54. Ibid.
55. For a detailed study see Parmanand, "India-Bhutan Friendship and Bhutan's problem of National Integration", *Strategic Analysis*, New Delhi, vol. 13, no. 12, March 1991, 1411-24.
56. Sunanda K. Datta-Ray, n.2.
57. For a detailed study see Parmanand, "Indo-Bhutan relations in the Nineties", in M. Rasgotra, V.D. Chopra and K.P. Misra, eds, *India's Foreign Policy in the 1990s*, Patriot. Publishers, New Delhi, 1990, 325-37.
58. See *The Hindustan Times*, 17 May 1985, 10.
59. *Indian Express*, Chandigarh, 16 August 1978, cited in Manorama Kohli, n. 45.
60. Sunanda K. Datta-Ray, "Return of the Dragon-II: Challenge for Indian Diplomacy", *The Statesman*, 18 July 1981, 6.
61. I.J. Bahadur Singh, "Introduction", in I.J. Bahadur Singh, ed., *Indians in South Asia*, Sterling Publishers Private Ltd., New Delhi, 1984, 13.
62. Ibid., 14.
63. Tapash K. Roychoudhury, "Indians' Settlement in Bhutan: Their History and Problems", in Ibid., 134.
64. See R.C. Misra, n. 49.
65. Michael Aris, n. 3, 164.
66. Leo E. Rose, "India and its neighbors in the region", in Francis Robinson, ed., n. 3, 240.

9

Retrospect and Prospect

I

Thus, Bhutan or Druk-yul (the land of the Thunder Dragon) has covered long distances and made great strides in a variety of ways in attaining first the status of a society and subsequently of a state. Its advancement in various spheres has been gradual but irreversible. Ever since it achieved the status of a society, various actors came to play, one after another, significant and substantial roles in its progress and development towards a state.

The roles played by Guru Padmasambhava, Shabdung Ngawang Namgyal, Ugyen Wangchuck, Jigme Wangchuck, Jigme Dorji Wangchuck and finally, Jigme Singye Wangchuck, during the various phases of the development of Bhutan cannot and should not be overlooked. These people completely identified themselves with Bhutan and never for a moment did any of them feel that his own interests were different from those of Druk-yul. This psychological phenomenon contributed immensely to the stability and all-round progress of the small South Asian Himalayan kingdom.

We have already seen how Guru Padmasambhava showed his political and diplomatic acumen by ensuring in his days that Bhutan and India did not war, for he knew and warned of the reality that if Bhutan were to succeed, all of India would have been conquered and if India were to win, all the Bhutan would have been conquered. This warning was, in actuality, an exhortion to peace. So long as Guru Padmasambhava's advice was adhered to, there was absolutely no problem between India and Bhutan. But as soon as either of them wavered and created hostile circumstances, one party suffered immeasurably. This is evident from the 1864 battle between the two. The 1865 Treaty was quite demoralizing for Bhutan. The violation of

Guru Padmasambhava's advice made Bhutan pay dearly.

The contribution of Shabdung Ngawang Namgyal to the unification, consolidation and system-building in Bhutan would remain immortal. It was his peculiar *modus operandi* of ruling, conflict-resolution and value-distribution that protected Bhutan from various kinds of turmoil—both internal and external—for a long time. It would, perhaps, be difficult to imagine the shape Bhutan would have taken in the absence of the then renovations made by the Shabdung. So great was the impact of the Shabdung on the politics and religion of the kingdom that his disciples and supporters for a long time continued to think that he was meditating, even when he was dead. It is not for nothing that even today he is held in very high esteem and remembered with exalted feelings.

The contributions of the Wangchuck *Druk Gyalpos* to the growth and development of Bhutan after 1907—when the first King, Ugyen Wangchuck, came to occupy the throne—have been tremendous and praiseworthy. The first two Kings—Ugyen Wangchuck and Jigme Wangchuck—contributed to the consolidation of the kingdom, which was badly needed during their reigns. They did not, on the other hand, forget the modernization of Druk-yul, which had been an isolated kingdom. Of course, they were chary of not going too far and too fast. Their attempt at modernization can, therefore, be seen and assessed only in the existing context.

The third and fourth Druk Gyalpos—Jigme Droji Wangchuck and Jigme Singye Wangchuck—however, reigned and ruled at a time when political and economic modernization and secularization of political culture could have been avoided only at a great cost. Therefore, they made Bhutan move towards the goals of increased specialization and differentiation of political structures and increased secularization of political culture. Truth to tell, this again has to be viewed in the existing nitty-gritty of Bhutanese politics and the milieu of the country. But there could be little doubt about their intentions. It seems obvious that they did not wish to take Bhutan on the path of modernization because of any compulsion either at home or abroad. They were indeed enlightened and imbued with a sense of social purpose. They had an earnest desire to create a welfare and service state in the small and beautiful Himalayan kingdom. They, of course, did not wish to go too far and too fast like their predecessors. But they certainly did not wish Bhutan to trail far behind in the regional and global contexts. Their attempts and efforts are there for everyone to see.

What is perhaps of the utmost importance is that rulers like Jigme Dorji Wangchuck and Jigme Singye Wangchuck did not resort to socio-politico-economic reforms because of any compulsion—either regional or global or even national. There was absolutely no threat to their throne in any manner. As such, whatever they did on the front of meaningful reforms and decentralization were mainly, rather exclusively, because of their enlightened attitude and motive.

It would be quite in order to mention here the fact that the acceptance of responsibility at quite a young age has been a common feature of the lives of the Bhutanese kings since the establishment of the monarchy in 1907. Ugyen Wangchuck, the first Druk Gyalpo of Bhutan, accompanied his father to battle at the young age of 15, and became Paro's Penlop when he was still 20. The second Wangchuck king, Jigme Wangchuck, received high official rank at the young age of 13, was made Tongsa Penlop at 17, and was crowned as Druk Gyalpo when he was just 21. Jigme Dorji Wangchuck, the third Druk Gyalpo, received his first high official rank at 17, became Paro Penlop and heir-apparent at 21, and was crowned as Druk Gyalpo at 23. The incumbent Druk Gyalpo, Jigme Sinye Wangchuck, was made Tongsa's Penlop and heir apparent at the age of 16 and occupied the throne even before he was 17. And, yet, youth was no hindrance to the efficiency of any of the Druk Gyalpo.

It is equally important to note that despite their enlightenment and desire for reforms, the Bhutanese monarchs retained their relations with the religious milieu of the Kingdom. This is clear from the fact that the ruling Wangchuck family in Bhutan traces its lineage from one of the most renowned Lamas. While this augured well for the Wangchuck dynasty, it also helped in maintaining the importance of religion in Bhutanese life. And it is also important to mention at this place that unlike the Shah kings of Nepal—who considered themselves as the incarnation of Lord Vishnu—the Bhutanese kings have never made any such pretensions. But without their being any incarnation, the Bhutanese people have given tremendous love and affection to their kings—making them "people's kings" in every sense of the term.

While discussing the significant and substantial roles played by personalities like Guru Padmasambhava, Shabdung Ngawang Namgyal and the 4 Wangchuck kings in strengthening and stabilizing Bhutan and encouraging progress, one should not lose track of the important role played by the disciplined and dedicated people of Druk-yul. Under the leadership of various personalities from time to time, the hard-working yet contented people of Bhutan have done everything possible for the development of their country. They are full of patriotic feeling and imbued with the feeling of helping each other. This has helped the kingdom in making great strides. By and large, the Nepalese segment of the Bhutanese population has also made significant contributions in various spheres of life. The Nepalese are basically hard-working people. The present crisis may also prove shortlived as there are reports that many among the Nepalese have started looking at the futility of an unjustifiable agitation. Nor is the Bhutanese government oblivious of the genuine problems of the Nepalese in the kingdom.

It goes to the credit of Bhutan that despite all changes made in the polity and politics of the country, it has been able to retain its cultural structure intact. This is no mean achievement in this fast-changing world. It also gives to Bhutan a special position in the comity of states. And, for this reason, among other reasons, it attracts a large number of visitors every year. It may not be wrong to say that Bhutan has, to a very great extent, been able to maintain its existence and independence because it has so seriously retained its cultural salience.

Once Bhutan decided to give up its seclusion as also the existent primitive political economy, and took to modernizing its economy, it has never looked back. Thanks to India's help in creating a viable and beneficial infrastructure and tremendous aid and assistance coming from various Western countries and aid-giving agencies, Bhutan has made great strides on the plane of political economy. In fact, it has today become one of the front-ranking states in Asia in terms of the per capita income. Of course, Bhutan is more concerned about the per capita happiness than per capita income. Perhaps it has succeeded on both these counts. The current state of affairs in Southern Bhutan is an exception.

Bhutan is one country which has been able to retain and maintain its religious-cultural structure despite making great strides in its political economy. It has also very largely succeeded in retaining a very pure environment, free from pollution. Not that Bhutan has no problem on the front of political economy. It lacks both skilled and unskilled manpower, and has to look to countries like India and Nepal for the supply of manpower for various public and private works in the kingdom. This in itself creates problems from time to time, for many who come from these countries tend to overstay. Needless to say, Bhutan provides them with plenty of facilities, making their desire to overstay in that country stronger. This has resulted in a variety of problems confronting the state apparatus in Druk-yul.

If Bhutan has been able to make notable progress on the front of domestic politics and economy, it has not lagged behind in presenting itself as a noticeable personality in global politics. True, because of a variety of factors—already discussed elsewhere—Bhutan cannot play a very significant role in global politics. In fact, because of the dismemberment of the Soviet Union and wellnigh conversion of the bipolar world into a unipolar one, not even the erstwhile important powers are able to play the same significant role they once played. But by taking independent stands on a variety of issues, Bhutan has proved its mettle. More importantly and relevantly, Bhutan has also shown that it can negotiate its problems with the giant Asian state, the People's Republic of China, without establishing diplomatic relations with the latter. Equally important in this context is the fact that Bhutan has shown that it can establish working relations with China, without in any way offending India.

Once Bhutan decided to give up its age-old seclusion, it has never looked back and there is no reason why it should do so in future. In this sense, it has proved itself to be completely different from another Buddhist state in this region, i.e. Burma. Moreover, Bhutan has shown that it is alive to international trends and public opinion. Bhutan attracted the attention of the world in a positive and praiseworthy manner by inviting a team of the Amnesty International to see for itself the state of human rights in the mountain kingdom. The Amnesty was not able to find any serious fault with the Royal Bhutan Government on the plane of human rights.

True, because of economic and other reasons, Bhutan has not been able to establish diplomatic relations with a large number of countries, but it has not trailed behind in interactions with relevant countries.

II

It is now time to attempt a projection of the politics of Bhutan in future, no matter howsoever imperfect it may be.

Bhutan has been making significant and meaningful reforms on the political front since the early 1950s, and there is no reason for those being abandoned at this stage. One could visualize that there would be further attempts at increasing decentralization and accountability in the kingdom's politics. This is not something new or unknown to the power-wielders and power-holders as also hoi polloi in the kingdom. There is absolutely no reason to feel that Bhutan's political system would act against the urges and aspirations of the people in the future. The contrived problems of nation-building and state-building may be solved to the satisfaction of most of—if not all—the Bhutanese in the near future. Many straws in the wind have indicated that those who are using catchy phrases to cover their real intentions, as also criminal and corrupt activities, would come a cropper sooner than later. They seem to be losing sympathies abroad rather fast.

Not that the government at Thimphu has learnt nothing from the politics of dissent and agitation adopted by a vocal segment of the southern Bhutanese. It is bound to move with more care and caution on this front. Bhutan, it is true, lacks skilled and unskilled manpower and would continue to confront this problem for a relatively long time. But that does not mean that it can allow itself to be a haven for economic refugees *ad infinitum*. It will have to distinguish between its citizens and non-citizens and this distinction has to be institutionalized further and farther. Bhutan seems determined to do so, lest the phoney crisis of national integration recurs.

Needless to stress, Bhutan is determined to take ambitious steps in the direction of building-up a very viable and strong economy. This is obvious from the objectives set for the 7th 5-year Plan, which the kingdom is going to launch in July 1992. Bhutan has never confronted the problem of funds: in fact, its problem has been how to avoid funds. But the perennial problem of manpower is bound to confront it once again. Mentionably, Bhutan has to be more careful on this front: it has learnt a lot from the recent agitations and disturbances. One hopes it would give a good account of itself and see that economic development does not lead to the phoney problems in the way of state-building and nation-building.

There is no reason why Bhutan should not tell more and more success stories in global politics in future. Of course, the seven rounds of talks the kingdom has had with China thus far, has not resulted in the final demarcation of borders with the latter or the return of its lost enclaves. But, then, other states, including India, too, have problems with China and there is no prospect of their being solved in the immediate future. Quite expectedly, Bhutan is doing a tightrope walk with China and would continue to do so successfully in future. It may not establish diplomatic relations with China in the near future. This would stand Bhutan in good stead. If the past is any guide, China's interference in the domestic politics of a friendly country has generally resulted in serious problems. Moreover, even if India succeeds in normalizing its relations with China, it may not like its other friends to do the same *vis-a-vis* China. Bhutan probably knows this complexity and moves with the utmost care and caution on this front. It would, in all probability, continue to do so in future. By not playing the China card *vis-a-vis* India, Bhutan has already proved its diplomatic mettle.

Strange to say, the King of Bhutan is pivotal in the kingdom's politics and polity, and yet, he is treated by his people to be above politics. This is a wellnigh impossible distinction to achieve. But through his tremendous responsiveness, King Jigme Singye Wangchuck could be said to have achieved it. Even his bitterest critics are unable to find fault with his honesty, integrity and responsiveness. Maybe it is because of these qualities of the Druk Gyalpo, around whom the present political system revolves, that the system continues and will continue. One hardly comes across any example where a ruling and reigning monarch—who enjoys both power and glory—offers to abdicate for the purpose of his country's integration and developmental activities. But the King did so only recently—in October 1991. And he chose no less a place than the country's national legislature—the *Tshogdu*—to do so. The response to this offer of the King was not unexpected: the entire people felt restive: the *Tshogdu* members insisted that the King never make such statements in future.

Needless to say, the monarchy has acted as the pivot of the existing political system in Bhutan. Almost all significant reforms have emanated from it. There is no reason why it should not happen in future. What should be remembered here is the consistent focus by the King on his people, whose welfare and service are always considered by him as his main objectives. If this *modus operandi* and *modus vivendi* continue—and there is no reason for any change in this—the interests of the people and those of the monarch would be protected simultaneously. Indeed they are not different from one another, as of today. Prospects of Bhutan's all-round progress remain bright against this background.

Appendices

The Treaty of Sinchula, 1865

APENDIX 1

Article 1: There shall henceforth be perpetual peace and friendship between the British Government and the Government of Bhootan.

Article 2: Whereas in consequence of repeated aggressions of the Bhootan Government and of the refusal of that Government to afford satisfaction for those aggression and of their insulting treatment of the officers sent by His Excellency the Governor-General-in-Council for the purpose of procuring an amicable adjustment of differences existing between the two States, the British Government has been compelled to seize by an armed force the whole of the Doars and certain Hill Posts protecting the passes into Bhootan and whereas the Bhootan Government has now expressed its regret for past misconduct and a desire for the establishment of friendly relations with the British Government, it is hereby agreed that the whole of the tract known as the Eighteen Doars, bordering on the District of Rungpoor, Cooch Behar and Assam, together with the Talook of Ambaree-Fallacottah and the Hill territory on the left bank of the Teesta up to such point as may be laid down by the British Commissioner appointed for the purpose is ceded by the Bhootan Government to the British Government for ever.

Article 3: The Bhootan Government hereby agree to surrender all British subjects as well as subjects of the Chiefs of Sikkim and Cooch Behar who are now detained in Bhootan against their will, and to place no impediment in the way of the return of all or any of such persons into British territory.

Article 4: In consideration of the cession by the Bhootan Government of the Territories specified in Article 2 of this Treaty and of the said Government having expressed its regret for past misconduct, and having hereby engaged for the future to restrain all evil-disposed persons from committing crimes within British territory or the territories of the Rajahs of Sikkim and Cooch Behar and to give prompt and full redress for all such crimes which may be committed in defiance of their commands, the British Government agree to make an annual allowance to the Government of Bhootan of a sum not exceeding fifty thousand rupees (Rs. 50,000) to be paid to officers not below the rank of Jungpen, who shall be deputed by the Government of Bhootan to receive the same. And it is further hereby agreed that the payments shall be made as specified below:

On the fulfilment by the Bhootan Government of the conditions of this Treaty twenty-five thousand rupees (Rs. 25,000).

On the 10th January following the 1st payment, thirty-five thousand rupees (Rs. 35,000).

On the 10th January following forty-five thousand rupees (Rs. 45,000).

On every succeeding 10th January fifty thousand rupees (Rs. 50,000).

Article 5: The British Government will hold itself at liberty at any time to suspend the payment of this compensation money either in whole or in part in the event of misconduct on the part of the Bhootan Government or its failure to check the aggression of its subjects or to comply with the provisions of this Treaty.

Article 6: The British Government hereby agree, on demand being duly made in writing by the Bhootan Government, to surrender, under the provisions of Act VI of 1854, of which a copy shall be furnished to the Bhootan Government, all Bhootanese subjects accused of any of the following crimes who may take refuge in British dominions. The crimes are murder, attempt to murder, rape, kidnapping, great personal violence, maiming, dacoity, thugee, robbery, burglary, knowingly receiving property obtained by dacoity, robbery or burglary, cattle stealing, breaking and entering a dwelling house and stealing therein, arson, setting fire to village, house, or town, forgery or uttering forged documents, counterfeiting current coin, knowingly uttering base or counterfeit coin, perjury, subordination of perjury, embezzlement by public officers or other persons, and being an accessory to any of the above offences.

Article 7: The Bhootan Government hereby agree, on requisition being duly made by or by the authority of the Lieutenant Governor of Bengal, to surrender any British subjects accused of any of the crimes specified in the above Article who may take refuge in the territory under the jurisdiction of the Bhootan Government, and also any Bhootanese subjects who, after committing any of the above crimes in British Territory, shall flee into Bhootan, on such evidence of their guilt being produced as shall satisfy the Local Court of the district in which the offence may have been committed.

Article 8: The Bhootan Government hereby agree to refer to the arbitration of the British Government all disputes with, or causes of complaint against, the Rajahs of Sikkim and Cooch Behar, and to abide by the decision of the British Government; and the British Government hereby engage to enquire into and settle all such disputes and complaints in such manner as justice may require, and to insist on the observance of the decision by the Rajahs of Sikkim and Cooch Behar.

Article 9: There shall be free trade and commerce between the two governments. No duties shall be levied on Bhootanese goods imported into British territories nor shall the Bhootan Government levy any duties on British goods imported into, or transported through, the Bhootan territories. Bhootanese subjects residing in British territories shall have equal justice with British subjects and British subjects residing in Bhootan shall have equal justice with the subjects of the Bhootan Government.

Article 10: The present Treaty of Ten Articles having been concluded at Sinchula on the 11th day of November 1865, corresponding with the Bhootea year Shim Lung 24 day of the 9th month, and signed and sealed by Lieutenant-Colonel Herbert Bruce. C.B., and Samdojey Deb Jimpey and Themseyrensey Donai, the ratifications of the same by His Excellency the Viceroy and Governor General or His Excellency the Viceroy and Governor General-in-Council and by Their Highness the Dhurm and Deb Rajahs shall be mutually delivered within thirty days from this date.

H. Bruce, Lieut. Col.
Chief Civil and Political Officer in Dabe Nagri
In Bhootea language

This treaty was ratified on the 29th November 1865 in Calcutta by me
John Lawrence, Governor General

25th January 1866

APPENDIX 2

Proclamation of Annexation of the Doars and other Territory of Bhutan (4th July 1866)

Whereas in the Proclamation issued on the 12th November, 1864, His Excellency the Viceroy and Governor—General in Council announced his resolution of occupying permanently and annexing to British territory the Bengal Doars of Bhootan and so much of the hill territory, including the forts of Dalimkote and Dewangiree, as might be necessary to command the passes and to prevent hostile or predatory incursions of Bhootanese into the Darjeeling District, or into the plains below.

And whereas in pursuance of that resolution, the British Government, under Article II, of a Treaty concluded on the 11th day of November 1865, has obtained from the Government of Bhootan for ever the cession of the whole of the tract known as the Eighteen Doars bordering on the districts of Rungpoor, Cooch Behar, and Assam, together with the Talook of Ambaree Fallacottah and the Hill territory on the left bank of the Teesta, up to such point as may be laid down by the British Commissioner appointed for the purpose.

It is hereby declared that the territory ceded by the Bhootan Government as aforesaid is annexed to the territories of Her Most Gracious Majesty the Queen of England.

It is further declared that the ceded territory is attached to the Bengal Division of the Presidency of Fort William, and that it will accordingly be under the immediate control of the Lieutenant Governor of Bengal, but that it shall not be subjected to the general regulations.

By order of the Governor General in Council

Simla (Sd) W. Muir

The 4th July 1866 Secretary to the Government of India

APPENDIX 3

The Treaty of Punakha, 1910

Whereas it is desirable to amend Articles IV and VIII of the Treaty concluded at Sinchula on the 11th day of November, 1865, corresponding with the Bhootea year Shing Lang, 24th day of the 9th month, between the British Government and the Government of Bhootan, the undermentioned amendments are agreed to on the one part by Mr. C.A. Bell, Political Officer in Sikkim, in virtue of full powers to that effect vested in him by the Right Honourable Sir Gilbert John Elliot-Murray-Kynynmound, P.C., G.M.S.I., G.M.I.E, G.C.M.G., Earl of Minto, Viceroy and Governor General of India-in-Council and on the other part by His Highness Sir Ugyen Wangchuk, K.C.I.E., Maharaja of Bhutan.

The following addition has been made to Article IV of the Sinchula Treaty of 1865:

> "The British Government has increased the annual allowance to the Government of Bhutan from fifty thousand rupees (Rs. 50,000) to one hundred thousand rupees (Rs. 1,00,000) with effect from the 10th January 1910".

Article VIII of the Sinchula Treaty of 1865 has been revised and the revised Article runs as follows:

> "The British Government undertakes to exercise no interference in the internal administration of Bhutan. On its parts, the Bhutanese Government agrees to be guided by the advice of the British Government in regard to its external relations. In the event of disputes with or causes of complaint against the Maharajas of Sikkim and Cooch Behar, such matters will be referred for arbitration to the British Government which will settle them in such manner as justice may require and insist upon the observance of its decisions by the Maharajas named."

Done in quadruplicate at Punakha, Bhutan, this eighth day of January in the year of our Lord one thousand nine hundred and ten, corresponding with the Bhutia date, the 27th day of the 11th month of the Earth-Bird (Sa-ja) year.

C.A. Bell Political Officer	Seal of Political Officer	Seal of Dharma Raja in Sikkim

Seal of His Highness the Maharaja of Bhutan
Seal of Tatsang Lamas
Seal of Tongsa Penlop
Seal of Paro Penlop
Seal of Zhung Dronyer
Seal of Timbu Jongpen
Seal of Punakha Jongpen
Seal of Wangdu Potang Jongpen
Seal of Taka Penlop
Seal of Deb Zimpon

8th January 1910

Minto
Viceroy and Governor-General of India

This Treaty was ratified by the Viceroy and Governor-General of India-in-Council at Fort William, on the twenty-forth day of March, A.D. one thousand nine hundred and ten.

S.H. Butler

Secretary to the Government of India, Foreign Department.

APPENDIX 4

The Treaty of November 1910 Between India and Bhutan Concerning Extradition and Other Related Matters

Whereas the Government of Bhutan have applied to the Government of India for a simpler form of procedure for the mutual surrender of criminals than that at present in force, Mr. C.A. Bell, Political Officer in Sikkim, in virtue of full powers vested in him by the Right Hon'ble Sir Gilbert John Eliott-Murray-Kynynnound, P.C. G.M. S.I., G.M.I.E., G.C.M.C., Earl of Minto, Viceroy and Governor General of India, and Rai Ugyan Dorzie Bahadur, Deb Zimpen, in virtue of full powers granted to him by His Highness Sir Ugyen Wangchuk, K.C.I.E., Maharaja of Bhutan, hereby agree as follows:

(1) The British Government shall, on demand being duly made in writing by the Bhutan Government, take proceedings in accordance with the provisions of the Indian Extradition Act, 1903 (of which a copy shall be furnished to the Bhutan Government), for the surrender of all Bhutanese subjects accused of any of the crimes specified in the first schedule of the said Act who may take refuge in British territory.

(2) The Bhutan Government shall, on requisition being duly made by the Government of India, or by any officer authorised by the Government of India in this behalf, surrender any British subject, or subjects of a foreign power, whose extradition may be required in pursuance of any agreement or arrangements made by the British Government with the said Power, accused of any of the crimes, specified in the first schedule of Act XV of 1903, who may take refuge in the territory under the jurisdiction of the Bhutan Government, and also any Bhutanese subjects who, after committing any of the crimes referred to in British territory, shall flee into Bhutan, on such evidence of their guilt being produced as shall satisfy the local court of the district in which the offence may have been committed.

Done in quadruplicate at Kalimpong this twenty first day of November in the year of our Lord one thousand nine hundred and ten, corresponding with the Bhutia date the twentieth day of the second ninth month of the Iron-dog year.

C.A. Bell [Seal of the Political Officer in Sikkim]
Political Officer in Sikkim

Seal of Deb Zimpen
Hardinge of Penshurst
Viceroy and Governor General of India

This Treaty was ratified by the Viceroy and Governor General of India-in-Council at Fort William on the thirteenth day of December AD one thousand nine hundred and ten.

J.B. Wood
Secretary to the Government of India
Foreign Department

APPENDIX 5

Treaty Between India and Bhutan, 1949

The Government of India on the one part, and His Highness the Druk Gyalpo's Government on the other part, equally animated by the desire to regulate in a friendly manner and upon a solid and durable basis the state of affairs caused by the termination of the British Government's authority in India and to promote and foster the relations of friendship and neighbourliness so necessary for the well-being of their peoples, have resolved to conclude the following Treaty, and have for this purpose, named their representatives, that is to say Sri Harishwar Dayal representing the Government of India, who has full powers to agree to the said Treaty on behalf of the Government of India and Deb Zimpon Sonam Tobgye Dorji, Yang-Lop Sonam, Chho Zim Thondup, Rin-Zim Tandin and Ha Drung Jigmie Palden Dorji, representing the Government of His Highness the Druk Gyalpo, Maharaja of Bhutan, who have full powers to agree to the same on behalf of the Government of Bhutan.

Article 1: There shall be perpetual peace and friendship between the Government of India and the Government of Bhutan.

Article 2: The Government of India undertakes to exercise no interference in the internal administration of Bhutan. On its part the Government of Bhutan agrees to be guided by the advice of the Government of India in regard to its external relations.

Article 3: In place of the compensation granted to the Government of Bhutan under Article 4 of the Treaty of Sinchula and enhanced by the Treaty of the eighth day of January, 1910 and the temporary subsidy of Rupees one lakh per annum granted in 1942, the Government of India agrees to make an annual payment of Rupees five lakhs to the Government of Bhutan. And it is further hereby agreed that the said annual payment shall be made on the tenth day of January every year, the first payment being made on the tenth of January, 1950. This payment shall continue so long as this Treaty remains in force and its terms are duly observed.

Article 4: Further to mark the friendship existing and continuing between the said Governments, the Government of India shall, within one year from the date of signature of this Treaty return to the Government of Bhutan about thirty two square miles of territory in the area known as Dewangiri. The Government of India shall appoint a competent officer or officers to mark out the area so returned to the Government of Bhutan.

Article 5: There shall, as heretofore, be free trade and commerce between the territories of the Government of India and of the Government of Bhutan; and the Government of India agrees to grant the Government of Bhutan every facility for the carriage, by land and water, of its produce throughout the territory of the Government of India, including the right to use such forest roads as may be specified by mutual agreement from time to time.

Article 6: The Government of India agrees that the Government of Bhutan shall be free to import with the assistance and approval of the Government of India, from or through India into Bhutan, whatever arms, ammunition, machinery, warlike material or stores may be required or desired for the strength and welfare of Bhutan, and that this arrangement shall hold good for all time as long as the Government of India is satisfied that the intentions of the Government of Bhutan are friendly and that there is no danger to India from such importations. The Government of Bhutan, on the other hand, agrees that there shall be no export of such arms, ammunition, etc. across the frontier of Bhutan either by the Government of Bhutan or by private individuals.

Article 7: The Government of India and the Government of Bhutan agree that Bhutanese subjects residing in Indian territories shall have equal justice with Indian subjects, and that Indian subjects residing in Bhutan shall have equal justice with the subjects of the Government of Bhutan.

Article 8(1): The Government of India shall, on demand being duly made in writing by the Government of Bhutan, take proceedings in accordance with the provisions of the Indian Extradition Act, 1903 (of which a copy shall be furnished to the Government of Bhutan) for the surrender of all Bhutanese subjects accused of any of the crimes specified in the first schedule of the said Act who may take refuge in Indian territory.

(2) The Government of Bhutan shall, on requisition being duly made by the Government of India, or by any officer authorised by the Government of India in this behalf, surrender any Indian subjects or subjects of a foreign Power, whose extradition may be required in pursuance of any agreement or arrangements made by the Government of India with the said Power, accused of any of the crimes, specified in the first schedule of Act XV of 1903, who may take refuge in the

territory under the jurisdiction of the Government of Bhutan, and also any Bhutanese subjects who, after committing any of the crimes referred to in Indian territory, shall flee into Bhutan, on such evidence of their guilt being produced as shall satisfy the local court of the district in which the offence may have been committed.

Article 9: Any differences and disputes arising in the application or interpretation of this Treaty shall in first instance be settled by negotiation. If within three months of the start of negotiations no settlement is arrived at, then the matter shall be referred to the Arbitration of three arbitrators, who shall be nationals of either India or Bhutan, chosen in the following manner:

(1) One person nominated by the Government of India;
(2) One person nominated by the Government of Bhutan;
(3) A Judge of the Federal Court, or of a High Court in India, to be chosen by the Government of Bhutan, who shall be Chairman.

The judgement of this Tribunal shall be final and executed without delay by either party.

Article 10: This Treaty shall continue in force in perpetuity unless terminated or modified by mutual consent.

Done in duplicate at Darjeeling this eighth day of August, one thousand nine hundred and forty-nine, corresponding with the Bhutanese date the fifteenth day of the sixth month of the Earth-Bull year.

Harishwar Dayal
Political Officer in Sikkim

Deb Zimpon Sonam
Tobgye Dorji
Yang-Lop Sonam
Chho-Zim Thondup
Rin-Zim Tandin
Ha Durung Jigmie
Palden Dorji

APPENDIX 6

Instruments of Ratification

Whereas a Treaty relating to the promotion of, and fostering the relations of friendship and neighbourliness was signed at Darjeeling on the 8th day of August 1949 by representatives of the Government of India and of the Government of His Highness of Druk Gyalpo, Maharaja of Bhutan, which Treaty is, word for word, as follows:

The Government of India, having considered the Treaty aforesaid hereby confirm and ratify the same and undertake faithfully to perform and carry out all the stipulations therein contained.

In witness whereof this instrument of ratification is signed and sealed by the Governor-General of India.

Done at New Delhi, the 22nd day of September, 1949.

C. Rajagopalachari
Governor-General of India

Whereas a Treaty relating to the promotion of, and fostering, relations of friendship and neighbourliness was signed at Darjeeling on the eighth day of August, 1949 by Representatives of my Government and of the Government of India which Treaty is, word for word, as follows:

My Government, having considered the Treaty aforesaid, hereby confirm and ratify the same and undertake faithfully to perform and carry out all the stipulations therein contained.

In witness whereof I have signed this instrument of ratification and affixed here to my seal.

Done at Tongsa, the fifteenth day of September, 1949.

J. Wangchuck
Druk Gyalpo

APPENDIX 7

The Constitution of the National Assembly

Rules and Regulations for Assembly Meeting

His Majesty the King has been pleased to command the following Rules to be observed by the Members of the National Assembly (consisting of the Members of the Royal Advisory Council).

It is the duty of every countryman to develop this beautiful country of ours in the political and religious fields; when our country is developed then every Dzong and the people living therein will be happy and prosperous.

Our Constitution may not be as big in comparison to other countries of the world but taking into consideration the welfare and the improvement of the living conditions of the people, all the Members have agreed to take up the measures necessary so His Majesty the Druk Gyalpo graciously established the National Assembly.

It is always wiser to arrive at a decision (to improve our country) in consultation with many intellectuals than to have one single person make that decision alone. This will prove beneficial not only for contemporary times but for posterity too. The National Assembly has been established with this aim in view.

The administration will be run according to the decisions taken by the National Assembly. Due to the Grace of God and the able steps taken by our previous rulers, we have maintained the independence, and national integrity of our country. But while preserving the gem of independence, we are still backward because of lack of education. We have not been able to improve much.

Other countries of the world have achieved rapid improvement because of rapid progress in education. Under the present circumstances, we too must bring ourselves to a point equal to that of these developed nations. As such, we must place greater emphasis on national development. This must be the foremost duty of all of us.

All Members, therefore, should work in unity to improve the country keeping in mind our culture, religious heritage and traditions of the past. We must thrust aside selfish attitudes and dedicate ourselves to the task of nation building. We must learn from our past follies. With these in view, the following 18 Rules and Regulations will be followed by the National Assembly.

Rule No. 1

His Majesty will nominate Members of the Royal Advisory Council from Government servants, the Monk Body will elect its Members from the Central Monk Body and the People's Representatives shall be elected by the People.

Rule No. 2

The Identity Cards of the Royal Advisory Council will be issued by His Majesty. Identity Cards of Members from the Monk Body will be issued by the Central Monk Body, and of People's Representatives, Identity Cards will be issued by the People's Body.

Rule No. 3

Members unable to attend the National Assembly sessions due to sickness or otherwise cannot send any other person on their behalf. The Speaker must be informed of any inability to attend in writing.

Rule No. 4

In accordance with Bhutan Law Book A(12), Chapter 2, the following persons shall not be eligible for Membership of the National Assembly

(1) A person who is not a Bhutanese National.
(2) A person who is less than 25 years old.
(3) A person who is mentally disabled.
(4) A convict.
(5) A person who has served a prison sentence.

Rule No. 5

A Member shall hold office for three years but should it be necessary for the Member to be changed, an application should be made to the Speaker.

Rule No. 6

Should a Member be found unfit to serve as a Member, the Assembly may decide in favour of his removal.

Rule No. 7

The number of Assembly Members shall be decided once every five years by the Assembly itself and the number decided upon shall be fixed—no more, no less.

Rule No. 8

Election of the Speaker: The Speaker shall be elected by the National Assembly every three years. Should the Speaker be unable to attend due to sickness or any other reason, then the Assembly reserves the right to elect another Speaker.

Rule No. 9

The Speaker has full powers to maintain proper order in the Assembly hall. No Member may object against him.

Rule No. 10

The Speaker shall fix the date of sessions of the National Assembly which shall be twice a year. But in emergencies and under extra-ordinary circumstances, the Speaker, with the Royal Command of His Majesty, may convene a meeting at any time.

Rule No. 11

Every Member shall have the full right and privilege to express his thoughts in the Assembly. No rule or law can interfere with a Member's freedom of expression.

Rule No. 12

Every Member shall be equal in the National Assembly and all Members may discuss any subject till a suitable decision is reached.

Rule No. 13

No Member shall raise a subject of any nature in the Assembly which is motivated with a desire to fulfil his own or that of his relatives self-interests. Such matters will not be permitted to be discussed.

Rule No. 14

Members may not contradict or take personal advantage of any decision that has been reached by the Assembly. Should any Member attempt to find fault with the decision, to start a quarrel or take the matter to court, he shall be termed a convict and be removed not only from service but also from society and ultimately from the country.

Rule No. 15

If a Member wishes to raise a point which is for the welfare of a particular person but not a Member of the Assembly, then that Member may come to the Assembly and petition the Speaker who can grant his consent.

Rule No. 16

No Member may reveal to an outsider any secret discussions that have taken place in the Assembly.

Rule No. 17

All the proceedings of meetings, be they large or minor, shall be passed by a two-thirds majority vote.

Rule No. 18

All Assembly decisions may be changed either by the Assembly or by the King. No one else can rectify these decisions.

APPENDIX 8

Bhutanese Citizenship Act, 1977

This Bhutanese Citizenship Act, approved by the 8th meeting of Lhengyal Shungtshog held on 22nd March, 1977, was framed on the basis of the Citizenship Act of 1958.

A. Eligibility for Citizenship

1. An employee of the Government can apply for Bhutanese citizenship after completing 15 years satisfactory service in the Government.
2. Any other private people will be eligible for citizenship only after 20 years stay in Bhutan.
3. All applicants of the above categories should be able to read and write the Bhutanese language and possess knowledge of Bhutanese history. Applications from such people will only be entertained by the Minister of Home Affairs. The Home Minister shall examine such applications for Bhutanese citizenship, and refer the same, if found acceptable, to His Majesty the King.

Without the above qualifications, one need not apply for citizenship.

B. Authority to grant citizenship certificate and qualifications

Citizenship certificate will be granted only in accordance with the approval of His Majesty. It shall not be every body's right to claim Bhutanese citizenship after putting 15 years service in the Government or 20 years stay in the country, and possessing the prescribed knowledge.

2. *Disqualifications*

i) One who has committed theft, robbery and murder in his/her private capacity and has undergone imprisonment for more than six months either in this country or in any other foreign country.

ii) Anybody related or connected to a person who has acted against the three Principles (to commit any act against the country, the King and the people) of the Government.

iii) People in this category shall not be considered for citizenship even though they may possess the requisite qualifications, mentioned in para 1 to 3 of the Clause A.

3. The name of the applicant shall be registered in the Government

records as a Bhutanese citizen on the very date of the grant of the citizenship certificate or approval of His Majesty.

4. If His Majesty approves the grant of citizenship to any foreigner the applicant will be required to take an oath of allegiance from the Home Minister in the following terms:

i) From this day onwards I shall be loyal only to His Majesty, the King of Bhutan.
ii) I shall abide by the laws of Bhutan and respect the King.
iii) I shall act and do according to the customs and traditions of the Bhutanese people.
iv) I will never do anything against the three principles of the Royal Government of Bhutan.
v) It shall be my endeavour to be one of the patrons of the Religious Lord of the Drukpa Kargyud sect (of Buddhism) serve the country to the best of my abilities.

I, therefore, swear in the name of the omniscent, Protector, Maha Kala.

C. Special Requirements

However, these rules will not be applicable to any foreigners of the following categories:

i) Good writers;
ii) Good technicians;
iii) Good scientists;
iv) Good artists and any other foreigner whose services are required for the country.

Citizenship certificate will be granted, with the approval of the His Majesty, to the above category of foreigners. But the rule relating to oath of allegiance will be applicable to them as in other cases.

D. Renòuncement of citizenship

1. Any Bhutanese who once goes away from Bhutan and whose name has been deleted from relevant Government records, and wishes to apply for permission to return home, will require two years continuous service for consideration, re-registering of his/her name with the Government as citizen, if he is not a rebel. If he is found satisfactory after two years, he will be treated as a Bhutanese

citizen.

2. If a foreigner, who acquired Bhutanese citizenship, wishes to renounce his citizenship and leave the country, with members of his family, the Government will not reconsider again an application for Bhutanese citizenship. But a grown up member of the family of a foreigner, who already renounced will be allowed to do so on application for Bhutanese citizenship. The Home Minister may consider to live in Bhutan as before.
3. In the event of a crisis in the country, the Government shall not entertain any application from Bhutanese nationals, or non-nationals, who acquired citizenships, for renouncement of Bhutanese citizenship till such period is over.

E. Who is a Citizen of Bhutan?

1. If a Bhutanese lady marries a non-national only she can retain her citizenship; her husband and children will not automatically be entitled to become citizens of Bhutan. If they wish to apply for Bhutanese citizenship, they can get it under the terms and conditions applicable to other foreigners.
2. In case a Bhutanese male marries a foreigner, his children will be legitimate Bhutanese citizens whereas his wife will be treated as a non-national under this Act.

Question from the Law

A-12-II

A Bhutanese citizen will be allowed to reside in a foreign country in order to carry on any official work assigned to him/her by the Government or do private business and studies and service.

Any Bhutanese, residing and serving in a foreign country, or staying in a foreign land after winding up his/her establishment in Bhutan or living as a citizen of another country, will not be treated as a citizen of Bhutan.

How to Register?

F.1 A Bhutanese should register the birth of his child, whether born in Bhutan or in a foreign country, within one year.

2. Children born in the country should be registered in their respective office of the Dzongda or S.D.O. Children born in a foreign country should be registered in the Bhutanese Missions Abroad. In case, a child is born in a foreign land where there is no Bhutanese Mission, the Ministry of Home Affairs should be informed in

writing accordingly.

3. If one fails to register the birth of a child within a year, he should write to the Ministry of Home Affairs, through the concerned district authority giving full reasons for delay in the matter. Then the concerned district authority shall consider such cases for registration.

Authenticity of birth certificate must be affixed with the official stamp

G.1 A birth certificate should be signed by an Officer of the rank of a Dzongda or otherwise it will not be honoured.

H.1 Enquiry about certificates so far granted. The Home Minister will make an enquiry into all the citizenship certificates so far granted to non-nationals except in cases which have the approval of His Majesty and submit a report on this subject to His Majesty.

Punishment

1. A subject of His Majesty the King of Bhutan is not permitted to do or talk anything which is against the interest of the State or to have contacts or carry on business and exchange or correspondence with the enemies of the Three Principles of Bhutan.

   If a citizen of Bhutan is found guilty of such activities he shall be debarred from Bhutanese citizenship.

2. The Government may cancel a citizenship certificate granted to a person who obtained it on false statement in his/her application for citizenship.

Commencement of the Act

The Citizenship Act has come into force with immediate effect. The Citizenship Act will supersede the 1958 Act in case of dispute.

APPENDIX 9
The Bhutan Citizenship Act, 1985

This Act may be called the Bhutan Citizenship Act, 1985. It shall come into force from Twenty-third day, 4th month of Wood Bull Year of the Bhutanese calendar corresponding to 10th June, 1985. In case of conflict betwen the provisions of this Act and the provisions of any previous laws, rules and regulations relating to citizenship, the provisions of this Act shall prevail.

2. Citizenship by Registration

A person permanently domiciled in Bhutan on or before 31st December, 1958, and, whose name is registered in the census register maintained by the Ministry of Home Affairs shall be deemed to be a citizen of Bhutan by registration.

3. Residence Permit

His Majesty the King was pleased to state that the Citizenship Act had been formulated and pased by the Naational Assembly, taking into account the present and future security and stability needs of a small country like Bhutan. Therefore, all the Assembly Members must recall this decision and ensure that there are no continuous changes in the important laws and regulations of the country.

His Majesty the King was pleased to note that in accordance with the Citizenship Acts promulgated in 1958, 1977 and 1985, the children of Bhutanese men married to non-nationals prior to 1985 would be automatically eligible for citizenship. In the case of the Bhutanese women married to non-nationals, her husband and children would according to the law not be considered as citizens. His Majesty assured the National Assembly that it was not the intention of the Royal Government to separate parents and children, husbands and wives from living together. In consideration of their welfare, His Majesty suggested that non-nationals married to Bhutanese and are not eligible to citizenship according to the provisions of the existing laws, could be granted special residence permit. They would also be entitled to health, education and other social benefits extended to citizens of the country.

According to Government's statics, marriages between Bhutanese and non-nationals have taken place during the last 20 years. As the number is not small, but runs into tens of thousands, it is necessary that the Ministry of Home Affairs, Department of Census, and the respective Dzongkhags, Gups and Chimis carry out investigations to ensure that the marriages are genuine and in conformity with the law. Marriages which have taken place according to necessary procedures could be given special residence permit.

If the Royal Government does not proceed strictly in accordance to the provisions of its laws, it is likely that non-nationals may come to the conclusion that irrespective of the clear laws of the country the Government would grant citizenship once inter-marriages have taken place. Under such circumstances, landless and unemployed non-nationals may resort to arrangement of marriages with Bhutanese nationals as a means of settling down in the country. If such cases take place in large numbers, as it has happened in many other countries, the peace and stability of the country will be affected. Therefore, even the granting of the special residence permits should be limited to those married prior to coming in force of the 1985 Act and should not be applicable to any individuals married thereafter.

His Majesty the King was pleased to state that marriages between Bhutanese and non-nationals are not prohibited, so long as they are carried out fully in accordance with the Citizenship and Marriage laws of the country.

4. Foreign Nationals Who Have Land & Property in Bhutan

The Deputy Minister Ministry of Home Affairs, reported to the Assembly that foreign nationals who have acquired land and property in accordance with the laws of the country should be permitted to apply for citizenship in accordance with the 1985 Citizenship Act. Those who have acquired immovable properties illegally shall not be admissible for citizenship.

5. Bhutanese Nationals Not Included in the Census

The Deputy Minister, Ministry of Home Affairs, reported that genuine Bhutanese Nationals not appearing in the census register shall be confirmed citizenship and included in the census after thorough investigations are carried out by the Ministry of Home Affairs, the Department of Census and respective Dzongkhags and Chimis. This must be undertaken within 1989.

His Majesty the King was pleased to state that in reveiwing their records of 9 Dzongkhags, it was found that 12,103 Bhutanese nationals have not been registered in the census. Thorough investigation would be carried out on each case. Those who have not been registered due to lack of knowledge or for justifiable reasons shall be permitted to be included in the census in 1989 and shall not be subject to any sanctions. Those deliberately avoiding to appear in the census for reasons of evasion of Woola and taxes, shall be subject to penalties depending on the seriousness of their actions. Further, appropriate punishment shall also be imposed on Government officials, Gups and other defaulters responsible for deliberate exclusion of people from the census.

APPENDIX 10

Author's Exclusive Interview with His Majesty Druk Gyalpo Jigme Singye Wangchuck at Thimphu on 21 October 1991

Q.1. How much foreign hand do you see in the movement launched by the ethnic Nepalese in the name of human rights? Do you visualize any country's or government's hands therein?

A. This movement is essentially a terrorist movement started by non-national immigrants and vested interests in southern Bhutan after the Royal Government initiated its census and immigration policy in 1988 to curb illegal immigration and also directed a cadastral survey to carry out proper indentification of all landholdings in Bhutan. While slogans of human rights and democracy have been used by the anti-nationals as a platform to gain international sympathy and support, large-scale terrorist activities have been simultaneously carried out against the government and the people. There appears to be no foreign hand behind the terrorist movement at present except that the anti-nationals have been seeking the assistance and support of the government and political parties of Nepal.

Q.2. How do you view the present state of relations between the two countries—India and Bhutan?

A. India is our closest friend and neighbour. The foundation of Indo-Bhutan relations was laid by Pandit Jawaharlal Nehru and my father, Jigme Dorji Wangchuck, in the 1950s. Since then Indo-Bhutan friendship has grown and flourished. Indo-Bhutan relations today provide an excellent example of how a large country like India and a small neighbour like Bhutan can co-exist in perfect peace, harmony and friendship based on mutual trust, understanding and cooperation.

Q.3. Are you satisfied with India's *modus operandi* and *modus vivendi* during the current terrorist movement in Druk-yul?

A. We are very happy with the unstinted support, cooperation and understanding extended by the Government of India to us.

Q.4. How do you view the attitudes of India's Assam and West Bengal Governments in the midst of the current disturbances engineered by the ethnic Nepalese in Bhutan?

A. The State Governments of West Bengal and Assam have shown complete understanding of the Royal Government's position on the terrorist movement in southern Bhutan. The Royal Government is keeping in close touch with both governments.

Q.5. What has been the attitude of the Sikkim Chief Minister in this controversy as per your information?
A. The Chief Minister of Sikkim has always expressed very warm sentiments towards me. We regularly exchange New Year greetings.
Q.6. Did India have any reservations about Bhutan establishing diplomatic ambassadorial relations with Bangladesh?
A. None whatsoever. As you know, Bhutan was the second country in the world to recognise Bangladesh. India was the first.
Q.7. Is there any problem of Indian workers overstaying in Bhutan after the end of their contract?
A. Contractual obligations have always been honoured by both parties. We have had no problems with Indian workers overstaying in Bhutan. Over the past three decades, Indian experts, technicians and workers have made tremendous contributions to Bhutan's development process.
Q.8. Are some Indians helping the Nepalese agitators in Bhutan?
A. The anti-nationals have been trying their best to undermine the excellent state of Indo-Bhutan relations with wild allegations of Indians being mistreated in Bhutan. However, as there is no truth whatsover to such allegations, this ploy has not worked. The only support they have managed to get is from the local Nepali population in the Duars region.
Q.9. What is your attitude to Bhutan People's Congress and other Human Rights Organisations functioning in Nepal or India?
A. As a Buddhist, and also as a member of the United Nations, I fully support the Universal Declaration of Human Rights and I respect all genuine human rights organisations. However, so-called human rights organisations such as the People's Forum for Human Rights (PFHR), which are merely a front for terrorist outfits, must be recognised for what they are. Perhaps it was in recognition of the bad reputation earned by the PFHR due to its dubious activities that its members have recently decided to make a cosmetic change and rename it the Human Rights Organisation of Bhutan.
Q.10. Has the Royal Government received any advice or suggestion in the form of letters/memoranda etc. from any reckonable leader of Nepal?
A. No. We have not received any such communication.
Q.11. Do you think that the genuine Southern Bhutanese (or ethnic Nepalese) have any genuine problems at all? If you think they really have some problems, how do you propose to go about their solution? For instance, Your Majesty's interviews to a section of the Indian

media had revealed the under-representation of the Nepalese in the *Tshogdu?*

A. I was fully aware that our people in southern Bhutan would face certain inconveniences with the promotion of the national dress and language. I had therefore repeatedly made it clear in all my public meetings that it was not necessary to choose "gho" and "kira" as the national dress as any dress that was different from those of other countries and could project a distinct Bhutanese identity was perfectly all right. However, our people in the south themselves chose to promote "gho" and "kira" as the national dress both during my public meetings with them and in the National Assembly. I still encouraged certain modifications in the dresses to make it more suitable during the hot summer months. Materials for the dresses were procured by the Royal Government and supplied to the people at subsidised prices.

We also took steps to remove the genuine problems of Southern Bhutanese who were married to non-nationals. All non-nationals married to bona fide Bhutanse have been given the Special Residence Identity Card which gives them permanent residence in Bhutan and practically all the rights and priviliges of citizenship. The Royal Government also registered and granted citizenship to 12,103 genuine Southern Bhutanese who had been left out from the previous census records.

Regarding representation in the National Assembly, I certainly agree that a careful review is necessary. Of course, it should also be kept in mind that the National Assembly was instituted in 1953 and the Southern Bhutanese were granted citizenship only in 1958 during its 11th Session. When the representation of the Southern Bhutanese was fixed at that time, the population in Southern Bhutan was considerably less than it is today. As their population has increased substantially since then, there is a case for reviewing the representation of the Southern Bhutanese in the National Assembly.

Q.12. What is the latest on the execution of the dress norms: gho and kira?

A. The national dress is required to be worn by Bhutanese citizens while visiting Dzongs, monasteries, government offices and institutions in the country and during formal functions.

Q.13. What is the recent controversy about the No-Objection Certificate?

A. The No-Objection Certificate was introduced in connection with transfer of students to other schools and appointments to new jobs. It applies to all Bhutanese equally. It was felt necessary, in the wake of the large-scale violence and terrorism unleashed last year, to ensure that persons having direct connections with known anti-nationals and terrorists are not given employment in sensistive posts or the opportunity to subvert fellow students in educational institutions.

Q.14. What is the state of inter-ethnic marriages in Bhutan especially in the light of the recent controversy?

A. Inter-marriages between Nothern and Southern Bhutanese had been encouraged with cash incentives of Nu. 10,000 to promote national integration. However, this programme has not been very successful.

Q.15. What is the state of ethnic Nepalese being encouraged to settle in other parts of the country?

A. The Royal Government encouraged Southern Bhutanese to settle in Northern Bhutan with incentives of land, cash and agricultural assistance. However, this effort at promoting national integration was not successful.

Q.16. What is the state of representation of the Nepalese in the Bhutanese police, army and bureaucracy? It is alleged that even though there is some representation, they are kept away from the decision making process.

A. The representation of the Southern Bhutanese in the police is about 22%, in the army about 25% and in the civil services about 40%. Many of them occupy senior posts and they are fully involved in all aspects of policy formulation and decision-making.

Q.17. What is the state of discipline in the Bhutan army and police?

A. The discipline and morale of both forces are very good.

Q.18. What is the relationship of the Bhutanese army with the Indian army?

A. The Indian Army has played a crucial role in the establishment and training of the Royal Bhutan Army. The Indian Army extends generous budgetary, logistic and training assistance to the RBA. The close friendship, understanding and cooperation between the Indian Army and the Royal Bhutan Army reflects the excellent state of relations between the two countries.

Q.19. What are your hobbies?

A. I like outdoor life and reading.

Q.20. What kind of books, journals or newspapers does Your Majesty like to read?

A. I read several leading Indian newspapers and magazines as well as some international periodicals. The books I read are mostly on politics, biographies and topical issues.

Q.21. What are the games that you enjoy and participate in?

A. Earlier I used to play golf and tennis. These days I play basketball for exercise.

Q.22. What are the foods that you like?

A. I have no particular favourite among Indian, continental, Chinese or Bhutanese cuisine.

Q.23. Is the Crown Prince also the Penlop of Tongsa? What was the significance of this when you were given this office before becoming the Druk Gyalpo?

A. The Crown Prince is normally conferred with the position of Tongsa Penlop when he comes of age. In my case, my father made me Tongsa Penlop when I was sixteen, less than a year before he died.

Q.24. How was the late Chogyal of Sikkim related to you?

A. The late Chogyal's father and my maternal grandmother were brother and sister.

Q.25. How does the Royal Government of Bhutan look at the Dalai Lama? Has he ever visited Bhutan?

A. The Bhutanese people deeply respect His Holiness the Dalai Lama as the reincarnation of Chenrezi the Bodhisatva of Compassion. He is traditionally considered the spiritual and temporal ruler of Tibet. His Holiness has not yet visited Bhutan.

Q. 26. How much does the state pay for the welfare or maintenance of the Buddhist monks in the kingdom?

A. Over the years, all the monastic centres in the country had acquired large tracts of lands and big herds of cattle and yaks that were donated by devotees. Between 1982 and 1984, the Monk Body surrendered these lands and animals to the government for distribution to needy and landless people. The Royal Government in turn gave cash compensation to the Monk Body for their noble gesture. This cash was then invested in various industrial projects. The returns from these investments are being used today to meet the everyday requirements of the Monk Body. The Royal Government subsidises whatever shortages are faced by the Monk Body from time to time.

Q.27. What is the latest outcome of the border talks between Bhutan and the People's Republic of China?

A. The boundary talks between China and Bhutan have reached an advanced stage. We have not encountered any serious problems so far. We are hopeful that the boundary talks will be concluded to the mutual satisfaction of both countries in the near future.

Q.28. You used to state stressfully in the early 1980s that your work has been reduced by 50%. Do you still hold the view in the present situation?

A. I have always endeavoured to decentralise the system of government in Bhutan. The Royal Civil Service Commission and District Development Committees in all the 18 districts of the country were established in the early 1980s. This greatly reduced the work load for all of us in the capital. This year, I have relinquished the Chairmanship of the Planning Commission. Gewog Yargye Tsohogpas (block development committees) have also been instituted this year to achieve further decentralisation and even greater participation of the people in the decision-making and planning process. Of course, the situation in Southern Bhutan today has brought more concern and responsibility to all of us.

Q. 29. How often are you present at the sittings of the *Tshogdu?*

A. I attend the National Assembly as often as possible and am present at most of the sittings.

Q.30. How often do you intervene in the discussions in the Tshogdu?

A. I do not intervene as such in the debates but participate in the discussions like any other member.

Q.31. Have you ever been criticised by the Tshogdu for any action or decision?

A. This normally does not happen. However, in the 69th session of the National Assembly, the members expressed strong reservations about the granting of amnesty to people involved in anti-national activities and they requested me not to grant amnesty to such people in future. In the 70th session which concludes tomorrow, I was taken to task for having granted amnesty to over 800 people arrested for anti-national activities since the 69th session. I also faced tremendous pressure from the majority of the National Assembly members to take a much stronger stand against the anti-nationals.

Q.32. What feeling do you get when you visit Southern Bhutan nowadays?

A. I have been visiting Southern Bhutan often. The feeling I get when I go there is one of deep sorrow and regret that all my personal efforts to bring our people in the south into the national mainstream has not succeeded. I feel very sad to see that many of the schools had to be closed down because of terrorist activities and that large numbers of the service facilities built at great cost have been destroyed. I view the situation in the south as a personal failure.

Q.33. With a view to paying the Southern Bhutanese in their own coin, would you think of allowing political parties and human rights groups to function in Bhutan?

A. I have always said that the future of Bhutan lies in the hands of the Bhutanese people. If the people feel there is a need for human rights groups or political parties or constitutional monarchy, it is for them to decide. As the King, my main concern and cherished wish is to ensure that the security and well-being of Bhutan will always be fully safeguarded. For me, the interest of the nation always comes first.

Bibliography

BOOKS

A. Dictionaries, Encyclopaedias and Atlases

Chambers English Dictionary, Allied Publishers Limited, New Delhi, 1991.

Collins Cobuild English Language Dictionary, Collins, London and Glasgow, 1988.

Laqueur, Walter, ed., *A Dictionary of Politics*, Pan Books Ltd., London, 1973.

Manorama Year Book 1991, Malayala Manorama, Kottayam, Kochi, Thiruvananthapuram, 1991.

Mini Atlas of the World, John Bartholomew & Son Ltd., Edinburgh, n.d.

Pears Cyclopaedia: 1982-83 (Ninenty-first edition), Pelham Books, London, 1982.

Roberts, Geoffrey K., *A Dictionary of Political Analysis*, Longman, London, 1971.

Robinson, Francis, ed., *The Cambridge Encyclopedia of India, Pakistan, Bangladesh, Sri Lanka, Nepal, Bhutan And The Maldives*, Cambridge University Press, Cambridge, 1989.

Scruton, Roger, *A Dictionary Of Political Thought*, Pan Books in association with the Macmillan Press, London, 1982.

The Atlas of Mankind, Mitchell Beazley, London, 1982.

The Blackwell Encyclopaedia of Political Institutions, Basil Blackwell Ltd., Oxford, 1987.

The Concise Oxford Dictionary Of Current English,(Eighth Edition), Oxford University Press, Delhi, 1990.

The New Lexicon Webster's Dictionary Of The English Language: Deluxe Encyclopedic Edition, Lexicon Publications, Inc., New York, 1987.

The Pan/Macmillan Encyclopaedia, Pan Books, London, 1989.

The Reader's Digest Great World Atlas, The Reader's Digest Association, London, 1984.

B. Government Publications

Agreement On Trade And Commerce Between The Government Of The Kingdom Of Bhutan And The Government Of The Republic Of India, Bengal Secretariat, *Political Mission To Bhootan*, Calcutta, 1864.

Central Statistical Office, Planning Commission, Royal Government of Bhutan, *Statistical Yearbook Of Bhutan*, Thimphu, 1989.

Department of Education, Ministry of Social Services, Royal Government of Bhutan, *A History Of Bhutan: 15th to 19th Century* (Course Book For Class VII), Thimphu, 1990.

Department of Information, *Anti-National Activities In Southern Bhutan: A Terrorist Movement*, n.p., 1991.

Department of Information, Ministry of Development, Royal Government of Bhutan, *Our Beloved King* (A Collection Of Speeches delivered by His Majesty Jigme Singye Wangchuck), Thimphu, 1979.

Facts On The Situation In Bhutan (Circulated by the Royal Government of Bhutan), n.p., n.d.

Planning Commission, Royal Government of Bhutan, *Bhutan: Round Table Meeting, 1992*, Planning Commission, Thimphu, 1991.

—— *Seventh Five Year Plan (1992-1997) Vol.I Main Plan Document*, Planning Commission, Thimphu, 1992.

Royal Government of Bhutan, Ministry of Foreign Affairs, SAARC Division, *Major Statements Made By Bhutanese Delegations On SAARC 1981-1991*, Thimphu, 1991.

Royal Government of the Kingdom of Bhutan, *Bhutan: Himalayan Kingdom*, Thimphu, 1979.

UNDP Development Cooperation Bhutan 1987 Report, Thimphu, 1988.

C. Others

Abrol, Mridula, *British Relations With Frontier States*, New Delhi, 1974.

Almond, Gabriel A., and Powell Jr., G. Bingham, *Comparative Politics: A Developmental Approach*, Amerind Publishing Co. Pvt. Ltd., New Delhi, 1975.

Appadorai, A. and Rajan, M.S., *India's Foreign Policy and Relations*, South Asian Publishers Private Ltd., New Delhi, 1985.

Aris, Michael, *Bhutan: The Early History of a Himalayan Kingdom*, Warminster and New Delhi, 1979.

——, *Views Of Medieval Bhutan: The Diary and Drawings of Samuel Davis, 1783*, London, Washington, D.C., and New Delhi, 1982.

[Bhutan] National Democratic Party Ideology, Manifesto And Organization Structure, n.p.,1992.

Bonn, Gisela and Wirsing, Giselher, *India And The Subcontinent: An Introduction To India, Pakistan, Bangladesh, Nepal, Sikkim, Bhutan*, Oxford & IBH Publishing Co., New Delhi, 1974.

Coelho, V.H., *Sikkim and Bhutan*, Indian Council of Cultural Relations, New Delhi, 1967.

Collister, Peter, *Bhutan and the British*, Serivedia, London, 1987.

Das, Nirmala, *The Dragon Country*, Orient Longman, New Delhi, 1973.

Deb, Arbinda, *Bhutan and India: A Study in Frontier Political Relations*, Firama K.L.M. Print Ltd., Calcutta, 1976.

Derbyshire, J. Denis and Derbyshire, Ian, *Political Systems ofThe World*, Allied Publishers Limited, New Delhi, 1990.

Dorji, Dasho Rigzin, *A Brief Religious Cultural And Secular History Of Bhutan*, The Asia Society Galleries, New York, 1989.

Dutt, V.P., *China's Policy: 1958-62*, Asia Publishing House, Bombay, 1964.

Edmunds, Tom Owen, *Bhutan: Land of the Thunder Dragon*, London, 1988.

Gupta, Shantiswarup, *British Relations With Bhutan*, Panchsheel Prakashan, Jaipur, 1974.

Hasrat, Bikrama Jit, *History of Bhutan: Land Of the Peaceful Dragon*, Education Department, Royal Government of Bhutan, Thimphu, 1980.

Hickman, Katie, *Dreams of the Peaceful Dragon: A Journey into Bhutan*, London, 1987.

Karan, Pradyumna P., *Bhutan: A Physical and Cultural Geography*, Lexington, Ky, 1967.

——, Jenkins Jr.,William M., *The Himalayan Kingdom: Bhutan, Sikkim and Nepal*, Princeton,1963.

Kohli, Manorama, *India And Bhutan: A Study in Interrelations 1772-1910*. Munshiram Manoharlal Publishers Pvt. Ltd., New Delhi, 1982.

Kolmas, Josef, *Tibet and Imperial China: A Survey of Indo-Tibetan Relations to the End of the Manchu Dynasty in 1912*, ANU *Canberra, 1967*.

Kyi, Aung San Suu, *Let's Visit Bhutan*, Burke Publishing Company Limited, London, 1985.

Labh, Kapileshwar, *India And Bhutan,* Sindhu Publications Ltd., New Delhi, 1974.

Mehra, G.N., *Bhutan: Land of the peaceful Dragon,* Vikas Publishing House, Delhi, 1974.

Menon, K.P.S., *China: Past And Present,* Asia Publishing House, Bombay, 1968.

Morgenthau, Hans J., *Politics Among Nations: The Struggle for Power and Peace*(fifth edition), Scientific Book Agency, Calcutta, 1976.

O'Malley, L.S.S., *Bengal District Gazetteers Darjeeling*, Logos Press, New Delhi, 1989.

Parmanand, *Political Development In South Asia,* Sterling Publishers Private Limited, New Delhi, 1988.

People's Forum For Human Rights, Bhutan, *Bhutan: Cry For Human Rights,* n.p., n.d.

Phadnis, Urmila, Muni, S.D., and Bahadur, Kalim, eds., *Domestic Conflicts In South Asia:vol.2:Economic and Ethnic Dimensions,* South Asian Publishers, New Delhi,1986.

Pommaret, Francoise, *An Illustrated Guide To Bhutan: Buddhist Fort Of The Himalayas,* The Guidebook Company, Hongkong, 1990.

Pommaret - Imaeda, Francoise and Imaeda, Yoshiro, *Bhutan: A Kingdom of the Eastern Himalayas,* Time Books International, New Delhi,1989.

Rahul, Ram, *Modern Bhutan,* Vikas Publications, Delhi, 1971.

——, *Royal Bhutan,* Motilal Banarsidars, Delhi, 1983.

——, *The Himalaya as a Frontier,* Vikas Publishing House Pvt.Ltd., New Delhi, 1978.

——, *The Rise of Nepal and Bhutan,* New Delhi, 1984.

Rasgotra, M., Chopra, V.D. and Misra, K.P., eds., *India's Foreign Policy in the 1990s,* Patriot Publishers, New Delhi, 1990.

Rathore, L.S., *The Changing Bhutan,* Jain Brothers, New Delhi, 1971.

Rennie, D.F., *Bhootan and the Story of the Dooar War,* London, 1866.

Rose, Leo E., *The Politics of Bhutan,* Cornell University Press, Ithaca, 1977.

Russell, Bertrand, *Power: A New Social Analysis,* George Allen & Unwin Limited, London, 1946.

Rustomji, Nari, *Bhutan: The Dragon Kingdom in Crisis,* Oxford University Press, Delhi, 1978.

——, *Enchanted Frontiers: Sikkim, Bhutan and India's North-Eastern Borderlands,* Oxford University Press, Bombay, 1971.

Sherubtse College, Kanglung, *Bhutan And Its Natural Resources,* Vikas Publishing House Pvt. Ltd., New Delhi, 1991.

Singh, Amar Kaur Jasbir, *Himalayan Triangle:A Historical Survey Of British India's Relations With Tibet. Sikkim and Bhutan, 1765-1950,* London, 1988.

Singh, I.J. Bahadur, ed. *Indians In the South Asia,* Sterling Publishers Private Ltd., New Delhi,1984.

Singh, Nagendra, *Bhutan: A Kingdom In The Himalayas,* (Revised second edition), Thomson Press India Limited, New Delhi, 1978.

Sinha, A.C., *Bhutan—Ethnic Identity and National Dilemma,* Reliance Publishing House, New Delhi,1991.

The Gurkha People Of Southern Bhutan Must Unite And Fight For Our Rights, n.p., n.d.

Third World Studies Centre, *Bhutan:Violations of Human Rights,* New Delhi, n.d.

White, J. Claude, *Sikkim and Bhutan: Twenty-One Years on the North-East Frontier, 1887-1908,* London, 1909.

ARTICLES

"A profile", *The Hindustan Times,* New Delhi, 17 December 1991, 21.

Abdi, S.N.M., "Rumblings of Discontent", *The Illustrated Weekly of India,* Bombay, 4-10 November 1990.

Aiyar, Swaminathan S. Anklesaria, "Anguished voices of a double tragedy," *The Sunday Times of India,* New Delhi, 7 October 1990, 17.

——, "Bloodshed In Bhutan-I: Simmering ethnic fury in Shangri-la", Ibid., *The Times of India,* New Delhi, 5 October 1990, 1-6.

——, "Bloodshed In Bhutan-II: King willing to hold talks with dissidents", Ibid., 6 October 1990, 9.

Anil, R.N.,"Bhutan's Dilemma", *Unity International,* New Delhi,vol.15, no.4, April 1991, 5.

——, "Bhutan's dilemma", *The Hindustan Times,* 17 December 1991,18.

——, "Mountain Shangri-la Bhutan:A Voyage of Friendship", *Unity International,* vol.15, no.4, April 1991,1-3.

——, "The Kings Of Bhutan", *The Hindustan Times,* 21 February 1985, 9.

Aris, Michael, "Bhutan: Internal development and relations with outside power to 1952", in Robinson, Francis, ed., op. cit., 161-64.

"Assurance on Bhutan" (editorial), *The Statesman,* Delhi, 26 October 1990, 6.

Bardoli, Utpal, "Human Rights in Bhutan-I: The issue has been grossly exaggerated", *Deccan Herald,* Bangalore, 1 June 1990, 1.

——, "Human Rights in Bhutan-II: Gorkha expansionism behind the furore", Ibid., 2 June 1990, 1.

Basu, Tarun, "Trouble in a Himalayan Kingdom", *India Abroad,* New York, vol. 22, no. 23, 6 March 1992, 25.

"Battle of Bhutan" (editorial), *The Statesman,* 3 October 1991, 6.

Bhanumathy, K.P., "Bhutan: Some Impressions", *Mainstream,* New Delhi, 18 August 1990, 25-26.

Bhattacharji, Romesh, "Bhutan: The land of the dragon", *Frontline,* Madras, 14 May 1988, 53-75.

"Bhutan and India Strengthen Economic Ties", *Unity International,* vol. 15, no. 4, April 1991, 9.

"Bhutan officials extradition sought", *The Times of India,* 11 September 1991, 9.

"Bhutan: Quiet Assertion", *Economic and Political Weekly,* Bombay, vol. 13, no. 37, 16 September 1978, 1571.

"Bhutan Under Siege" (editorial), *The Statesman,* 26 September 1990, 6.

"Bhutan's bid to save Shangri-la image", *The Hindu,* New Delhi, 24 February 1991, 21.

"Bhutan's latest philatelic marvel", *The Statesman,* 11 March 1992, 8.

"Bhutanese influx posing problems", Ibid., 24 January 1991, 5.

Biswas, Soutik, "Bhutan: Shattered Silence", *India Today,* New Delhi, 31 December 1991, 177-80.

——, "Refugee Camps: Tales of Terror", Ibid., 177.

"Bloodshed in Bhutan" (editorial), *The Times of India,* 27 September 1990, 8.

Bose, Shikha, "Anti-ULFA Drive: Bhutan Wary of Joining in", Ibid., 28 January 1992, 4.

Breetveld, Jim, "Bhutan: Land of the Peaceful Dragon", *The Illustrated Weekly of India,* 30 January 1977, 36-39.

Chadha, Kumkum, "Bhutan: The tremors within", *The Hindustan Times Magazine,* New Delhi, 17 November 1991, 1.

——, "Drukpa Banam Nepali: Bhavisya Ke Garbh Men Palta Toofan", *Saptahik Hindustan,* New Delhi, 1 December 1991, 12.

——, "We are not fighting for the throne" (being an interview with King Jigme Singye Wangchuck), *The Hindustan Times Magazine,* 17 November 1991, 2.

Chakrabarti, Ashis, "Bhutan stir shadow in Darjeeling", *The Hindustan Times,* 5 May 1991, 19.

Chaudhuri, Kalyan, "A Captive ruler: Peace intrigues in restive Bhutan," *Frontline,* 6 December 1991, 30-32.

Chophel, Karma, "Democrats' Terror In Bhutan", *The Statesman,* 15 January 1991, 6.

Choudhury, Savitri, "Democracy for dragon kingdom", *The Sunday Times of India,* 16 February 1992, 14.

Clad, James, "Bhutan I: Nepali threatens the hermit kingdom: The kukris edge", *Far Eastern Economic Review,* 20 December 1990, 22-25.

——, "Bhutan 2: Monarch stresses dialogue to resolve conflict:The King speaks out", Ibid., 26.

Das, B.S., "Economic Development and Social Change in Bhutan", in Phadnis, Urmila, Munis, S.D., and Bahadur, Kalim, eds., op. cit., 82-99.

Datta-Ray, Sunanda K., "Diplomatic Realism: New Look At Aims Aboard", *The Sunday Statesman,* 21 July 1991, 6.

——, "Druk Past & Present-I: Catching Up With The 20th Century", Ibid., 10 July 1983, 6.

——, "Druk Past & Present-II: Strategies For Survival", *The Statesman,* 11 July 1983, 6.

——, "Flight Of The Dragon-I: Bhutan's Three-Pronged Strategy", Ibid., 27 April 1984, 6.

——, "Flight Of The Dragon-II:Challenge Of Settlement With China", Ibid., 28 April 1984, 6.

——, "India's Closest Friend:Ancient Oath On Ties With Bhutan", Ibid., 20 July 1983, 6.

——, "Influx By Treaty: Pressure Of Nepal's Diaspora", *The Sunday Statesman,* 6 October 1991, 6.

——, "Return Of The Dragon-I: Bhutan Prepares To Talk To China," *The Statesman,* 17 July 1981, 6.

——, "Return Of The Dragon-II: Challenge For Indian Diplomacy", Ibid., 18 July 1981, 6.

——, "Return Of The Dragon-III: Economic Progress Without Hurrying", Ibid., 20 July 1981, 6.

——, "The Phoney Crisis: Propaganda War Against Bhutan", Ibid., 2 September 1990, 6.

Desmond, Edward W., "Stirrings in the Himalayas: Stony look tranquility is shattered by ethnic and political unrest", *Time*, 29 October 1990,13.

Dutt, Srikant, "Bhutan's International Position", *International Studies,* New Delhi, vol. 20, nos. 3-4, July-December 1981,601-23.

——, "Scholarship On Bhutan", *China Report,* Delhi, vol, 17,no.5., September-October 1981,58-62.

"Gair Bhutananion Ke Dwara Hamarae Upar Rajnaitik Badlao Thope Nahin Ja Sakte:Bhutan Naresh", *Saptahik Hindustan,*1 December 1991,12.

Ghosh, Manash, "Bhutan's survival at stake:Tsering"(an interview with Foreign Minister Lyonpo Dawa Tsering), *The Sunday Statesman,* 26 June 1992,10.

Gupta, Anish, "Destination:Unknown: Bhutanese refugees languish without hope in Nepal", *Sunday,* Calcutta, 8-14 March 1992, 26-27.

——, "Inside Bhutan: An ethnic bomb is ticking away in the Himalayan kingdom", Ibid., 22-27.

Gupta, RAkesh, "Small not smaller is beautiful", Link, New Delhi, 29 September 1991, 20-23.

"Interview of The Fortnight:Jigme Singye Wangchuck:A Neighbour Without Problems", *India Today,* 1-15 March 1980, 90.

Katyal, K.K., "Ties with neighbours:positive signs", *The Hindu,* 30 December 1991,8.

Kohli, Manorama, "Bhutan's Strategic Environment:Changing Perceptions", *India Quarterly,* New Delhi, vol.42, no.2, April-June 1986, 142-53.

——, "Chinese Interest In Bhutan: Evolution Of the British Indian Perspective", *China Report,*vol.19, no.4,July-August 1983, 37-45.

——, "Dragon Kingdom's Urge For An International Role", *India Quarterly,* vol.37.no.2, April-June 1981, 227-49.

Kottary, Sailesh, "The Last Shagri-la", *The Illustrated Weekly Of India,* 20 October 1985, 44-45.

Kumar, Arun, "Bhutan:Shant Ghati Men Vikas Ki Halchal", *Ravivar weekly,* Calcutta, 7 May 1978, 20-23.

Kumara, D.P., "Appeal to Bhutan terrorists", The Statesman 14 October 1990, 7.

——, "Bhutan Today-I: Road to two countries two peoples", Ibid., 25 October 1990,1-8.

——, "Bhutan Today-II: Terrorists disguised as democrats:", Ibid., 26 October 1990, 7.

——, "Fear still haunts South Bhutan", Ibid; 18 October 1990,1-9.

——, "Warning to Bhutan terrorists", Ibid., 13 October 1990, 1-7.

Kumar, Narendra, "Uneasy Lies The Head....," *The Sunday Statesman Miscellany,* Delhi, 14 July 1991, 4-5.

Labh, Kapileshwar, "Bhutan's International Position Prior to 1947", *International Studies,* vol.13,no.1, January-March 1974.

——, "King And Country-I: Why Bhutan Needs Peace", *The Statesman,* 4 January 1991, 6.

——, "King And Country-II:Need For Drukpa-Nepalese Unity", Ibid., 5 January 1991,6.

——, "Monarchical System Of Bhutan:Challenges Of Modernization", in Phadnis, Urmila, Muni, S.D., and Bahadur, Kalim,eds., op cit., 182-95.

Mazumdar, Sundip, "Bhutan: Once upon a time: There was a nice king", *Newsweek,* 18 June 1990, 21.

Menon, Ritu, "Bhutan:the dragon stirs", *Indian Express,* New Delhi, 17 September 1991,8.

Misra, R.C., "Bhutan-China Relations", *China Report,* vol,17, no.2, March-April 1981, 43-50.

——, "Scholarship On Bhutan", Ibid., vol. 18, no.4, July-August 1982, 59-61.

——, "Tibetans in Bhutan: Problem of Repatriation", Ibid.,vol.18, no.5, September-October 1982, 25-32.

Nanda, Prakash, "Foreign Affairs: Is Bhutan likely to do a Nepal on India?" *The Times Of India,* 11 May 1989, Agenda-3.

Nerayan, Hemenddra, "Bhutanese refugees in Nepal: Caught between frying pan and fire", *India Expres,* 19 February 1992,12.

"Our neighbour, Bhutan"(editorial), *Patriot,*New Delhi, 5 November 1991.

"Outlawed Bhutan Congresh resurfaces", *Sunday Mail,* New Delhi, 6 October 1991, 2.

Pal, Samir, "A significant upswing", *The Hindustan Times,* 17 Deacember 1991,18.

——, "Bhutan's cultural dilemma", Ibid.,17 September 1990,13.

——, "PM: India will financae part of Bhutan plan", Ibid., 1 October 1985.

Pandey, Kedar Nath, "Bhutan Today:anguished voices of a double tragedy", *Alive,* New Delhi, June(Second) 1991, 20-22.

Parekh, Navnit, "A Journey Through Bhutan", *The Illustrated Weekly of India,* 1 April 1979, 29-31.

Parmanand, "Bhutan:Badrang Hota Chehra", *Hindustan Ravivasariya,* New Delhi, 16 December 1990, 6.

——, "Bhutan Ka Rajnaitik-Arthik Paridrishya", *PTI Feature,* Bombay 528kh, November 1991.

——, "Bhutan Men Rajnaitik Halchal ", *PTI Feature,* 29kh, December 1990.

——, "Bhutan: Misguided discontent", *Patriot,* 16 November 1990,4.

——, "Bhutan: Monarchy, Modernization and Internationalization", *Rising Nation,* New Delhi, vol,2,issue 5, May 1987, 56-59.

——, "Bhutan: Phoney Crisis of Integration", *The Times Of India,* 20

November 1991, 6.

——, "Bhutan suffers interference", *Link*, 10 November 1991, 17-18.

——, "China-Bhutan Varta Ka Arth", *Dainik Hindustan*, New Delhi, 2 July 1987, 6

——, "Dakshin-Bhutan Ki Rajnaitik Halchal Ko Nepali Netaon Ki Shah", Ibid., 21 December 1990, 6.

——, "Friendly Neighbours: India And Nepal Come Closer", *The Statesman*, 17, December 1991,7.

——, "India-Bhutan Friendship and Bhutan's Problem of National Integration", *Strategic Analysis*, New Delhi, vol.13, no.12, March 1991, 1411-24.

——, "Indo-Bhutan Relations in the Nineties", in Rasgotra, M., Chopra, V.D., and Misra, K.P.,eds.,op. cit., 325-37.

——, "Rashtriya Ekta Ka Kritrim Sankat", *Yugvarta Feature*, New Delhi, vol.24,no.135,28 November 1990.

Parmar, Suresh Kumar, "Bhutan Men Chhota Tibet Panap Raha Tha", *Ravivar* weekly, 4 March 1979, 19-20.

Phadnis, Urmila, "Ethnic Conflicts In South Asian States", in Phadnis, Urmila, Muni, S.D., and Bahadur, Kalim, eds., op. cit., 100-120.

"Planned development", *The Hindustan* Times,17 December 1991, 21.

"Plight of Bhutanese refugees in Nepal", Ibid., 20 December 1991, 6.

Pubby, Vipin, "Bhutan asks immigrants to leave", *Indian Express*, 15 January 1991, 9.

——, "Is Bhutan next", Ibid., 3 May 1990,1.

——, "King replies with an edict", Ibid., 4 May 1990, 9.

——, "The King may seek India's help", Ibid., 5 May 1990, 9.

Rabgye, Sonam T., "Current developments In Bhutan and its implications", *Unity International*, vol.15,no.4,April 1991,7-8.

——, "Statement" at the India International Centre, New Delhi on 16 October 1990.

Rahul, Ram, "Making Of Modern Bhutan", *International Studies*, vol. 19, no.3, July-September 1980, 515-28.

Rai, Ram Bahadur, "Dakshin Bhutan Ki Sthiti:Rajshahi Ke Khilap Bagawat Ki Awaj", *Navbhart Times*, New Delhi, 17 September 1990, 1-8.

——, "Dakshin Bhutan Ki Sthiti:2:Rajshahi Ko Chunauti Bharat Ki Dharti Se", Ibid., 18 September 1990, 1-7.

——, "Dakshin Bhutan Ki Sthiti:3: Bhutan Ke Andolankari Daldal Men Khare Hain", Ibid., 19 September 1990, 1-5.

——, "Dakshin Bhutan Ki Sthiti 4: Bharat Harara Ghanist Mitra: Bhutan

Naresh", Ibid., 20 September 1990, 1-6.

Ramachandran, S., "The spirit remains the same", *The Hindu*, 18 April 1992, 19.

——, "We are restrained in dealing witah Nepali subversives: Bhutan King", Ibid., 25 April 1992, 6.

Rattan, Kamaljeet, "Bhutan: Between two Worlds", *India Today*, 15 September 1989, 134-37.

——, "Jigme Singye Wangchuck: Haste to develop erodes our traditions", Ibid.,134.

Rose, Leo E., "Bhutan", in Robinson, Francis, ed., op.cit, 231-32.

Roychoudhury, Tapash K., "Indians' Settlement in Bhutan:Their History and Problems", in Singh, I.J.Bahadur, ed., op.cit.,125-35.

Sanghvi, Hemen C., "Images Bhutan:A Photo-Essay on a Never-Never Land", *Destination South Asia,* New Delhi, vol.1, no.1, October-December 1987, 41-43.

Sen, Antara Dev, "Neighbours: Troubled hills", *Sunday,* 28 October 1990, 22-26.

——, "The people will decide "King Jigme Singye Wangchuck on the futere of Bhutan", Ibid., 28.

Sen Gupta, Bhabani, "Bhutan: Slow, steady pace of change", *The Hindustan Times,* 8 January 1988.

——,"Shant Bhutan Ko Shikayat Hai Bahar Valon Se", *Nav Bharat Times,* 8 July 1988.

Sengupta, Uttam, "Bhutan: Cracks in Paradise: Ethnic strife threatens kingdom's peace", *India Today,* 30 September 1990, 159-60.

Sharma, L.K., "No diplomatic ties with China-Bhutan", *The Times of India,* 16 May 1985,16.

Sonwalkar, Prasun, "Trouble brewing for Bhuran King", Ibid., 21 March 1990, 4.

Sriram, K., "India, Bhutan for world peace", *Indian Express,* 30 September 1985,1.

"Thimphu—least bustling capital in Asia", Ibid., 7 March 1992,11.

Victor, Cecil, "Bhutan and Greater Nepal", *Patriot* 8 November 1991.

Vinayak, M., "Unrest in Bhutan: The voice of a people uprooted", *Frontline,* 27 April 1991, 109-11.

"When crooks become patriots", *The Statesman,* 6 September 1991, 5.

Index

Attention: Readers/Authors

This includes all recent titles in the field of History, Political Science and Philosophy.

We welcome your comments which will be valuable to us to improve the quality of publications.

Invitation to authors: If you are working on a manuscript now or planning to write one in near future – maybe a textbook or a monograph – we shall be glad to receive your proposal for its publication.

If you want to receive our publication information sheet regularly please send your name and address indicating your areas of interest.

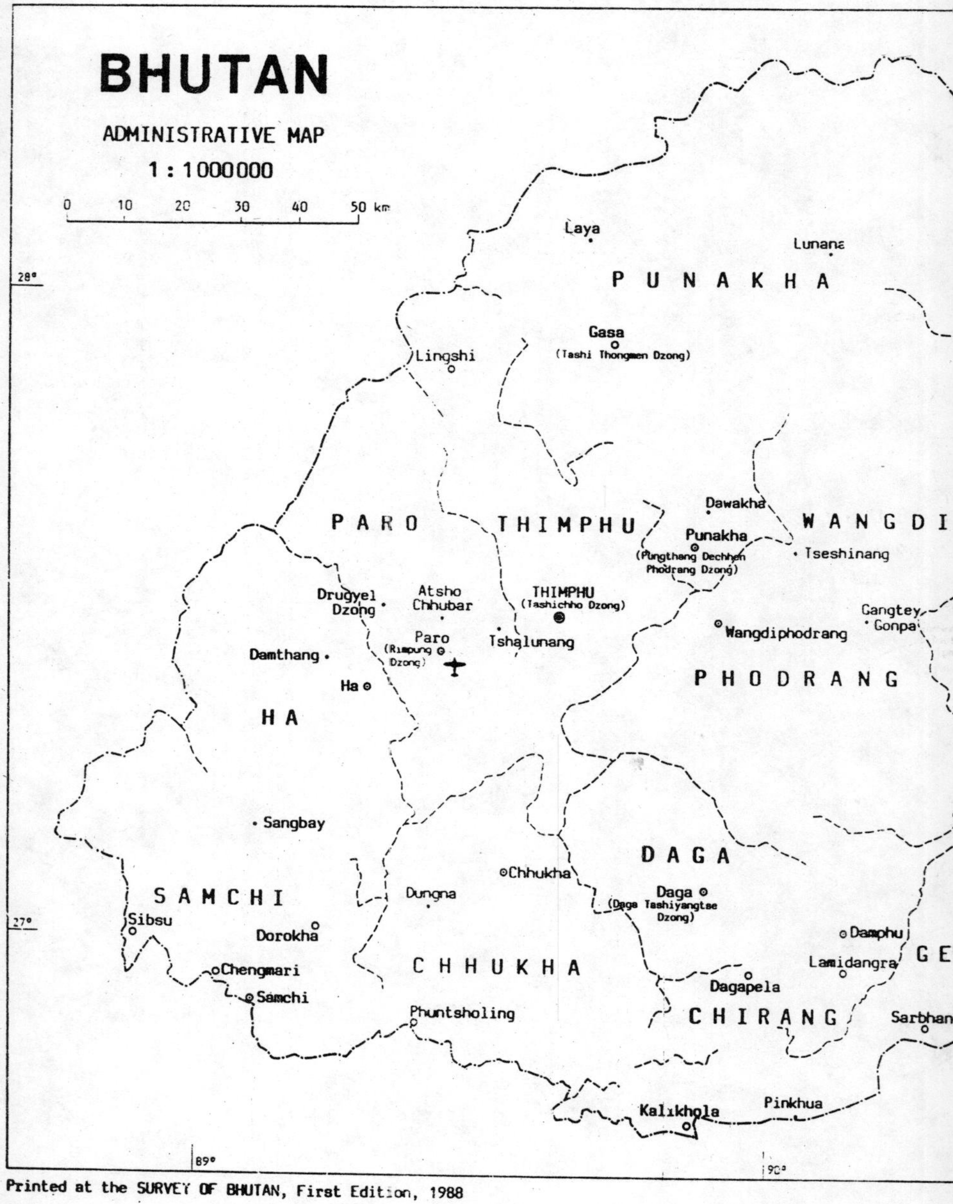

Printed at the SURVEY OF BHUTAN, First Edition, 1988